Praise for The Fragile Dragon

"The US and China need each other economically and geopolitically. Having spent years engaging China at the highest levels, I know how easy it is to mistake size for strength and confidence for stability. Ker Gibbs brings rare credibility to this conversation, grounded in decades of experience at the intersection of trade, diplomacy and business. He shows that China is neither collapsing nor invincible, but a complex system marked by real achievements and real vulnerabilities. As he understands better than most, strong commercial ties help stabilize the broader relationship. This book is essential reading for anyone who wants to understand where China is headed, and how the United States should respond."

—Max Baucus, US Ambassador to China (2014-2017)
US Senator (1978-2014)

"Few relationships are as complex as that between the US and China. *The Fragile Dragon* offers a realistic and sobering guide to how history, politics, and commerce intertwine. Drawing on deeply personal experience from someone who lived through China's rise, the book presents trenchant yet balanced views of the growing tensions between Washington and Beijing. Readers with China experience will appreciate its tour de force through China's transformation, while newcomers will gain a clear understanding of what it means to do business in China."

—Till Vestring, former Senior Partner
Bain & Company in Asia

"*The Fragile Dragon* by Ker Gibbs is a colorful and instructive book about US-China relations with a special focus on a key driver of the bilateral relationship that still doesn't get enough attention—business ties. From his arrival in China in 1985, and through the subsequent decades, Mr. Gibbs had a front-row seat at one of the most remarkable dramas of our times: China's amazing economic development, the impressive growth of US companies in China, and the subsequent deterioration of US-China bilateral ties. The book is filled with fascinating examples of how this evolution played out in real life, as Mr. Gibbs taps into his rich experience as a banker, investor, business chamber president and eyewitness to how China's rise has contributed to a redefinition of US-China relations."

—Kenneth Jarrett, former US Consul General, Shanghai

"I read *The Fragile Dragon* with great interest and admiration. It is lively, personal, and rich in detail. The book traces a long and unusual journey through China's reform era and the evolution of US–China relations. The author's firsthand experiences give the narrative an immediacy and texture that few accounts can match."

– Weijian Shan, Executive Chairman of PAG

"*The Fragile Dragon* offers a clear-eyed and deeply informed examination of China as both a formidable competitor and a profoundly vulnerable system. It reminds us that power built on control, fear, and opacity carries inherent limits. Nowhere is this clearer than Taiwan, where Beijing's inability to tolerate a free Chinese society reveals the fragility beneath its strength. As the United States navigates an era of heightened risk with China—across trade, technology, and potential military conflict—this book is essential reading. It challenges simplistic narratives and helps policymakers, business leaders, and citizens understand the real stakes of competition with China, and the dangers of miscalculation."

– James Stavridis, Admiral US Navy (retired)
Supreme Allied Commander at NATO (2009-2013)

"President Jimmy Carter normalized the relationship with China in 1979, and American business leaders went to China with the hope of selling American products and making profits. Gibbs' book provides information that is crucial to sustain American business engagement with China – it is no longer just a marketplace; its leaders are both dreamers and agitators, its people harbor both love and hate toward things American, and the national goal may collide with the American way of doing business and conducting politics. But Americans must stay — selling merchandise and services the American way is vital, as is figuring out a way to interact with the "fragile dragon" so both can peacefully compete and prosper."

– Yawei Liu, Senior Advisor on China, The Carter Center

"Ker Gibbs's book is a gem. Admirably, it is not the typical punditry and never pedantic. The reminiscences and journeys told in the book are unvarnished, and made all the more interesting by Ker's novelist eye for relevant details. It is a book for people with a casual interest in China and US-China relations as well as those with a deeper interest. For me, it is an engaging read which presents at times different and challenging, but instructive, perspectives."

—Bob Ching, Founding Partner (retired)
The Boston Consulting Group in China

THE FRAGILE DRAGON

China's Strengths and the Limits to its Power

KER D. GIBBS

EARNSHAW BOOKS

The Fragile Dragon
By Ker D. Gibbs

Trade Paper: 978-988-8904-96-9
Hardback: 978-988-8904-98-3
Digital: 978-988-8904-97-6

POLITICAL SCIENCE / International Relations / Diplomacy

EB272

Published in Hong Kong by Earnshaw Books Ltd.

For my parents, Donald A. Gibbs and
Loretta Li Yun-zhen

Contents

Author's Note

China is complicated, as is talking and writing about it. I made a number of choices when writing this book that I would like to explain. Readers will note that I often refer to the Chinese Communist Party, or the CCP, and might take the view that I'm over-stressing the term "communist," a loaded word to people from the West, or that it is inaccurate because China is not really communist at all. Both are true to some extent, but my reason for using the term is to be precise about who said and did what. From a distance, it may be easy to think of China as a monolith, and we may use the word "China" to represent broadly held views within the country. But while China is a highly centralized state with one ruling party, there are people in China with a range of opinions on all topics, and no absolute equivalence between the people of China and the party that governs them. This book, among other things, explores the diversity and evolution of their views, especially toward the United States.

As for the CCP, one must bear in mind that in China, the party stands for something very different from political parties in America. The CCP plays a central, all-encompassing, and, so far as we can see now, long-lasting role. The party is a central character in this book, and could be the subject of a book by itself. In fact, it is the subject and the title of Richard McGregor's book, *The Party*. First published in 2012, I have yet to find a more detailed and insightful description of the CCP and its inner workings. McGregor explains that in order to understand the level and extent of the party's control over China, one would have to imagine a world in which the head of America's Republican

Party, for example, also had the power to appoint the heads of the *New York Times*, ExxonMobil, and JP Morgan. In the Chinese system, where the only media that matters is the state media, and state-owned enterprises reign supreme, the party exerts its power in exactly this way. In a liberal market-based system, the separation between state authority and private commerce has been a foundational principle, with governments avoiding encroachment upon corporate autonomy and entrepreneurial discretion.

Several American presidents are referred to in this book, alongside their Chinese counterparts. Xi Jinping holds that title as the head of state, but his role as president is largely ceremonial, and his real source of power is his position as the Communist Party's General-Secretary.

The book contains many stories and anecdotes, and I've done my best to let people tell their own stories in their own words. I'm not a journalist and I made no recordings when these conversations took place, but I did keep notes and have recalled the details and wording as best I could. In some cases I checked back with individuals to get their help filling in details, and secured their consent to use their names. In others, I've obscured their identity while preserving the facts of the stories.

This book recounts a number of conversations with government officials, both Chinese and American, which were not public but also not expressly secret. In most instances there would have been an assumption that I would share the content of meetings with others, and certainly with the members of the American Chamber of Commerce. It was my job to do so. In some cases, I am taking a bit of liberty by recounting the conversations, but I don't believe I'm violating anyone's trust. I've used real names and titles where I felt it was appropriate, but in some cases naming government officials could cause problems for them with no actual benefit to readers.

Some of the conversations described in this book were in English, while others were in Mandarin. Unless it was relevant to the narrative, I have not always specified which language was used. If interlocutors used my Chinese name—Ji Kaiwen—then readers can assume the conversation was in Mandarin. In some meetings I was joined by colleagues, but in others I was alone. There are a few meetings described where I was not alone, but I have not named the other participants in order to protect their privacy.

Chinese names and terms are expressed using the standard *pinyin* system. In some cases, Chinese names have become well-established in English using a different system for Romanization. The late leader of the Republic of China, for example, is well known under the spelling Chiang Kai-shek. I have chosen not to change it.

My experience is mostly with American companies, and as head of the American Chamber of Commerce in Shanghai I was the spokesperson for the Americans only. In most instances, the term "foreign companies" and "American companies" are interchangeable, but not always. Facing the Chinese government, American and European companies were treated largely the same and dealt with similar issues, although the industry mix is quite different. The German companies lean toward manufacturing, whereas more American companies are in the service sector. The French have many large food companies, as do the Italians. The diversity of Europe is reflected in the industry mix.

The text will sometimes refer to AmCham, or "the chamber", or the American Chamber of Commerce. Unless specifically mentioned, all references to AmCham refer to the American Chamber of Commerce in Shanghai.

China's official currency is the yuan, but it is more commonly referred to as the renminbi, meaning "the people's currency." It is abbreviated as the RMB, and all these terms mean the same thing.

This book is part family history, and part commentary on foreign policy, current affairs, and US-China relations. As such, it moves roughly in chronological sequence, but it is also organized according to episodes and themes. The episode on the Global Financial Crisis, for example, also describes related events that took place a decade later. I have therefore broken the book into several parts, with episodes within each Part moving roughly in chronological order.

For example, the clock resets for the part covering Taiwan, so readers can more clearly follow the events that led to the situation the island finds itself in today. Trying to weave the Taiwan story into the overall timeline and narrative about China as a whole would be confusing.

As I set out to write this book, I spoke with two publishers who asked me the same thing: "Are you planning to return to China?" The implied question is whether I expect anything in this book to impact on my ability to be allowed to return, or whether I have censored myself in order to avoid trouble. The answer is yes, I do plan to return to China, and no, I don't know if there will be objections to anything I've written here. I have many friends in China. I love living in China, and I spend as much time as I can in my home in Shanghai.

The title of this book, *The Fragile Dragon,* invokes an important symbol of Chinese culture. I also happened to write most of the book during the Chinese Year of the Dragon. The dragon symbolizes power and strength. The Chinese emperor was known as the "True Dragon Son of Heaven," and the Kung Fu Panda from the DreamWorks movie transformed into the formidable "Dragon Warrior." Chinese stories describe dragons that are powerful, but they can also bring prosperity and abundance.

Chinese state media introduced the idea that 2024 should be known as the year of the *loong*, instead of using the English word "dragon," because Western dragons are mean and destructive. According to this narrative, Chinese dragons, or *loong*, are benevolent and noble, often bringing good luck. The two should not be confused. But an argument about the characteristics of two mythical creatures is of course ridiculous, and if anything, could be a metaphor for the relationship between China and the West. We can't seem to agree on anything, and have even taken our disputes into the realm of fantasy.

This book is about the former—the world we actually live in—and the very real disputes that threaten to disturb our peace. With this book, I hope to explain how the dragon is strong, but at the same time fragile, not so that it can be destroyed, but so that the dragon's behavior and motivations can be better understood, or perhaps to help readers decide if there truly is a difference between a dragon and a *loong*.

Introduction
Getting Started in China

My mother looked across the dinner table at me as my father cleared the remains of our meal and began loading the dishwasher. The whirlwind of activities marking my college graduation were behind us and we were discussing my future.

I grew up on the university campuses where my parents both taught—the University of Washington, Harvard, and finally UC Davis. Graduate students constantly visited our home, arguing about Confucian philosophy, Marxist economics, and the inherent tension between human rights and national sovereignty. People like Victor Mair and Perry Link were frequent guests in our home on their way to becoming renowned scholars in the field of China studies. As much as I enjoyed growing up in that environment, an academic career didn't seem right for me.

"You should go to China." My mother stated it as a fact, not a command or suggestion, and she offered no argument to support her claim. She simply informed me that this was something I should do. Unlike other Asian "tiger moms" she had guided my upbringing with a light touch and made few demands, but it was clearly important to her that I go to China, so I went.

I arrived in China for the first time in 1985, when China's economy was about the size of Portugal's economy today. The main form of transportation was the bicycle, and most people ate meals of pickles and rice cooked over a brick of coal. Average income was $300 per year. British Prime Minister Margaret Thatcher had just announced that Hong Kong would be handed back to China, but at the time it was still a British colony. It was also the main point of entry into mainland China, so that's where I went. From Hong Kong, I took a train to Lo Wu and joined throngs of people walking across the border into mainland China.

The train on the Hong Kong side was sleek and modern, but as I walked with the crowd of people across the bridge to the Chinese side of the border, time seemed to move backward and colors faded from the landscape. I was one of few Western travelers; most people were locals hauling goods, straining under the enormous loads on their backs. Some wore flip-flops. I suspected the boxes contained consumer products purchased in Hong Kong and carried across the border tax-free as personal items. The cameras, radios, and TVs would be quickly sold on the black market. My first impression of China was that it was dirty and disorganized, with too many people and not enough goods. China in the mid-1980s was poor.

Before the revolution in 1949 my mother's family was relatively well off, highly educated, and owned a bit of land. I suppose they would have been called capitalists, and as the revolution ended, the class warfare began. Anyone with wealth, connections, or enough good luck to obtain a plane or boat ticket used it to get to Hong Kong, Taiwan, or simply anywhere but China.

My mother managed to get to Taiwan before Shanghai fell to the communists in May 1948. She was sixteen at the time. Her older brother had previously been posted to Taiwan and was well-established there long before the exodus, so he was able to arrange for her to join him. The rest of the family, including my mother's sister and her children, were left behind. When I got to China, my mother was eager for me to reconnect with her side of the family, especially my aunt.

My aunt's children—my cousins—grew up under Mao and lived through the Cultural Revolution. They experienced the worst excesses of ideology run amok. Educated people were sent to the countryside to "learn from the peasants." People of the wrong class background (like ours) or with relatives overseas (like me) were persecuted mercilessly and accused of being "capitalist roaders" or not supporting Chairman Mao with sufficient enthusiasm.

The Cultural Revolution was a disaster for China. Mao Zedong initiated the movement in 1966 as a means to restore the ideological purity of the party, but he soon lost control as it evolved into a culture war. In Mao's name, groups of young "Red Guards" attacked local government officials, teachers, and public intellectuals for allegedly betraying revolutionary ideals.

A rumor or accusation was enough to prompt mobs to drag neighbors from their homes and into the street where they were humiliated and beaten, sometimes to death. Family members turned on each other, and children were manipulated into denouncing their own parents. My aunt was forced to divorce the father of her children in order to save herself, and another of my relatives was driven to suicide. One of my cousins was pulled out of her middle school and sent to Chongming Island—now an eco-tourist destination about an hour from Shanghai—to slop pigs and work in the fields. My aunt also had two sons, both of whom suffered various kinds of abuse.

Estimates vary widely, but by the time it ended with the death of Mao, at least a million people may well have been killed by their own colleagues, friends, and neighbors. Millions more were persecuted, their careers destroyed.

Xi Jinping, now the paramount leader of China, was a teenager during the Cultural Revolution. His father, a high-ranking government official, was purged from the party leadership amidst the furor, and the young Xi was pulled out of school and sent to the countryside to experience hard labor alongside his fellow students. He famously ran away from the grueling work and living conditions, but he was sent back by his own mother.

It's hard to say what Xi's view is on the Cultural Revolution today, or how much responsibility the party has accepted internally for what happened. Among young people in China, born after about 1970, any mention of the events that rocked the nation during that period draws mostly blank stares. Information is tightly controlled, especially regarding anything that might suggest mistakes or flaws in the way the CCP governs the country. On the other hand, Xi Jinping has suggested that China's youth need to "toughen up," as he did himself during the Cultural Revolution, and he has revived the rhetoric about "ideological struggle" that was popular during Mao's era.

The Cultural Revolution effectively ended in 1976 with the death of Mao Zedong, China's autocratic leader. A cult of personality had formed around the man who thrived on chaos and deliberately engineered destruction and disorder as he clung to power. He famously declared: "the world in great disorder, situation excellent!"

It is tempting to think that the Cultural Revolution was unique to China, and that this level of self-harm could never happen elsewhere. But elements of its political style have seeped into other countries, even in Western-style democracies. In the United States, President Donald Trump may not have uttered the words "chaos under heaven," but his governing style has been described as chaotic, not dissimilar to Mao's.

When appointing lieutenants, both leaders have prioritized loyalty and ideology over competence and experience. During the first part of his second term, Trump employed young people to attack the establishment and dismantle institutions like the Department of Education and USAID (US Agency for International Development). He didn't actually close the schools, as was done in China for a decade, but Trump has withheld billions in federal funding and attacked institutions of higher learning. Intellectuals and "elites" have been labeled as enemies, while the president panders to the working class and others who see themselves as having been disenfranchised.

Trump's "Make America Great Again" movement has very different roots from the Cultural Revolution, but the parallels are striking: vilifying opponents, undermining established institutions, and cultivating a personality cult. Chairman Mao can easily be imagined saying: "I alone can fix it." The history of Mao's China shows how such tactics can destabilize a nation, even one as wealthy and powerful as the United States.

My mother had arranged for me to teach English at a university in Beijing. I took the summer to get myself settled, then had full teaching responsibilities in the fall, so it was winter before I had the opportunity to visit Shanghai and meet my relatives for the first time. I arrived just before the Spring Festival, when the Chinese New Year is celebrated, and families typically gather for meals and exchanging gifts. It was cold and the air smelled of coal as I walked along the Bund with my cousin, admiring the European style buildings.

I called her *"biaojie"* because she was older than me by a few years. The Chinese language has specific terms for older cousin, younger cousin, cousin on the father's side or mother's side, and male or female cousin. Li Hong was the daughter of my mother's older sister. By the mid-1980s people were shedding the blue Mao suits, but she still dressed plainly for a young woman, and wore no make-up or jewelry.

We paused at the old Hongkong & Shanghai (HSBC) bank building, a magnificent neoclassical structure topped with an enormous dome. It was once known as the most luxurious building in all of Asia, decorated with marble on the inside. Outside it was grey, caked in soot from decades of burning coal for cooking and heat. The smell of coal was a permanent and pervasive fixture in the city.

After the revolution of 1949, the Bank's building fell victim to the new regime's desire to take down symbols of capitalism and foreign influence. Business with the West collapsed, and the building was confiscated from HSBC and became for more than thirty years the municipal government headquarters, effectively city hall. I looked east across the Huangpu river at Pudong. Decades later it would later become China's gleaming new financial center, built up with banks and insurance buildings pushing up the sky, but on that day it was not much more than a mud flat.

We walked north along the Bund, and crossed over Suzhou Creek. The creek was smelly back then, and the boats that used it as a vital waterway had to push through garbage as they made their way inland. Years later, a massive redevelopment effort would clean up the creek and transform the area, to the delight of tourists and local residents alike. The walking paths, greenery, and art installations became the pride of the city.

We crossed a bridge and arrived north of the creek in Hongkou, an area which before the war was a part of the International Settlement, with a substantial Japanese presence. As the Nazis swept through Europe, thousands of persecuted Jews found their way to Shanghai, where the International Settlement did not require visas for arrivals. Many of them settled in Hongkou.

My cousin escorted me through narrow streets lined with shophouses until we arrived at the home where our family lived until the building was confiscated after the revolution. It was a Western-style villa with a stucco exterior, wooden shutters, and a portico that residents were using to park their bicycles. Laundry hung on poles poking out of the windows, and debris was piled against the side of the house. Beneath the clutter, I could see that it was a magnificent building, and I had a hard time imagining that my family used to live there. "Who lives here now?" I asked my cousin as she took me past the gate, up a long gravel driveway, and through the main entrance.

"Oh, many people live here because it's so large," she explained, pointing to the row of electrical boxes connected to twists of wires that ran haphazardly along the wall of the common area just inside the main door. "Each family gets one room. They pay for their own electricity, so each one needs a meter. This is a big house so there are probably fifteen families living here."

That explained the smell of cooking that permeated the house. Each family cooked in their own room, or in the unventilated hallway. It also explained why the hallways and common areas were dark, where nobody paid for the electricity.

"After liberation, our family had to move out of this house." My cousin was born a few years after the 1949 communist victory, so she would not have had any memory of it. She spoke with no remorse or resentment for losing the magnificent house.

Many Chinese people still refer to 1949 as "*jiefang*," meaning liberation, which carries a great deal of meaning. *Jiefang* marked the end of a brutal civil war, and a departure from the Nationalist-led government, but it also meant liberation from a feudal system that allowed landlords to exploit peasants who worked the land. Local warlords fought amongst themselves before power was consolidated in a central government. To many, *jiefang* meant liberation from oppression at the hands of foreign powers and the end to China's "century of humiliation." And to others, it meant the end of dreams for a different kind of China, the confiscation of assets, hardship and even exile.

Finally, after our tour, my cousin brought me to see her mother. We met in the lobby of my hotel, a 1930's Art Deco building on the north bank of Suzhou Creek. We were not far from the famous Broadway Mansion, where foreign residents watched from the balconies as Japanese soldiers took over much of the city in 1937 (the remainder fell in 1941 after Pearl Harbor). Later, the magnificent building, the luxury residence of diplomats, business people and journalists, became Japan's military headquarters in Shanghai. Given China's turbulent history, it's remarkable that any of these buildings were left at all in 1985, but here we were. My aunt looked like an older version of my mother, yet her life experience could not have been more different. This woman had suffered.

She gazed at me, the distant foreign relative, a part of her family that had been split off when her little sister boarded a boat and disappeared, separated by war and ideology for three decades. Now here I was, a young kid obviously foreign and out of place, standing before her with a lost look and a lot of questions. The lines on her face and her bent posture told a story of hardship, but her eyes were bright and flashed as she looked me over.

Moments earlier, she had been hopping up and down, unable to contain her excitement. Chinese people have no tradition of hugging or embracing each other in public, leaving them with few tools available for emotionally charged situations like this. My aunt's solution directed the energy vertically until she regained her composure.

She finally settled down but still held both my hands in hers as if I might slip away and disappear if she released me. I'm at least a foot taller, so she looked upward, searching my face for the Chinese element that connected me to her.

My aunt looked around the room, then lowered her voice and said to me, "Kaiwen…" She called me by my Chinese name, speaking in Mandarin. At home, she would normally speak in Shanghainese but could use standard Mandarin just as easily. I addressed her as "*yima,*" the word for mother's older sister. She spoke no English. "…if America and China go to war, which side will you be on?"

The question left me stunned. She was deadly serious and wanted an answer. I grew up during the Cold War and understood something about Mao Zedong, enough to know he was no friend of the United States. But even before a team of ping-pong players were used to break the ice in the early 1970s, I never saw China as a threat or war between our nations as a real possibility. Our concern was the Soviet Union. China never had missiles pointed at us from an island ninety miles off our shore, as Russia did in Cuba. As a child growing up in the 1960s, I experienced air raid drills and learned to get under my desk in case Russia decided to drop THE BOMB. It wasn't China that launched a spacecraft that drove us to a Sputnik moment.

Back home growing up, my image of China was formed mostly during family dinners in Chinatown, and I had no strong opinions except that it was an odd and isolated country. China was poor, I knew that much, and it posed no particular threat to the United States. Was it even capable of attacking us? More importantly, why would they do that? Cold War ideology was certainly an issue. I knew that China was "communist," which supposedly made it a threat to our way of life, but that didn't mean an actual war was likely.

My aunt saw things the other way. She was not suggesting that China might attack the United States. She was worried that the United States would attack China. This idea was preposterous and fantastical to me, but later I would learn more about China's recent history and more importantly, how many Chinese have a very different interpretation of the same set of facts and events. My aunt's point of view was, in a way, understandable—the party had for decades cast America in the role of a threatening adversary.

My father, a first-generation American of European ancestry, was involved in the conflict that was in a way the root of my aunt's concern. He fought in the Korean war as a code breaker in army intelligence. The army sent him to the Defense Language Institute in Monterey, where he was taught to speak Chinese, not Korean. He spent the next eleven months living in a bunker north of the 38th parallel.

Like many combat veterans, my father never spoke much about the war, but I had always assumed it was fought between Americans and Koreans, or at least between Koreans in the north and south, but that was wrong. Most of the fighting was between Americans and Chinese. In China, it wasn't called the Korean war at all. The Chinese government calls it *"kang mei yuan chao,"* or "War to Resist American Aggression and Aid the Korean People."

I came to China because of my family, then returned for my business career. Eventually, I landed in a position situated between the two governments and the foreign business community. The American Chamber of Commerce in Shanghai is a group that includes CEOs, entrepreneurs, bankers, and lawyers. It hosts officials from both governments, including ambassadors and congressional delegations. Over the years, I have met with Chinese and American government officials, including House

Majority Leader Paul Ryan, Federal Reserve Chair Janet Yellen, and even Supreme Court Associate Justice Samuel Alito, among others. From this perch, I have dug into almost every issue that confronts the United States and China, and heard the arguments from both sides.

Membership in the delegation was highly selective, mostly made up of C-level executives. Citizenship or ethnicity was not a factor. Our Chinese friends and colleagues were often shocked to discover that ordinary people could have access to such a high level of government. Having said that, security can be an issue, and not all meetings in every building would be open to "non-AmCits," as the State Department refers to American citizens. Our meetings with the US Trade Representative, Commerce, and other departments were open to citizens of all countries, but for meetings with the National Security Council and the Treasury, we needed to show a US passport.

As a bi-racial person in a nation of immigrants, my citizenship has never been questioned, unlike the Eurasian superstar Aileen Gu, the Olympic skier who became a citizen of the People's Republic of China in order to compete on the Chinese team in the 2022 Beijing Olympics. She had to go through contortions to explain her allegiances. In a press conference, the spirited and charismatic eighteen-year-old quipped, "I'm American when I'm in the United States, and I'm Chinese when I'm in China." Clever, but I'm quite sure that if I tried that tactic on my visits to the Ministry of Foreign Affairs in Beijing, the powers-that-be would not be amused! (My citizenship is American, full stop).

In China, people often have a hard time understanding AmCham, and are skeptical when I tell them it is not a branch of the US government. The absence of any functional equivalent in their own country makes it hard for the Chinese to understand. There are hundreds of business organizations in China of course, and many of them perform functions similar to AmCham's. Invariably, these groups are connected to some branch of the Chinese government, usually the Ministry of Commerce, and are very much under the direction of the government. AmCham is different. AmCham maintains a dialogue with both American and Chinese government officials and advocates on behalf of business, but as an organization it is independent of both governments.

The significance of AmCham is not just as a platform for senior business executives to discuss issues and exchange information, but as a vehicle to communicate publicly. Foreign business managers are notoriously reluctant to speak publicly about China. Even in closed-door meetings it can be difficult to get them to say anything that could be interpreted as critical, and for good reason. The Chinese government can be sensitive, petty, and vindictive. Therefore the Chamber speaks on behalf of members as the "voice of American business in China." Still, even the Chamber can land in trouble with the authorities because of public statements.

Fear of retribution stops some foreign business leaders from criticizing China, but others are willfully naive about China's Communist Party and the direction the country is now headed. Some of these people are quite willing to criticize the United States and a few have become social media stars in China for doing so.

In Shanghai, an AmCham member challenged US government policy during a Consulate briefing, saying "we don't believe there's any forced labor in Xinjiang." She had no experience in such matters and could not possibly have covered the vast region sufficiently to make such a statement.

I therefore pointed out that any "we" in that statement would have to mean her and her company or associates. She could not speak for AmCham or the business community as a whole. Even I, as the president and spokesperson for the Chamber, was kept on a short leash by my Board and stuck carefully to our talking points and core messages. Still, many business people in that room would have agreed with her desired outcome, even if they were wise enough not to sign on to the perspective she put forward. Many foreign business leaders in China would prefer that the US government not rock the boat.

Many of today's long-term resident expats arrived in China and established themselves when it was a very different place. To be sure, China in the 1990s and 2000s was authoritarian and tightly controlled by the party, but much was overlooked or forgiven because the country was moving in a more liberal direction. Foreign business people accepted a similar equation as the Chinese people themselves: give me stability and a successful growth model so I can get rich, and a sense that the direction is right. We care about where we are going, not how we got there.

Also, most business people are only exposed to the CCP and China's government at a level where the system works mainly toward commercial objectives. At the provincial and municipal level, the government is very much focused on investment, jobs, and taxes. Surveillance and interference in personal lives are not entirely absent, but the sub-national level is generally not where these characteristics come into play. But China is always shifting under our feet, and many in the foreign business community are too invested in their own narrative and are not willing to adjust their thinking when it comes to the party and what's happening now. *This is not the China of the 1990s.*

China's political and economic system makes it different from those of Western countries and in some ways incompatible. China's history of conflicts with the West, and its alternative interpretation of them, have left the system obsessed with competing with America, and hypersensitive about that which Beijing cares about most: national security, sovereignty, and respect.

Conversations with ordinary people in China also reflect these priorities, although its difficult to distinguish official messaging from what people truly believe. Xi Jinping has been pushing "socialist values," but people in China care about the same things as people everywhere—creating wealth and a better life for themselves and their families.

Many of us believed these differences would diminish over time, but instead China is moving in the opposite direction, and quickly. Those of us living in China have felt the shift. This is a very different nation under Xi Jinping than it was under Deng or those who came after.

In September of 2019, members of the American Chamber of Commerce traveled to Washington to speak with Congress. We especially wanted to meet with Senator Steve Daines because he had a reputation for being fair, and we believed he would be open-minded as he had worked in China before his political career, as an executive with Procter & Gamble, based in Guangzhou in the late 1990s.

Our group filed into the senator's conference room and took seats at the large, square table. It was too big for the room and left little space to maneuver. Also too big for the room, an enormous buffalo head was mounted on a wall high above, as if looking down on us. "I guess you can take the senator out of Montana," quipped one of our members, "but you can't take Montana out of the senator." The remark drew chuckles, but it also reminded me that we would be discussing beef. American beef exports had been restricted in China.

Senator Daines came in a moment later, shaking hands and collecting business cards. These meetings were often with staffers, with the member of Congress dropping in for a few minutes between floor votes, but Senator Daines took a seat and invited us to begin.

"Thank you for your time, senator," I said, speaking quickly so as to leave as much time as possible for the other members of the delegation. "We've been eager to meet with you, as one of the few people on the Hill who knows China."

The senator immediately parried: "There is nothing more dangerous than a senator who's been to China… five years ago!" Daines was making the point that China changes dramatically, and referring to the danger that exists if we fail to understand a nation that is quite literally changing the world around us. Despite increasingly tense bilateral relations, Senator Daines had maintained his diplomatic engagement with Beijing. This commitment to firsthand understanding positioned him as the first person from Congress to visit China as President Trump's envoy following his return to the White House.

Chinese society has indeed changed. The Chinese people who so eagerly came to work for US companies typically now prefer employment with local competitors, companies like Alibaba and Midea. Some of the younger generation especially are not impressed with America. They see it as a spent power that has accomplished little during their lifetimes that would justify such swagger on the world stage, a swagger they want for themselves and believe they deserve. This is of course the view promoted by the state media system, and it has an impact. The global financial crisis is seen as a clear example of America's failure, say some, and point to our messy politics, racial strife, and inconsistent foreign policy as examples of what China seems to do better. But the US has a transparency that China lacks, and the Chinese response to the global financial crisis created a mountain of debt that put a drag on the economy. China's highly controlled media environment obscures the diversity of views that exists within the country, especially positive opinions about America and the freedoms we enjoy. Chinese people are still lining up for green cards, after all.

China does many things well. Investments in infrastructure have given China transport and logistics networks that are second to none. China's political system is highly centralized and very unforgiving of alternative views, but for certain narrowly defined goals the system works well. A centrally planned economy indeed creates inefficiencies, but China's mixed model has produced spectacular results in the past few decades, starting from a low base. Even foreign companies have benefited, as long as they conform to the plan. But the desire for self-sufficiency and the extensive use of state subsidies especially has put China out of compliance with the global trading system and World Trade Organization (WTO) rules, and created tensions with many of its trading partners.

Even as our disagreements become more inflamed, our commercial interests continue to bind us together. China is the world's largest growth market for everything from cars to cat food, and American companies will never abandon the market willingly. China's strict regulatory environment has already caused many foreign firms to rebalance activities away the market. Google, LinkedIn, Facebook, and many others have either been blocked or exited in response to government actions. Other foreign companies have left because of local competition, exacerbated by an uneven playing field and the presence of giant state-owned companies with inherent advantages. But the market opportunity of 1.4 billion consumers is too important for most American companies to ever leave China voluntarily.

China has benefited tremendously from its relationship with the West over the past half-century, even though the nation is usually too proud to admit its accomplishments were not achieved entirely on its own. The industriousness and drive of the Chinese people fuel the system's competition with the United States. In America, long-running complaints about unfair practices and a lack of reciprocity have grown steadily louder in recent years, even as the voices of foreign businesspeople operating inside China are noticeably muted, in part through self-interest, wanting to avoid rocking the boat that, in good times, can enrich bottom lines and accelerate careers. The party has absolute control over every aspect of life inside the People's Republic, and is increasingly trying to exert influence abroad. Everyone has to be careful about everything they say and do, or risk consequences that can take many forms. Smaller nations are the usual target of China's actions, but apologies have been extracted from companies, movie actors, and even the American Chamber of Commerce in Shanghai.

China, in the eyes of many, has become pushy. A number of its neighbors feel the pressure, and even distant powers have become concerned. It now has a formidable military, which reports directly to the party, and has growing influence and interests throughout the world. China has abandoned the policy of the Deng years of staying low-key and avoiding confrontation, and seems to be attacking the very systems and institutions that enabled its success.

China may seem powerful, like a dragon, but its often pugnacious posture masks deeper vulnerabilities. The system has achieved remarkable progress—transforming infrastructure, lifting hundreds of millions from poverty, and demonstrating an impressive capacity to mobilize resources through centralized control. Yet beneath this surface lie structural weaknesses: a lack of institutional diversity and transparency that erodes confidence, demographic decline that is already shrinking the population, and massive local government debt that constrains flexibility.

The challenges are mounting. A property market crisis threatens the foundation of household wealth and local government finances. Weak consumer spending reflects a crisis of confidence about the future. The banking system remains opaque and fragile, with no independent checks to prevent miscalculation. Inequality between rich and poor, urban and rural, continues to widen. Youth unemployment is rising even as the state tightens its grip on the economy. And looming over it all are geopolitical pressures, with Taiwan representing perhaps the most consequential uncertainty.

The party works hard to push the narrative that China is a victim, and that a strong, unchallenged central government is essential to defend against its enemies, both internal and external. The "black hand" of the West is everywhere, according to this line of reasoning, and the US is coordinating with its allies to prevent China's rise. This narrative explains that the United States feels threatened as it faces inevitable decline, a result of its "inferior political and economic system."

The best lies are based on an element of truth. The United States is not on the verge of collapse, but Beijing's concerns do not come out of thin air. Also, two stories can be true at the same time. The CCP uses China's tragic and contentious history to bolster its legitimacy, but it's also true that Western powers have, through history, taken actions that have harmed China. Even if we are sure that the United States has no plan to attack China, the perception on the other side has concrete consequences.

I am American, but I am also Chinese, giving me the advantage of being able to look at both sides of these issues. The

United States and China were allies in World War II, so why does Beijing view the US military presence in Asia with suspicion? To what extent do China's own vulnerabilities drive behavior, and its weaknesses actually motivate what others perceive as aggression?

Stories from the past provide a context for business activities, and can help equip individuals with knowledge necessary before embarking on ventures in China. As an introduction to the issues, and how foreign businesses can navigate them, Part I of this book provides an overview of the US-China relationship in recent decades, while offering a perspective on how some of the key events can be viewed. Parts II and III explain the role that foreign companies have played in China's economic development and how their position in the economy has changed over time. Parts IV, V, and VI shift the focus to the role of government, both in the US and China, and how the relationship began to deteriorate, concluding with a discussion of the potential for conflict. China may be more vulnerable than it appears.

China is very much in transition. The country has shifted dramatically even in the relatively short time since I first arrived in 1985. Back then, Chinese people still wore Mao suits and knew little about the world beyond their borders, or how to run a business. They were curious and optimistic, and eager to cooperate with new friends from the West. China was opening up and they were experiencing more freedom than they ever thought possible, and there was every reason to believe the country would continue on that trajectory. It did not.

Xi Jinping, in his effort to "rejuvenate" China, is shaping the country in a new direction that suggests it wants to be a superpower in all areas, on a par with the United States. And even then, from a Confucianist hierarchical perspective, parity is not a comfortable arrangement. China's history has never been smooth, and the current period is no exception. It's a complicated place that is changing fast. With this book, I hope to explain the parts I know and have experienced myself, with the goal of helping readers form their own opinions.

PART

1

KNOW BEFORE YOU GO

"With bronze as a mirror, one can correct their dress; with the past as a mirror, one can understand the rise and fall of states."
— Emperor Taizong, Tang dynasty

Chapter 1

Imperial Weakness Invites Barbarian Intrusions

My great-grandfather was addicted to opium. In Chinese I would have called him *"wai zeng zufu,"* the specific term for my mother's mother's father. He owned the Golden Lion bicycle company as well as several properties in Shanghai on Anfu Road, in the same neighborhood where I would own an apartment myself, roughly a century later. His addiction caused him to lose everything he owned, including his business, plunging the family into poverty. He even sold off his own daughters to support his habit.

"It has a sweet smell," my mother told me. "I could smell it everywhere in Shanghai." Her aunt, a woman she called "Ya," was also addicted to the drug.

British traders brought opium into the market after they became frustrated with their relationship with China. They imported tea, silk, and porcelain from China, but China bought practically nothing in return. In the 18th century, Qing dynasty China was the dominant Asian power and maintained diplomatic and commercial relationships with its neighbors. It was not, however, fundamentally a trading nation, and the Manchu rulers famously rebuffed the Europeans looking for new markets, completely missing the shift in economic power between Europe and Asia that was underway.

The spectacular failure of George Macartney's delegation on behalf of the British crown has received much attention from historians, but less has been written about the first visit by an American. As the story has been told and re-told, in 1793 Lord Macartney spent a year negotiating for an audience with the emperor. His mission was to secure permission to have a resident ambassador in Beijing and open trade between Europe and China. The mission failed. Emperor Qianlong thought little of the so-called technological advancements from the West and saw no use for the clocks, telescopes, and other items the delegation presented. China, except for certain periods, most notably during the Tang Dynasty (618 to 907 AD), was never a trading nation. It was always large with a diverse economy, and relations with its neighbors were never on equal terms. The Qing dynasty court in Beijing often received visiting state representatives, but the items they brought were viewed as tribute to a superior power. China already commanded respect from its neighbors, which is what the emperor cared most about, and saw no need to buy goods from other nations.

The Son of Heaven, as the emperors were called, also saw no need for a foreign ambassador to be resident in Beijing and sought to get the foreigners out of China as soon as possible. All of Lord Macartney's demands were rejected, including the request to open up trade. This refusal to engage on commercial terms fostered widespread smuggling and invited military coercion, ushering in what later became known as the "century of shame."

The first American to visit the emperor took a slightly different approach, involving a juicy lie, but the result was the same. As described in Bill Hayton's book, *Invention of China,* a Dutch-born American by the name of Andreas van Braam saw an opportunity in the aftermath of the British envoy's visit. He was an entrepreneur, and like foreign businesspeople in China today, he was a practical person and unconstrained by diplomatic protocols or aristocratic niceties. Like Macartney, he brought gifts to the emperor, but he also complied with the traditional protocols required by the Qing court. Moreover, he delivered an obsequious message from the Dutch king, recognizing the emperor's "peerless reputation," exalted status, and "China's civilizing influence" on the world. How did a Dutch-American businessman extract such a flattering statement from a European sovereign? Because he didn't exist! In 1795 there was no Dutch king. Van Braam had simply made it up, but to the Chinese court, form mattered over substance.

As time went on, China's trading relationship with Europe became increasingly lopsided, especially with the British. Through the British colonies in India, British traders had access to opium, which they began smuggling into China. After a series of conflicts, all of which China lost, opium was legalized, trade routes were opened, and China was forced to cede control of territory to the Europeans and later to the Japanese as well.

The British were by far the dominant players in opium, as the architects and enforcers of the trade. The British East India Company had a government sanctioned monopoly on the cultivation of poppies in India, and companies like Jardine Matheson and the Hongkong & Shanghai Bank (now HSBC) controlled trade and financing. American companies were involved as well, although never on the same scale. They were opportunistic participants and lacked political backing, despite the fortunes made by families such as Delano (maternal grandfather of Franklin D. Roosevelt), Russell, Perkins, and Cabot.

The Qing government of China at the time was too weak to

stop the trade. Lin Zexu was the Commissioner assigned by the emperor to deal with the matter. In 1839, just before the outbreak of the Opium War, he wrote the following "Letter of Advice to Queen Victoria," edited here for brevity:

> "Our Celestial Empire takes the whole world as its domain. The Great Emperor's benevolence is as vast as Heaven itself, extending over all without distinction. Even the most distant and remote lands are within His care. Since trade was opened in Guangdong, merchants of your nation and our inland people have long enjoyed peaceful and profitable exchanges for hundreds of years. Products such as rhubarb, tea, and silk—treasures of our realm—your country cannot do without, for they sustain your people's livelihood. Yet Our Celestial Empire, treating all equally with generosity, has permitted their export overseas without restriction. This has been done purely out of grace, sharing the heart of Heaven and Earth. However, there are some deceitful foreigners who manufacture opium, secretly smuggle and sell it, seducing foolish people and destroying their bodies for profit. In the past, few smoked it, but now it spreads contagiously, its poison growing deeper by the day. In our prosperous and populous Central Plains, even though these foolish people ruin their own lives out of greed for pleasure, that is their own misfortune. Yet in a great unified empire, it is our duty to correct morals and purify hearts; how could we allow the people under Heaven to perish by poison? Therefore, the empire now severely punishes both sellers and smokers of opium, to eradicate its spread forever.

We understand that this poisonous substance originates among certain

subjects of your nation—wicked and crafty men who make it privately, not under your royal command. Even among all nations, only a few produce it; it is not common to all. We have heard that your own country forbids its people to smoke opium, and violators are punished—clearly, you know its harm, hence your prohibition. But if you forbid smoking, you must also forbid making and selling it; only then is the principle of fairness upheld. If you prohibit its use yet continue to produce and sell it, enticing our foolish people, then you seek your own life by causing others' death; you seek your own profit by bringing harm to others. Such conduct is detested by human conscience and condemned by Heaven's law.

The Celestial Empire, whose power commands both its citizens and foreigners, could easily enforce its will by force. Yet, in the magnanimity of the Emperor's benevolence, We first issue this proclamation as warning and persuasion. Previously, official communications have already been sent to your King urging joint prohibition; how then can ignorance be claimed? Now, We make this agreement with your King: that this harmful opium shall henceforth be utterly cut off. Within our realm, smoking is prohibited; within your dominions, manufacture must cease. For all opium already made, your King must order it to be thoroughly searched out and thrown into the sea, so that under Heaven no trace of this poison remains.

By doing so, not only will our people be spared its harm, but even your own subjects will be protected—

> for if they make it, how can you be sure they will not also smoke it? To forbid its manufacture is to the benefit of both nations. Would this not bring shared peace and prosperity, and further demonstrate your King's sincerity and respect? Thus, Heaven will witness this righteousness and will not send calamity; humanity will approve it, and even sages would bless it.
>
> The Celestial Empire rules the myriad nations by awe-inspiring power beyond measure. Do not say this warning comes too early. When your King receives this document, he should promptly report what measures will be taken to prohibit and eliminate the source of this evil. Do not delay or make excuses. We await your swift reply."

The letter was delivered to the British Commissioner in Guangzhou, Charles Elliot, who passed it on to the Foreign Office, but scholars doubt that it was ever read by the queen. The boundaries of the realm were loosely defined, and the emperor's authority was conceived not in geographic terms but in moral and cosmic ones. He ruled "*tian xia*"—literally "all under heaven"—giving him broad reach and authority.

The British were not impressed. The opium trade persisted, and only added to the humiliation of the Qing Dynasty losing territory to the outsiders.

While the Western powers continued to encroach on Chinese territory and establish settlements and trading centers, the Russians also participated in the "unequal treaties." Unlike the European powers, Russia had a land border with the Qing empire (which consisted of Manchuria, China and Mongolia), and proceeded to take advantage of the Qing dynasty's weakness by moving the border to the north of the Amur river basin, seizing territory all the way to Vladivostok, which Russia holds as its own territory even today. Russia currently occupies over one million square kilometers (about twice the size of Texas) that previously belonged to the Qing. Chinese maps show Vladivostok, Russia's treasured naval base and deep water port on the Pacific, as "Haishenwai." The clashes were brutal, with the history very much unforgotten by the people who live near the border. Stories of Russian soldiers forcing local residents at bayonet point into the river to drown have been passed down through generations.

Russia—later the Soviet Union—is indirectly responsible for additional Chinese territorial losses. The country of Mongolia, landlocked and uncomfortably situated between China and Russia, was joined to China for centuries. China's Yuan dynasty (1271 to 1368) was founded by the Mongols and was a part of its empire that stretched from Poland to Korea, under the great ruler Genghis Khan and his descendants. Mongolia was then linked to China again in 1644 when the Manchus conquered both and created the Qing dynasty. When that dynasty fell in 1911, the Mongols quickly declared independence over the objections raised by China's new leaders, who argued that the Republic of China was the heir apparent to all territories ruled by the Qing emperor. Bolshevik Russia disagreed and supported the establishment of Mongolia as an independent state. Today, the Mongolian people are divided, with more ethnic Mongolians living within the borders of the People's Republic of China than in the independent nation of Mongolia across the northern border.

China's relationship with Russia has long been volatile and violent, with few signs of real affection between the two peoples. As we will see later on, China's leaders have at times found relations with Moscow to be useful, but not always. Moscow has provided leverage as China's relations with the West ebbed and flowed, but there is one nation with which China has had a particularly damaging relationship for more than a century, and that is Japan.

CHAPTER 2

Warlords, Chaos, and Compromises

Long before the bombing of Pearl Harbor, which is the event that put Japanese aggression into the consciousness of most Americans, the Japanese empire had been expanding in Asia. In 1895 Japan won a brief and one-sided war and forced the Qing government to cede the island of Taiwan as reparation. The Japanese emperor and his armies also took over the Korean peninsula and from there made their way into Manchuria, which is now known in China as *dongbei,* meaning the Northeast. A puppet government was set up to rule "Manchukuo," or "the country of the Manchus."

Japan's involvement was decidedly unhelpful as China struggled to transition its governance from a hereditary monarchy to a republic. The Republic of China, founded in 1911 with the fall of the Qing dynasty, inherited a country suffering from abject poverty, weak institutions, and rampant corruption. It also needed to put down infighting between regional warlords while contending with foreign powers happy to take advantage of China's weakness.

My great-grandfather, the opium addict, had several daughters, one of whom joined the Li family and became my mother's mother. The head of the family was a lawyer from Anhui Province, Li Cishan, who became an activist and revolutionary just as the new nation was being formed. He advocated for a strong and independent China, but eventually became alienated from both the Nationalists and the Communists.

While living in Shanghai, I managed to uncover some of his writings from when he was still a member of the Nationalist Party. This passage is dated February 11, 1933, not long after the Mukden Incident that Japan used as a pretext to seize control of Manchuria:

> "I firmly believe that resistance against Japan is the only way out for China, and leading the people in resisting Japan is the only way out for our party. I believe that being Chinese means having the obligation to resist Japan. Therefore, I have made resistance against Japan my life's work. No matter what happens in the future, I will never leave the anti-Japanese front line. Even in prison, I can write for the anti-Japanese cause; even if my head is cut off, I can become a heroic ghost for the anti-Japanese cause."

My grandfather's wish to become a ghost was nearly granted. Li was a Chinese nationalist in the sense that he wanted his country to be strong and independent. He opposed the Japanese occupation and criticized the government's corruption and incompetence. He wanted a China run by and for the Chinese, which at that time it very much was not, and he advocated for a form of government accountable to the people, which those in power did not want.

Yuan Shikai, an important figure during the Qing dynasty, became president of the Chinese Republic in 1912 as a result of a political compromise. But what Yuan really wanted was to become the next emperor, which he ultimately declared himself to be. My grandfather opposed this. He was arrested by the police in Shanghai's French Concession, but managed to escape before being handed over to Yuan's men, who almost certainly would have killed him.

A system of government that places too much power in the hands of one person is often unpopular, and Yuan Shikai was soon overthrown. This was not the end of troubles for the country, however, or for my grandfather. The Japanese ruled the northeast from 1931 and became increasingly embedded in other parts of the country, skillfully utilizing Shanghai's gangsters, who possessed the weapons and organizational infrastructure to impose control in an otherwise lawless land. But one of Shanghai's most notorious gangsters, Du Yuesheng, resisted and famously decamped to Hong Kong in 1937 when most of Shanghai was occupied by the Japanese, leaving his empire of drugs, gambling, and prostitution behind. When Hong Kong was also captured by the Japanese, Du moved to Chongqing, the wartime Chinese capital, in December 1941 and returned to Shanghai in 1945, only to leave again for Hong Kong in 1949 when the communists took over.

The Japanese also found ways to collaborate with the person some called the biggest gangster of all, Chiang Kai-shek, and the KMT. To his credit, Chiang managed to hold together a fragile coalition of warlords and kept China in the fight against Japan. He also maintained—with considerable help from his wife, Soong Mei-ling—international recognition for his government. However, he was often criticized as an ineffective leader presiding over a corrupt government.

Li Cishan spoke out against corruption and foreign influence. Chiang took umbrage with his criticism and sentenced him to death. I asked my mother about this and she explained the politics: "My father was a patriot, determined to fight against the Japanese. He went from warlord to warlord trying to persuade them to fight. Chiang Kai-shek was a southern warlord who favored resistance but elected not to fight, instead leaving the fighting to the Western foreigners. That's why Chiang ordered the assassination of my father."

Li Cishan apparently got word of the plot through a friend and immediately made plans to escape to the northern city of Tianjin, which was controlled by foreigners. He would be safe there, beyond the grasp of Chiang's henchmen.

Li would have departed from the Shanghai North Railway station, a bustling nexus that was the site of other political assassinations.[1] The assassin most likely planned to kill my grandfather on the station platform, then escape into the crowd and disappear. He apparently missed that opportunity, and as my grandfather boarded his train, the man assigned to kill him slipped on behind him. Looking to get close to his mark for another opportunity, he took the seat next to my grandfather, and the two fell into amiable conversation. The would-be assassin then broke into Li's cabin and found several documents, which he read. He became impressed with Li's point of view, and the two became friends.

My grandfather escaped death on the train, but some years later his criticisms landed him in trouble again with the powers that ruled China, and he was expelled from the KMT on February 11, 1933 (the 22nd year of the Republic) and feared that he would again be targeted for assassination. Li appealed directly to Chiang Kai-shek, addressing him as the chairman of the KMT political party:

---

1 March 20, 1913 Chinese Premier Song Jiaoren was assassinated by gangsters believed to be under orders from Yuan Shikai, the first president of the Republic.

> "Chairman Chiang, please carefully consider the following letter. The sender, Li Cishan, is a party member recently expelled from the Shanghai party headquarters, a lawyer whose license has been revoked by the same party, and rumored to be a suspect wanted under your orders. I do not know where my guilt lies regarding the party. I do not know where my wrongdoing as a lawyer lies. And I certainly do not know the reasons for which I should be wanted. But I dare to straightforwardly declare: I am a loyal and diligent party member, and at the same time, I am a loyal and diligent citizen. Furthermore, I wish to inform you, Chairman Chiang, that I am a career-oriented legal scholar, a politician with purely Chinese ideals, and a determined anti-Japanese fighter with a strong sense of national consciousness, state concept, and revolutionary sentiment. I firmly believe that resistance against Japan is the only way for China, and leading the people in resisting Japan is the only way for our party. Therefore, I consider anti-Japanese resistance as my life's work."

We don't know Chiang's reaction to this letter, but we do know that none other than Chen Duxiu, a co-founder of the CCP and its first general secretary, came to my grandfather's aid. Chen had his own complicated relationship with the various powers that were vying to control China, and he would later be jailed by China's Nationalist government, but at the time he had enough influence to get my grandfather's death sentence lifted. My grandfather died after a long illness in 1936. A year later, Japan finally dropped any pretense of being a peaceful neighbor and formally invaded China on July 7th, 1937.

China was an important component of Japan's ambitions. With its enormous landmass and population, China was the key to dominating all of Asia and the entirety of its resources. The United States and the allies understood this clearly and helped to defend China against the invaders even before formally entering the war. For that reason, the American fighters were designated as "volunteers." Before 1941, when the Japanese attack brought the United States into the war, Americans trained in neighboring Burma and fought alongside Chinese troops defending their country against the Japanese. A group of American pilots joined these volunteers and became known as "The Flying Tigers," playing a key role defending supply routes and slowing the Japanese incursions. With the United States still diplomatically neutral, the planes carried no markings that would identify them as American. Pilots sewed Chinese flags on the back of their flight jackets that would identify them as friendly in case they were shot down. By all accounts, the Americans stationed there fought heroically along aside the Chinese army until the Japanese were ultimately defeated.

Hollywood made the Flying Tigers famous with epic films depicting the heroics of pilots commanded by Claire Chennault. However, the Chinese flag shown in these movies—that of the Republic of China, still used in Taiwan today—creates contemporary political sensitivities in Beijing, despite being the national flag when American pilots sewed it on their jackets. Beijing interprets this history differently, often reshaping historical facts to serve present political narratives.

China has always been a complicated place, but the 1930s and 1940s saw twists and turns that have echoes in the geopolitics of today. The central government was weak. There were power struggles, accusations of corruption, and an ideological split between the Nationalist Guomindang (KMT) and the Chinese Communist Party (CCP). The internationally recognized government of China was led by Chiang Kai-shek and the KMT. Diplomatically, America had no choice but to work with Chiang to defeat Japan, but this was never a comfortable relationship.

Mao and the CCP, throughout the war against Japan, focused on fighting the KMT. Western historians generally agree that Mao's strategy at the time was to keep his armies well away from the conflict with Japan. According to Adam Cathcart, a University of Leeds historian, "While Mao had written some important anti-Japanese treatises in 1937 and 1938, by the time the Cairo Declaration came around, he was primarily concerned with expanding his inland base area against Nationalist government resistance and calculating his best chances to overtake Chiang Kai-shek after the Japanese surrendered."[2] Sure enough, as soon as World War II ended, the civil war began, with the followers of Mao holding the advantage. Chiang's government forces were exhausted and the Soviet Union occupied the Northeast straight after Hiroshima and refused to hand it over to anyone but the Communists.

For the American businessmen who returned to Shanghai after the Japanese surrender in August 1945, this was a confusing time, and they were ambivalent. During those four years, the Nationalist government bumbled and mismanaged the economy and squandered much of the war materiel provided by the United States. The foreign business community was frustrated with Chiang and many saw his government as damaging to their interests. Some in the US government disparagingly called

2 *The Guardian*: "Bloggers ridicule Chinese film placing Mao Zedong at key wartime conference," by Tom Phillips, August 17, 2015.

Chiang "the peanut"[3] even as he propped himself up with the title "generalissimo."

By 1949, the American business presence in China was once again substantial. The American Chamber of Commerce, founded in Shanghai in 1915 with just a handful of members, grew as Coca-Cola, General Motors, and other industrial giants came into the market. China also became home to hundreds of American entrepreneurs and adventurers, some of whom created industrial giants of their own, or what we might today call unicorns. AIG, the enormous American insurance company, was founded in Shanghai by a twenty-seven year old American, CV Starr. He started out by selling business insurance, protecting cargo sent by ship across the Pacific. From there he branched into life insurance and opened offices throughout Asia and, eventually, New York.

Other businesses thrived, some legit and some not. American and other foreign companies found ways to navigate the complicated landscape and deal with gangsters and warlords, tapping into China's vast market. China was chaotic, with a central government weakened by war.

The historian Graham Hutchins, in his book *China 1949: Year of Revolution,* describes the situation faced by the Americans as the Republic fell apart and was replaced by Mao and his peasant guerrilla fighters. Hutchins points out that in 1949, many Americans actually *welcomed* the communist revolution.[4] They viewed the KMT as corrupt and incompetent and expected a change that would be good for business. Hutchins quotes US Consul General John Moors Cabot who said, after meeting with the American Chamber of Commerce, "The rejoicing couldn't have been greater if the city had been liberated by

3 *New York Times,* "The Life of Chiang Kai-shek," by Alden Whitman, April 6, 1975.
4 Graham Hutchins: *China 1949: Year of Revolution.* Page 176.

American forces. American and British businessmen were convinced—I can't think why—that they would do better under the communists."

Echoes of this sentiment can be heard today, with American businesspeople generally giving high marks to the CCP on issues of control and management, especially through the 2000s and the early 2010s. China's economy did well enough through the 2008 global financial crisis, and its army of economic bureaucrats have generally proven to be good stewards in their management of the economy, building infrastructure and other public services. The turn inward after 2012, when Xi took office, has disappointed the business community, but for at least twenty years, China's economy hummed along, and the party got credit for that.

Similarly, with Mao's victory in 1949, US government officials were horrified that American executives, well aware that US policy backed Chiang Kai-shek, were celebrating his departure and welcomed the communists taking over. Or at least, they did at first. Consul General Cabot said they would regret it soon enough, and he was right.

Mao quickly brought an end to overt capitalist activities, foreign elements were purged, foreign businesses were closed. The odd optimism among some in the foreign business community proved to be misinformed, even though in the early days, the CCP and brought welcome stability to the situation. The CCP soldiers, most of whom came from the countryside, were prevented from looting or appropriating resources the way KMT soldiers had done. The honeymoon was short-lived. After driving the KMT—and soon after, foreign businesses—from the mainland, Mao consolidated his power and built a new national identity around the Communist Party. People like my aunt were inculcated with the idea that the nation and the party are one and the same. There is no China without the CCP, and supporting the party is the same as supporting China. In this world, any aid to an entity not aligned with the CCP was tantamount to working against China, even if those individuals were Chinese. America's military support for the KMT definitely fit this category.

By this logic, the United States gets no credit for helping China win the war and driving the imperialist Japanese out of the country. It was a messy time in China to be sure, but Chiang Kai-shek and the KMT were the legitimately recognized government and the Americans quite rightly worked with them. Nevertheless, seen from the perspective of the CCP, the Americans were China's enemy from the start because they supported Chiang and not Mao.

The logic seems twisted and facts get in the way, but the CCP has a solution for that. The party is famous for changing facts to fit a certain conclusion. A 2015 film called *Cairo Declaration* produced by the Chinese military portrayed Mao at the 1943 Cairo Conference with Churchill and Roosevelt, although Chiang Kai-shek—not Mao—was the Chinese leader actually present.

CHAPTER 3

China's War to Resist "American Aggression"

My father grew up in northern California, the son of immigrants from Europe. They arrived penniless. The family settled and scratched out a living in the area known today as Silicon Valley, but in the 1930s and 1940s the sunshine and fertile soil made the region ideal for growing prunes and apricots, not making silicon wafers. Bill Hewlett and Dave Packard had just graduated from Stanford and hadn't yet found the garage that would become the birthplace of HP. Bill Shockley was still toying with transistors at Bell Labs and hadn't yet made the move to California, where the defense industry was already well established. The military would later become key to the development of the semiconductor industry, and important to my father.

He made good money picking and packing apricots, but the skinny, geeky kid from a working class family wanted more out of life. His father earned a steady paycheck and a pension as a railroad worker, but that was equally unappealing. My father was determined to get a college education.

The family had no savings for tuition, but fortunately my father had one special skill: he could run fast. Very fast. After distinguishing himself in high school, becoming the Northern

California Scholastic Federation champion as a mid and long-distance runner, he secured a scholarship to attend college at Idaho State. At first, all went well both on and off the track. But he was unprepared for the altitude. In his first season with the track team he damaged his lungs. The injury wasn't debilitating but it made him uncompetitive, and he lost his scholarship.

With nowhere else to turn, he joined the army. Getting accepted into officer training or West Point was out of the question, but in 1944 Congress passed the GI Bill, which would cover the cost of his four-year college education in exchange for military service.

Throughout World War II, Hollywood pumped out propaganda that glamorized military service, and boys like my father gobbled it up. Therefore the thought of getting shot at as an infantry soldier on the front lines was far from his mind as he signed his papers. He was immediately given a series of tests, and again fortune smiled on my father by giving him skills: the test revealed an extraordinary aptitude for breaking codes. He was great at recognizing patterns, which was also important for learning languages.

In military intelligence he was given a choice, which is rare in the army. He could study Russian, Arabic, or Chinese. By chance, he had walked past a restaurant on his way to the recruiting office and wondered about the peculiar writing scrawled on the window. He chose Chinese.

The Defense Language Institute, known as DLI, was in the coastal town of Monterey. My father remembers little of the rugged California coastline, the cypress groves, or sun-washed hills. The deal was this: the army needed twenty Chinese speakers. Therefore they enrolled seventy men into the program. Each week an exam would identify the weakest candidate. That man would immediately be removed from military intelligence and sent to the front lines. Life expectancy on the front lines of any war was low, giving the men powerful motivation to study.

"We were under constant pressure that sticks in your gut," my father recalls. "None of us wanted to fail. We would listen to Chinese phrases over and over on a phonograph. At lights out the power was cut, so I would put the player under my arm and walk back to my quarters in the dark." Week after week, the exam placed him near the bottom of his class, just above the cut line. But a year on he had climbed to the top. As a reward, the army shipped him to Korea.

Like many Americans, my understanding of the Korean war and the impact it had on US-China relations was murky before going to Asia. Most of what I knew about what happened in Korea came from the TV series MASH, which was about an American field hospital treating soldiers in what I thought was just a civil war on the Korean peninsula. It was more than that.

Korea has a tragic history and Koreans suffer even today as a result of misunderstandings and miscalculations not of their own making. To be clear, the war started because North Korea invaded the South, but the split between North and South Korea happened because of mistrust between the Soviet Union and the United States, having little to do with the Koreans, or with the Chinese who did most of the dying in the conflict.

In the closing days of World War II, there was little trust between the Soviet Union and the United States, despite having fought as allies against the Nazis and the Japanese. Stalin and Truman couldn't agree on which side would accept Japan's surrender in Korea. Instead they took a Solomonic approach and divided the peninsula in two, along the thirty-eighth parallel. The United States controlled the south and supported a puppet government under Syngman Rhee. The Soviets had a puppet of their own, one they found more difficult to control. Kim Il-sung, the grandfather of today's North Korean leader Kim Jong-un, was a brash young leader with grand ambitions.

Kim Il-sung was a guerrilla fighter. Details about his personal history are murky and contested by academics, but it is generally believed that whatever name he made for himself as a military man came from his experience fighting the Japanese in Manchuria. In 1950, Kim got Stalin's permission to invade the south and unify the peninsula under a communist banner and in a surprise attack, he was almost able to accomplish that militarily. Seoul, the capital of the south, fell in the first few days and Kim pushed the South Korean army to Pusan at the far southern end of the peninsula before American forces arrived in sufficient numbers to provide support.

American forces were experienced and well-equipped, and used military tactics that were honed fighting the Japanese. General Douglas MacArthur's "Incheon landing" became legendary for its audacity, and its success. Incheon lies on the coast just west of Seoul, and was thought to be impenetrable because of its natural defenses. The seawall, currents, and extreme tides make an amphibious landing nearly impossible and extremely dangerous. If an initial invasion failed before the tide went out, then ships stuck in the mud would be easy targets for North Korean gunners. MacArthur chose Incheon anyway, gambling that it would be poorly defended for exactly those reasons. He was right.

MacArthur's attack was an unambiguous success, and within a month over 135,000 North Korean troops had been killed or captured. Stalin had permitted Kim to invade but he did not promise any real support, and he declined to send reinforcements. Stalin was concerned about engaging the Americans directly with ground troops, and although he eventually sent a few MIG fighter aircraft, his support for the war was half-hearted at best.

The Americans, fighting under the banner of the United Nations, decimated the North Korean army.

The United Nations condemned North Korea's attack, and the Soviet Union was at that point boycotting the organization for continuing to recognize the Republic of China (by then moved to Taiwan) instead of the communist People's Republic of China. Therefore, North Korea's only allies were not present when the vote was taken for the United Nations Security Council on sending troops to the peninsula.

From Beijing, Mao Zedong observed what was happening with horror. He had been preparing his own assault on Taiwan, where Chiang Kai-shek was holed up. He knew that Chiang was still protected and supplied by the Americans, but now he saw the Americans move even closer to the land border on his northern flank. American troops, in an awesome show of force, recaptured the entire Korean peninsula and could easily move across the Yalu River into northern China.

Back in the United States, President Truman was a staunch anti-communist, but he was also cautious about provoking China. Beijing had already signaled that American troops moving north of the 38th parallel would be an issue. Truman's military commander, Douglas MacArthur, had political ambitions of his own and pressed his boss for permission to attack China. Truman refused.

Today, the declassified documents show that the US never had any intention to invade or conquer China. The military had no operational plan to do so, and President Truman's private statements were consistent with his public pronouncements that he would not widen the war beyond Korea, which would have also been politically unpopular. Invading China would almost certainly have drawn the Soviet Union into the conflict, and legally, any attack or effort at regime change in China would have violated the UN resolution that only authorized "restoration of international peace and security in Korea."

However, Washington's actions created enough ambiguity for Beijing to misread US policy. UN forces pushed all the way to the Yalu River, and MacArthur's public rhetoric—at odds with the president's actual policy—further muddied the picture, much as assertive statements from Congress members can do today, a structural feature of the American political system. The result was a dangerous gap between American intentions and Chinese perception—an ambiguity that convinced Beijing that it faced an existential threat.

As a result, China entered the war. The North Korean army had already been neutralized, so for the next two years, foreign troops from the United States and its allies and China fought each other on Korean soil. Troops from twenty-two countries including Turkey, Canada, and the United Kingdom fought under the United Nations Command. And also the Republic of China, which by then meant Taiwan.

My father worked alongside soldiers from Taiwan, some of whom he knew were spies for China. Mao sent men to infiltrate Chiang's forces in Taiwan. Some of them took the opportunity to switch sides, and joined up with the Americans. Others pretended to but didn't. Separating friend from foe was nearly impossible, since they all spoke the same language. Some of these men tattooed their bodies to demonstrate their allegiance. "The soldiers from Taiwan were Department of the Army Civilians, or DACS, but we called them 'ducks'," my father explained. "They didn't seem to mind. The British and Americans called each other much worse. It's what soldiers do."

Mao knew that men were switching sides, and distrusted his own troops who were captured in Korea. According to reports, some were executed after they were returned to China at the end of the war. I don't know if this is true or not, but the repatriation of prisoners was a major sticking point in negotiations to end the war. Mao wanted prisoners returned to China, but the Americans demanded that they be given a choice. This prolonged the fighting, but the American position was finally accepted. Most Chinese prisoners chose not to return to China.

By the time the fighting stopped, over 30,000 Americans and more than 100,000 Chinese were dead, and millions of Koreans were left homeless and impoverished. The war left the entire peninsula, north and south, in ruins. There was no winner, only death, destruction, and misery.

Chinese propaganda describes this as a victory, but it was actually a draw. My father believed that was the result of orders that restricted the ability of the UN forces to engage. "Our orders were to not engage the enemy with a force larger than a platoon," he told me. He primarily worked as a decoder in the field, but the Army also assigned him to Washington for duties in Special Intelligence at Arlington Hall, where the National Security Agency supported functions in addition to cryptography.

Washington restricted the military commanders in the field, directing them to hold positions at the 38th parallel and limiting offensive engagements that would have pushed the Chinese troops further north. America in the early 1950s had no overwhelming enthusiasm for the war, having just finished fighting the Nazis and imperial Japan. Full occupation of North Korea was not the objective, as that was politically unpalatable to American voters at the time.

Washington politicos thought they had solved the problem by placing limits on the activities of US forces in Korea, but the strategy caused massive casualties in the field. My father said: "Mao's basic principle in battle was to attack only with overwhelming force and surprise. On the MLR (main line of resistance), the Chinese would quietly shift units to concentrate their strength. They would launch sudden attacks that penetrated to some depth, remove whatever equipment they had surrounded, then withdraw."

This tactic partly accounts for the high death toll in the Korean War. It took the war in Vietnam ten years to kill as many Americans as were killed in Korea in three, but the human wave tactics on the Chinese side caused far greater numbers of casualties.

"Radio transmissions were unencrypted back then," my father told me. "We could hear everything, even though it was hard to understand with the profanity and dialects mixed in. We broke their codes and figured out their positions by creating action, then listening to how they reported it. Working at night in Korea was frightening and none of us liked it but we did it."

An armistice was finally reached in July of 1953 with South Korea preserved as an independent non-communist state, which later flourished into a prosperous democracy. The People's Republic of China, meanwhile, achieved its goal of retaining North Korea as a buffer state while also ending what it *incorrectly perceived* as an existential threat. Over the decades following the war, an uncomfortable armistice has remained in place with 35,000 American troops more or less permanently stationed in South Korea. Added to that were troops stationed in Japan and, until 1992, the Philippines. The United States had as many as 5,000 troops stationed in Taiwan until President Nixon's visit to Beijing. The Chinese government felt threatened and vulnerable, and for most of the three decades after the PRC was established, the primary enemy was perceived to be the United States, with the Soviet Union taking top spot for much of the 1960s. Today, Beijing continues to view North Korea as a strategic barrier, and consequently tolerates, and provides much support to the country, despite many efforts by the US over the decades to get Beijing's support to rein in Pyongyang.

I came to China because of my family, but the growth opportunities in the region continued to lure me back to Asia throughout my business career. I started in management consulting, but most of my work has been at the intersection of finance and technology. I worked for Apple, managing operations across Asia, from Australia to India, and other regions. As a tech banker with HSBC, I covered markets in Asia with a particular focus on mainland China, Taiwan, and Hong Kong. Before China's incredible growth, Japan was the major market in Asia, especially for American technology, but South Korea was fast catching up.

I learned a lot from my colleagues overseas. I learned about their cultures and traditions, their food, and their business practices, but I also learned to see things from different perspectives. Not everyone lives in a country that is a superpower and has little to fear from its neighbors.

Conflicts often arise from differences in perspective. Beijing claims that certain territories "are and always have been part of the Chinese nation," referring to Tibet and other regions that were part of China, except when they weren't. Whether we accept these arguments as valid, The United States is a relatively new nation forged from land that was already occupied by others. Huge pieces of America's land were purchased and fought over and Americans have a very practical and some might say transactional view of land. China does not. China's borders have shifted considerably over thousands of years, but most Chinese people have a strong sense of the territory that they believe belongs to them.

America is confident about where it stands, perhaps at times too confident, and the role our nation plays in the world. As a nation, China seems at times obsessed with competing with the United States, and perhaps this is part of the reason why China, once a powerful and much-admired nation that led the world in economic activity, art and science for most of human history, is still looking for where it fits in the world of nations.

From Beijing, for reasons that perhaps relate to a dearth of self-confidence, Western influence is not necessarily seen as benign. The US Navy operates in international waters not far from China's coast and throughout the South China Sea, as it operates in international waters around the world. Its ships dock at friendly ports from Singapore to Sydney, extending north to Japan and South Korea, and haven until recently regularly visited Hong Kong, and occasionally Shanghai. According to the US Indo-Pacific Command, based near Honolulu, approximately 375,000 American military and civilian personnel are stationed in the Asia Pacific region,[5] including forces stationed in Alaska, Hawaii, and Guam. Of these, the number based in Japan, South Korea and a smattering of other locations is about 80,000, a number that has not changed much since the late 1970s. Of course, the area of responsibility for these forces encompasses far more than just China, but seen from Beijing they can appear threatening.

My father, for whom the Korean peninsula was a war-torn wasteland, couldn't believe his son was doing business there. My trips to South Korea became more frequent after my job changed to a regional role, covering markets throughout Asia. The team in each market had distinct characteristics and personalities. The

5 According to US Indo-Pacific Command, approximately 375,000 American military and civilian personnel are stationed in the Asia Pacific region. U S Indo-Pacific Command, "Headquarters, United States Indo-Pacific Command."

crew in South Korea was all male, with a "work hard, play hard" mentality, but they were deadly serious about the business of winning.

"Did you see the news this morning?" My country manager, normally a very serious person, practically bounced into the lobby of his office to greet me. Kevin Yi, a former professional baseball player, was a charismatic leader who pushed his team to the limit for results. "It was awesome. We have done well." I was confused, but I soon realized he was referring to the video footage on the TV that morning from the Middle East.

It was March of 2003. The much-anticipated war in Iraq had finally begun, and CNN was broadcasting live images of smart bombs hitting targets the size of garbage can lids from 30,000 feet. My country manager was right: the combination of precision and power was truly awe-inspiring.

His use of "we" was the same "we" that is used when the home team wins a big game. Every touchdown, each caught pass, and all the made plays belong to each of "us" as if we had made that tackle personally. South Korea is a fiercely independent country, but on this day my Korean friends basked in the collective glory of a resounding military accomplishment and victory for the home team. South Korea was very much on Team USA.

South Korea does a great deal of trade with China and has major investment projects there, but from a military and security point of view it is aligned with—and dependent on—the United States military. With 35,000 American troops stationed on the peninsula, there is no question about who will be involved if the South is attacked.

China has no reason to attack South Korea, although it supports its rival North Korea with food, oil, and other commodities despite international sanctions prohibiting such shipments. Beijing is, however, very uncomfortable with South

Korea's security alliance with the United States. In July 2016, following increased missile threats from the North, South Korea announced a decision to deploy a Terminal High Altitude Area Defense (THAAD) anti-missile system, supplied by the United States. Beijing was furious, stating that the move "undermines China's strategic security interest." For the next year or more, prompted by the government, Chinese consumers boycotted and harassed South Korean businesses, targeting everything from Lotte department stores to K-pop stars. (Samsung's semiconductor business in China was left untouched.)

The war in Iraq did not involve China or South Korea directly, but the Koreans were proud and impressed with the United States as their military partner. The view of the war from Beijing was entirely different, as I would come to appreciate in the years that followed. In hindsight, the war in Iraq contributed significantly to the shift in US-China relations. By invading Iraq the United States not only demonstrated awesome military capabilities, but also a willingness to remove a regime that was deemed dangerous to the region or to Western interests. From that point forward, Beijing included this in calculations involving its own security.

A conclusion possibly drawn in Beijing was that the United States had the capability and willingness to bend countries to its will, and that what happened to Saddam Hussein and his Ba'ath party could conceivably happen to the CCP.

The relative peace between the United States and China starting in the 1970s did not come easily or by accident, and it had everything to do with the Soviet Union. Similar to China's current leader, Xi Jinping, Mao looked to Moscow immediately after taking power and quickly established a rapport with his ideological brethren. In fact, Mao made several trips to the Soviet Union, which was unusual for a man who otherwise never traveled abroad. After Stalin's death in 1953, Mao and Khrushchev differed on policy and ideology, and Sino-Soviet relations deteriorated. Tensions increased throughout the 1960s, resulting in a border war in 1969 and thousands of Soviet experts leaving China.

Mao continued to distrust the leadership in Moscow, probably largely due to the paranoia that grew on him with age, but that didn't immediately translate into warm feelings toward the United States. However, as it became clear that the United States would not prevail in Vietnam, which would have put an occupying force on China's southern border, a thaw in the ice became possible and Mao felt comfortable opening discussions with America's president. For both parties the primary reason for establishing a relationship was a concern about the Soviet Union.

Getting the Americans out of Vietnam was helpful, but it didn't solve all of China's problems. China has land borders with fourteen countries, and to this day, it has either historical conflicts or outright border disputes with many of them.[6] In addition, China has maritime disputes arising from its claims in the South and East China Seas. Mao knew that China needed friends, and decided to test whether a relationship with Washington could provide a counterbalance against Moscow.

His timing was good. America's anticommunist fervor of the 1950s had died down, and animosity was pointed more directly at Moscow rather than communism per se. In the 1960s Americans were becoming more curious about China, although reports trickling out about the Cultural Revolution presented a

6 Some are historical conflicts going back to the ROC. Only three are actively pursued by the PRC. Sea disputes are more numerous .

confusing picture. Mao had empowered a radical faction within the party that created havoc, but in general Americans knew little of that, and saw China as a simply being poor, isolated and far away. Certainly nowhere near as threatening as the Soviet Union.

Richard Nixon, as he prepared his campaign to run for president, wrote in *Foreign Affairs* that "There is no place on this small planet for a billion of its potentially most able people to live in angry isolation."[7] Circumstances had shifted, bringing the United States and China back to the table and eventually to diplomatic recognition, but the relationship has remained fragile and often fraught.

Therefore, when an American Secretary of State makes a speech about China, as Mike Pompeo did in the final days of the first Trump administration, and talks about the legitimacy of China's government and the possibility of the Chinese people rising up against the CCP, these are not taken as idle words. Pompeo's speech in 2020 on US-China relations, made at the Nixon library, came to within an inch of calling for regime change in China.[8]

For various reasons not unrelated to fragility and levels of self-confidence, there were people in Beijing who took those remarks seriously and as more than simply American election year rhetoric. The party has its own justifications for keeping China's historical conflicts with Japan and the West fresh in the minds of the general public. Having an enemy to point to is a powerful motivator and can justify all manner of actions if need be. Lingling Wei, the China-born author of "Superpower Showdown," describes the military exercises she was required

7 *Foreign Affairs:* "Asia After Viet Nam," by Richard M. Nixon. October 1, 1967.

8 Richard Nixon Foundation: "Event Recap: Secretary Pompeo at the Nixon Library." July 29, 2020.

to do as a schoolgirl. "Imagine the target is an American," her shooting instructor told her.[9]

Ironically, as the Chinese government defends what it sees as national honor, it comes across as weak and insecure even as the country uses its enormous market power to bend smaller nations to its will. Today, the sight of a country as large and powerful as China constantly plays the victim is puzzling, but official spokespeople in Beijing throw fits in response to any minor infraction that "harms China" or "hurts the feelings of the Chinese people." "China doesn't want war." A woman in the back of the room put up her hand to speak. I was giving a talk at Books by the Bay, a shop in Sausalito near my home in San Francisco. She apparently objected to my answers as I replied to questions about why China was using navy destroyers to ram Filipino fishing boats and sending as many as fifty fighter planes a day into Taiwan's airspace. Xi Jinping has reportedly instructed his military to be prepared to take Taiwan by force by the year 2027.

"China has always been peaceful and never starts wars," she added, explaining that her ancestors were from China, but she had never actually lived there. This was a familiar refrain, often repeated from the dais at China's Ministry of Foreign Affairs, as the United States was criticized for yet another military adventure.

First, I asked what she meant by "China," because this could mean the CCP, which makes decisions and takes actions on behalf of the country, or the government, or PLA military leaders or the people of China. China is not a monolith, and there is a diversity of views within the country, but I had no problem agreeing that nobody wanted war. No sane person would. Not only that, if by

9 Lingling Wei and Bob Davis, "Superpower Showdown," page 6.

"China" she meant the Chinese people, and specifically Chinese people from the countryside where most soldiers come from, then she was absolutely correct. Families with only one son would never want to risk going to war.

On other facts, and the idea that China has never attacked other countries, I had to correct her. China fought a war with Vietnam in 1979. Beijing creatively described it as the "Self-defensive counterattack," and it's a fact that Chinese troops crossed the border into Vietnam, not the other way around. China fought Russia in a border conflict in 1969, and with India in 1962. According to Beijing's view, Tibet has been a part of China since the beginning of time, but in 1951 it was the PLA which brought the territory under the control of the CCP.

Great powers use great force, and the United States and China are the same in this aspect. The US has effected regime change in various countries over the past few decades, and it has had an impact on politics in South Korea and Japan at various points since 1945. Yet countries in Asia, including China, have ultimately benefited from the security and prosperity afforded by the American-led order, Pax Americana.

President Carter's National Security Advisor, Zbigniew Brzezinski, summed up this view in his foundational book, *The Grand Chessboard*, writing:

> "For China, America across the Pacific should be a natural ally since America has no designs on the Asian mainland and has historically opposed both Japanese and Russian encroachment on a weaker China. To the Chinese, Japan has been the principal enemy over the last century; Russia, the "hungry land" in Chinese, has long been distrusted; and India, too, now looms as a potential rival. The principle 'my neighbor's neighbor

> is my ally' thus fits the geopolitical and historical relationship between China and America."

My aunt had asked me, "If we have a war, which side will you be on?" She wanted to know where I stood, as a person with both Chinese and American roots. I thought a long time about the answer before saying to my aunt: "If your mother and father get into a fight, do you want one side to win? Or do you just want the fight to be over?"

PART 2

CROSSING THE RIVER BY FEELING THE STONES

"I believe it to be the duty of everyone to unite in the restoration of the country and the reestablishment of peace and harmony."
— Robert E. Lee

Chapter 4

Shanghaied by the Boston Consulting Group

It was a blazing hot August day in Shanghai. The compound of the Shanghai First Works of Electrical Apparatus Company, a leading producer of electrical switches in China at the time, was deserted as workers went to find shade and cool off wherever they could. The sprawling industrial complex composed of cement buildings of indeterminate age or purpose belonged to a state-owned enterprise under the Shanghai Mechanical and Electrical Industries Bureau. The temperature dropped at least five degrees as I stepped out of the sun and into a workshop. I had started the day in a suit but managed to shed the jacket. I could retrieve it later from the conference room where we had begun our tour. The shift supervisor, a tiny little man of uncertain age, accompanied me through the compound. His skin was dark and leathery. He wore a white short-sleeved shirt with a collar, with several pens tucked into the breast pocket. His baggy pants were held up with a belt that was too long by at least a foot, so it wrapped almost twice around his thin waist. He seemed unbothered by the heat.

Boxes of metal parts were scattered around, and a half-assembled machine was shoved in a corner next to a work table, but the tools had been removed, perhaps locked up so they wouldn't disappear. A mission to clean the shop floor was left abandoned, with a push broom dropped on the floor next to a pile of trash and dirt. My companion guided me through the buildings as I looked for ways to improve the operational efficiency of the sprawling, lethargic enterprise.

The year was 1990, and I was touring factories because after two years of business school I still had no clear direction for my career. I reckoned that a year or two in management consulting could help me find one. On my first day in the San Francisco office of the Boston Consulting Group, I met Bob Ching. He was the senior partner, and I learned later he was revered throughout the firm, earning him the right to do as he pleased, and at that moment what pleased him was sending new associates to China to help reconstruct a new nation. Bob was born in Shanghai but left for Taiwan after the communists took over. His career with BCG, as the firm is known, took him all over the world, advising CEOs and helping governments. And now he had the opportunity to return to China and deliver what the country so badly needed: management advice.

Bob was tall and soft spoken, which are unusual characteristics for a southern Chinese. A physicist by training, he was more of a philosopher than a businessman, and he tended to answer questions with more questions, an annoying habit to a young man looking for answers. Today he often sports a white, wispy beard that gives him a Gandalf-like aura. He was clean-shaven back then, but the aura was already there.

Bob knew that China would need to move step by step to modernize its systems and business practices, and managers would eventually need to find their own way. He was there to help, but he doled out the building blocks of modern business only when his client had learned enough to know what to ask for. To this day, my conversations with Bob are like trying to change the shape of a cloud, as his answers push me to ask better questions.

Bob sifted through the resumes of dozens of new associates who had just joined the firm and plucked out anyone with relevant language skills, which landed me on his team. He put me on a plane to Shanghai and sent me walking through factories looking for how we could make improvements.

Using lecture notes from courses I had completed only months before, I got busy giving talks on management theories and business methodologies to the managers at the Shanghai First Works of Electrical Apparatus Company. It was slow going, hampered by the fact that I had never done this even in English, much less Chinese, and we had few common points of reference. China had been isolated for decades, and information about capitalist societies was actively kept out of the country. How could we work through a case study about Volkswagen when nobody had actual experience with a car?

It was hard to know where to begin, but harder still to believe that places like this would soon become the world's factory for every kind of product imaginable, from umbrellas to underwear. In the 1990s, China was ramping up quickly, mostly making products to meet domestic demand. At that time, the country with a fifth of the world's population produced less than three percent of global manufacturing output.[1] China's economy was still primarily agrarian, but it was on its way to becoming an industrial manufacturing export-oriented economy. Enterprises like the Shanghai First Works of Electrical Apparatus Company had a long way to go before it could aspire to making iPhones or

1 *The Economist:* "Made in China?" March 12, 2015. "In 1990 it produced less than 3% of global manufacturing output by value; its share now is nearly a quarter. China produces about 80% of the world's air-conditioners, 70% of its mobile phones and 60% of its shoes."

semiconductors.

My guide, the shift supervisor, brought me to a room with a tall ceiling that echoed and amplified the sound of machines and steel. A metal stamper stood in the middle of the room. It was narrow, about thirty feet high, and functioned by using a motor to lift a large, heavy object and then slamming it down on a metal sheet. An old man—he looked ninety but was probably in his forties—crouched at the base, moving the sheet of metal slightly after each impact.

The supervisor pointed around the room, trying to explain the stamping process but with the noise I could make out only one word out of ten. We were in the room for less than three minutes, but when we left my ears were ringing and I'd lost the ability to hear anything but dull sounds.

"How long is that guy's shift?" I asked, pointing back at the room while trying to get away from the noise as quickly as possible.

"Same as the others," my guide said, waiving an arm, "but he gets a break every three hours because of the noise."

"I wonder what he does when he goes home from work? Do you think he enjoys Peking opera?" I asked, facetiously. My ears still rang from the brief exposure. The old man would be there for three hours, continuously. Throughout my tour I saw not a single person wearing ear protection. There was no sign of gloves, hard hats, steel-toe boots, or protective gear of any kind.

"Of course not!" The supervisor laughed. "He can't hear a thing!"

"Exactly..." I muttered to myself as we walked away. I wondered how many more workers became deaf or otherwise maimed, and what became of them if they could no longer work.

Our next stop was a room labeled "Parts Supplies." Shelf after shelf contained boxes of oddly shaped gizmos and widgets.

Some boxes were opened or had a few parts taped to the top of the box, indicating its contents.

"This is amazing!" I was impressed with the size, but I was curious about the haphazard way in which everything was stored. Unlike the other rooms, it was clean but there seemed to be no structure, with boxes of pipes stored next to copper wires, placed amidst jugs of unlabeled but toxic-looking chemicals. "What's your inventory management system?" Again, the supervisor gave me a blank look so I tried again. "How do you find things here?"

He lit up with a proud grin. "Oh, we have a very good inventory management system." He emphasized the word *system,* using the term he had just heard from me, which I'm fairly sure he didn't use often. "Our system is very good. We have an old man. He's the only one with the keys to this room, and he knows where everything is!" After my sarcastic remark about Peking opera, I wasn't going to ask what would happen if the man didn't come into work. Or how old he was. That would be a problem for another day.

We moved to a different part of the workshop where wires were carefully placed into a plastic harness that was then baked into a single unit. It was a standard operation to assemble low-voltage switches. "What's your yield from this machine?" I had looked up the Chinese word for "yield" along with other terms I would need to ask questions about the business. The supervisor understood the meaning of my words, but he couldn't make sense of my question and gave me a puzzled look.

"Yield. How many of these units work, and how many fail?" After a long pause, I pressed on. "Out of a thousand units that come off this line how many can you ship to a customer?"

The supervisor brightened. "All of them!" I gazed at the parts flying by on a conveyor and wondered how that could be possible.

I had done similar work in Taiwan, where we measured and tested everything. We measured the time it took to work down inventory, how long machines were idle, and we spot-tested to make sure products worked properly before they were shipped to a customer or moved to the next stage of assembly. We tested semiconductor packages, ensuring the diodes were connecting. I once interviewed a woman whose job was to take one of every twenty units out of work in process inventory and connect it to a device that ran current through it. A light went on if the device worked. If not, her job was to pull a cord to stop the machine and call a supervisor. She kept meticulous records, which she showed me with great pride. Taiwan, with its manufacturing quality standards and business practices, was decades ahead of Shanghai.

I stood in front of the machine that cranked out one piece every three seconds and dropped it from the conveyor into a plastic bin. "All of them? So you have 100% yield off this machine? That's very impressive. Can I see the test results?"

"What tests?" My guide was uncomfortable being asked questions for which he had no answer and I could sense he was getting irritated.

"The tests showing that all your switches work. Where are the records?"

"Oh, these things are very flimsy. Of course they don't all work. How could they? They are made of the cheapest material, and the workers who assemble the wires just throw them together. We don't test. Our job is to ship everything!"

The supervisor was right about one thing. The switches cost about three cents each to make. The problem was the switches would be built into much larger machines that cost tens of thousands of dollars, and they needed reliable switches. If one switch failed the entire machine could malfunction, bringing an even larger process to a halt, which is why quality control is so important. In advanced manufacturing environments quality control workers often wear white hard hats, indicating a special status on the factory floor. It's one thing to hang a sign at the entrance that says quality matters; it's another to empower "white hats" to bring the entire operation to a halt if they see something that could adversely affect the quality of the end product. In 1990, factories in China hadn't even put up the sign yet.

Scheduled maintenance was another area where Western business practices clashed with Chinese sensibilities. The Chinese are a frugal people, perhaps by nature, but maybe as a result of decades of scarcity and making do. These habits have changed over time, but when I first arrived in China I saw factory workers toil away in the dark rather than turn on the lights. Naturally, this created quality and safety issues but they were able to save on electricity. I pointed this out and always got the same response: *"women xiguan le!"* We're accustomed to it!

Workers in China tended to ignore instructions about scheduled maintenance, preferring to use things until they break. In some circumstances their reluctance to waste could be seen as a virtue, but China now makes airplanes and high-speed trains. Each component has a specific function and an expected life span. A fuel pump in a jet engine, for example, might be designed to work for a certain number of flying hours before needing to be replaced. A maintenance worker would know this, but they might pull out the pump, look to see that it appears to be working, and put it back in the plane instead of replacing it. That's not a problem for a tractor, since a tractor won't fall out of the sky when the engine fails. Chinese managers learn quickly, but the presence of Western companies—and people like Bob

Ching— accelerated the process.

Our factory tour concluded, and we made our way back to the conference room for a discussion about marketing. Several of the shift supervisor's colleagues were waiting for us, drinking tea and chewing on watermelon seeds. A chubby fellow sitting toward the middle of the room seemed to delight in using his mouth to skillfully separate the seeds from the husk, which he was spitting on the floor. He seemed like the boss.

I took a seat across from him and began sifting through the stack of papers they had prepared for me. "How can you be so precise with your estimates of future sales?" I asked. Volume estimates going out five and ten years were listed down to three decimal points. I asked about best case and worst case scenarios, but my questions drew blank looks. "Are you sure about the market conditions going out five years? What about competition?"

"Competition? What do you mean?" The chubby boss grinned as he took a sip of tea. "The government assigns us this much to produce, so that's what we do!"

In the 1990s, running a business according to market principles was still a new idea in China. The Chinese had spent decades believing capitalist ideas were harmful to society. They had no playbook, no methodology, and no experience with basic concepts like supply and demand.

While children in America set up lemonade stands, experimenting with costs and pricing, Chinese children were learning to quote Mao Zedong and recite Marxist-Leninist slogans. Deng Xiaoping famously coined the phrase *"mo shi guo he,"* meaning "to cross the stream by feeling the stones." Deng admitted that he had no idea how China's giant, lumbering, economy would respond to his policies, but he went forward anyway. He learned as he went, putting in place policies that would shape China for the next decades. Similarly, business managers were also learning as they went.

Lack of experience and the absence of a common vocabulary presented challenges, but our job as foreign consultants was made even more difficult when we found that skills enabling managers to thrive in a state-owned enterprise environment were the exact opposite of what we were looking for to modernize and improve the business.

In the 1990s, a job at a state-owned enterprise, or SOE as they are commonly called, was a major prize (and has become so again today as the economy plateaus). An SOE provided steady pay, opportunities for growth, and most important, status. A climb up the ladder required managers to be obedient, not innovative, following orders without question. The idea was to conform, to blend in, to be a cog in the giant wheel that was China's political and economic system at the time.

The idea, then and now, was control. The SOEs have always been instruments of political control, allowing the party to steer the course, manage employment, and guide the economy. Now, after decades of market driven growth and productivity gains and in a new era in which control and national security are paramount concerns, the SOEs have been assigned a stronger role in the economy.

Before 1978, when China's reforms started to be put in place, nearly three-fourths of industrial production was produced by state-owned enterprises.[2] In the 1990s China was still very much a centrally planned economy, although the policies put in place by Deng Xiaoping were changing that on an almost daily basis. Deng's policy of "reform and opening up" had to undo decades of bureaucratic thinking, although it should always

2 Congressional Research Service: "China's Economic Rise: History, Trends, Challenges, and Implications for the United States." June 25, 2019

be remembered that the party's ultimate control was him of paramount importance. With his encouragement, in the sectors opened up, China's entrepreneurs began to wake up.

Foreign companies were also encouraged by the policies, even though they continued to be highly restricted. Companies entering China in the 1980s and early 1990s understood that everything was prohibited, except what the government explicitly allowed. It would take three decades for China's policymakers to at least formally reverse course and shift to a "negative list" for foreign investment. In 2018 the National Development and Reform Commission (NDRC) finally declared all sectors in China to be open to foreign investment except for those that were expressly prohibited. The list was long, but it represented a shift in thinking toward a market-oriented approach.

Looking back at the 1990s and the early 2000s, the years on either side of China's accession to WTO, what were Beijing's true intentions? Was there a genuine commitment to integrate with the global economy led by the West, and could that have led to reciprocal benefits and a long lasting relationship? Or was "reform and opening up" simply a pragmatic expedient and temporary measure for China to get what it needed? The answer depends on which China you're talking about—the country is not a monolith. Undoubtedly there were people who saw China's future as being inextricably linked with the West—exchanging students, sharing technology, and participating in each others' markets. But as we will see in later chapters, there has always been those party who could not abide the dilution of control this would involve. Once China achieved a certain level of development, they pushed the door shut. Xi Jinping personifies—and now leads—this group, taking the rest of the country with him.

Chapter 5

Built on Borrowed Strength

The BCG methodology was best known for its matrix that categorized businesses into "cash cows" to be milked for profit and "rising stars" that were worthy of investment. But in Shanghai, our focus was on people. I continued learning from my boss and mentor, Bob Ching, as we searched for people we could work with to break the mold, do things differently, and shake up a sclerotic system that rewarded workers who spent day after day producing, packaging, and shipping products that they knew didn't work. We found many such people. In a country as large and diverse as China it was possible to find nearly anything, and even in 1990 there existed people who somehow passed through China's educational system without completely losing their ability to challenge the status quo or think critically.

China's educational system is optimized for something very specific, and different from what Western liberal education endeavors to do. Throughout history, the Chinese people have often suffered from chaos and instability, whether from foreign intrusions such as the Mongols and the Japanese or internal weakness or strife, typified by the Taiping Rebellion. Either way, *"pa luan"*—the fear of chaos—is burned into the minds of ordinary Chinese, making them willing to put up with a lot in order to enjoy stability, including an educational system that serves them poorly.

China's educational system works well for the purpose for which it was designed—obedience. It is much easier to control a group of people who have been taught that there is such a thing as the correct opinion, and the best answer is the one the teacher is looking for. The goal is to remember and repeat it.

The author Lenora Chu describes this in her book, *Little Soldiers*. She enrolled her son in one of Shanghai's finest local schools, and conducted five years of research on the system. Chu, a Chinese-American journalist and author, describes many of the positive aspects of Chinese education, including discipline, perseverance, and teamwork. Her son was also well-schooled in the fundamentals of math, science, and of course Chinese and English. But was the spark of self-expression ever allowed? While Chu was observing classes at another Shanghai kindergarten, she saw that all the children were taught to draw rain in exactly the same way. Those of us who have experienced the joy of being around small children know there is no such thing as a "correct" drawing, and that children have limitless ways to interpret the world around them and express what they see. This is the seed of creativity, which is precisely what the Chinese educational system dampens.

Chu describes how the teacher demonstrated that "rain falls from the sky to the ground and comes in little dots," and required all students to populate their pages methodically from top to bottom. In a Chinese classroom, Chu writes, "Rain does not blow sideways, nor does it hurtle to the earth in sheets. There are no hurricanes or monsoons. There is no figurative rain, such as raining tears, or raining frogs, or raining cats and dogs. There is no purple rain."

This system is successful in many ways, and some graduates still manage to be incredibly creative, although skeptics would say these people have succeeded in spite of the system and not because of it. The accomplishments in math and science are irrefutable, but for the most part the system results in discipline, conformity, and obedience, producing disciplined workers but stifling creativity and critical thinking—a major weakness in today's knowledge-based global economy.

Our goal at BCG was to find people who had been through this system, but for whatever reason could still generate new ideas and put into practice alternative ways of doing things. Ideally, they could promote change from within and bring others along on a path toward market-driven practices. This way, our small team of consultants could create leverage and help to transform the giant state-owned enterprises into more efficient and productive entities.

Unfortunately, whenever we identified such a person on the staff of the SOE, we found that their goals didn't match ours. We wanted them to embrace a new role, leading task forces and working groups. In our consultant-speak vocabulary, they would become the "lighthouse" that would guide others who were willing to follow. We worked hard to make that path as rewarding as possible, but the managers we identified as potential lighthouses turned out not to be interested. In the early 1990s, bright ambitious people weren't excited about reforming SOEs or cooperating with management consultants. They only wanted one thing—to get out of China.

They were looking for sponsors who could help them apply for admission to American graduate schools where they would acquire advanced degrees. Many of these people stayed in America after graduation, contributing to an already highly educated and productive workforce. They joined companies or started their own, significantly contributing to the economy and the tax base in the United States.

But this has been a boon for China as well. Many of these former students, having worked abroad and acquired new skills, experience, and a Western way of doing things, have been recruited to return to China to work for American and Chinese companies. There are in fact so many of these people that a term has been added to the Chinese language to describe them. The term *hai gui* is a pun, which literally means "sea turtle," *hai* meaning "sea," and *gui* meaning "turtle." But *gui* with another character can also mean "return," and *hai* of course refers to overseas, giving the term additional meaning. Those who are familiar with the habits of sea turtles will be even more impressed with the cleverness of the term, knowing that sea turtles are among those species that eventually return to the place of their birth.

Chinese is an amazingly adaptable language that has specific terms for all manner of people. The *hai gui* is a term generally of admiration since this group for many years generally commanded a high salary and position, but the Chinese cleverly created an antithetical definition with the term *tu bie.* A *tu bie* is a tortoise, which is the land-bound relative of the sea turtle. As such, the term refers to someone who not only lacks overseas education but is, to put it politely, more earthy in his habits and outlook on life. The *tu* part of *tu bie* means "earth." Calling someone *tu* is the equivalent of calling them a country bumpkin.

There are other terms to describe people of Chinese ancestry who live outside China. The most common term is *hua qiao,* or "Chinese person abroad." Adding *meiji,* meaning American, gives us "*meiji huaqiao,*" for American-born (or long-term resident) Chinese. Even this term has a modification, *lao huaqiao,* which is a person of Chinese ancestry living overseas but who failed to come back to China, and therefore missed out on the opportunity to participate in China's spectacular growth years and presumably get rich in the process.

As if they haven't had enough fun with these terms already, in recent years Chinese people have turned the *hai gui* term around to describe people who studied overseas, returned to China, then left China again. These people are called *gui hai,* a term that carries with it a tinge of disloyalty. In a sign of how quickly reversals can occur in China, even the *hai gui*—the talented individuals with overseas experience who were so sought after in the 2000s and early 2010s—are sometimes now viewed with suspicion in the new hypersensitive political environment and no longer necessarily favored as executive leaders.

This may seem like an excess of energy going into the creation of these terms, but these groups of Chinese people have played an extremely important role in China's history and development, and the differences between them are meaningful in terms of skills, experience, and degree of loyalty. And tracking their movements provides important insights into the direction that China is headed today. For years, Western-educated Chinese returned home to start firms and share expertise. Today, heavy-handed political control, censorship, and career limits are driving talent out of China, just as they did in the early 1990s.

I left China myself around the mid-1990s, returning to the San Francisco Bay Area where businesses in Silicon Valley were playing around with a new toy called the World Wide Web. I took a job with Apple, working in the Macintosh System Architecture Division. In the 1990s, Apple sold no products at all in China, but my attention was still drawn to Asia. I found a home in an obscure corner of the company and began working on multilingual software. Today, computers can display any language using any script[3] in any document, but the 1990s the technologies that enabled this—protocols like Unicode and Worldscript—were just being developed. Our solutions became a big hit in Japan. For the next few years, I shuttled between Tokyo and Cupertino, then finally got myself posted to Hong Kong just as the British were about to hand the colony back to China in 1997.

My years in Hong Kong were amazing. The city was an intoxicating mix of East and West, and functioned with the consistency and precision of a Swiss watch. The government, directed from London, was believed to be highly competent, and incidents of corruption were rare. By and large, I saw few signs that Hong Kongers were dissatisfied with British rule, but still, many disliked the idea of living in a colony and pointed out the hypocrisy of not being allowed to vote for their top leadership. The British had introduced elections in India, Malaysia (Malaya), and Singapore before they became independent, but in Hong Kong they waited until a few years before the handover to implement reforms.

In 1992, a few years before I arrived, Chris Patten, a career politician, was appointed Governor of Hong Kong. He immediately introduced a number of reforms that significantly broadened the voting power of Hong Kongers by eliminating appointed seats on the Legislative Council, expanding functional constituencies to include virtually all working Hong Kongers, and lowering the voting age to 18. The reforms were popular, and the first elections demonstrated that democracy could work in the

3 A script refers to the writing system, which is different from language. Some scripts, like Hebrew, are written right to left instead of left to right, as the Roman alphabet does. Language like Arabic and Mongolian use contextual formatting, so certain letters might change shape depending on their position within the word.

majority Chinese British colony. Pro-democracy candidates won landslide victories in 1994 and 1995. The 1989 protests in Beijing and subsequent crackdown had increased Hong Kongers' sense of concern about the 1997 handover and how much autonomy they would retain. They were not wrong. Beijing was furious about the reforms, accusing the British of reneging on the terms of the handover agreement. Chinese officials labeled Patten the "sinner of a thousand years" and warned that the elected legislature would not be allowed to continue. True to their word, Beijing dismantled the entire structure immediately after reclaiming the territory in 1997, replacing the elected Legislative Council with an appointed Provisional Legislative Council.

Feelings about the handover in Hong Kong were decidedly mixed, encompassing a range of emotions, including hope, ambivalence, anxiety, distrust and regret. Many residents of Hong Kong had fled the mainland due to poverty, chaos, or political persecution, and were deeply skeptical of Beijing's commitment to keep Hong Kong "unchanged for 50 years" under the framework of one country, two systems. As it turned out, they were right. The business community was generally more optimistic, thankful for stability and a peaceful transition, and viewed unification as an opportunity for market growth and investment, which it also did. But some residents took to the streets to cheer as PLA soldiers marched across the border into Hong Kong and Prince Charles lowered the Union Jack for the last time.

Today, the overhaul of Hong Kong's governance structure in recent years has fundamentally altered its political and economic role. The National Security Law, the dismantling of independent institutions, and the reengineering of elections have ended the city's semi-autonomous status and removed many of the legal and political firewalls that once distinguished it from the mainland. This consolidation reminded everyone that nowhere within the PRC is beyond the reach of the central authority, giving rise to uncertainties on the rule of law, regulatory predictability, and protection of civil liberties. The result has been a decline in investor confidence, an accelerated outflow of talent and capital, and the weakening of what had been China's most credible and trusted interface with global markets. Hong Kong's transformation thus underscores a broader pattern: in the current era, political control takes precedence over economic openness, even at the cost of undermining China's own strategic assets.

In 1997, the Hong Kong handover was a significant event, and the landscape was changing quickly in other ways; China's entry into the World Trade Organization in 2001 was the big bang. Suddenly, China became a legitimate member of the global trading community, opening up trade and investment in a way that people like Lord Macartney and the American businessman, van Braam, could only dream of.

Many of the people who left China in the 1980s and 1990s began coming back, bringing with them skills and experience from working in the United States, Europe, and elsewhere. These *hai gui* returnees made up a significant share of the talent pool that multinational companies relied upon to manage their growth.

In 2002, after almost a decade away, I returned to Shanghai. I kept strong ties to Silicon Valley, and managed the operations in Asia-Pacific for various tech companies from my base in China. The changes to the quality of life were obvious. The chaos of the Mao years were a distant memory, as China embraced a more open economy and a forward-looking society. Even before China joined the World Trade Organization, China's global trade volume shot up, increasing from about $140 billion in 1990 to

roughly $510 billion a decade later. China's GDP was growing by double digits in this period, and incomes grew exponentially.

China was building up substantial foreign currency reserves, putting upward pressure on the value of the renminbi. Normally, if global markets are functioning properly then interest rates and currency values adjust, prompting foreign currency reserves to flow between countries and balance each other out. But Beijing kept its capital account closed, even after joining the WTO, leaving the government with a huge foreign currency surplus and an appetite to invest overseas.

Jiang Zemin, China's supreme party leader for two terms between 1993 and 2003, understood this and made moves to bring his nation's currency into line. Jiang was an enthusiastic, vivacious, and engaging leader who deftly navigated through numerous diplomatic challenges. He was also curious, both intellectually and culturally, and known for his ability to sing operas and recite the Gettysburg address—in English. He was also the originator of China's policy of *zou chuqu*, or "Going out Strategy." Chinese investors were eager to implement his plan.

Around this time, I was invited to speak at an outbound investment conference in Shanghai, which is where I met Frances Sun. The ballroom was already full when I arrived, and as I waited backstage I noticed a woman chatting with another foreigner in near perfect English. When it was my turn to speak, I took the stage and delivered some remarks about venture capital and trends in Silicon Valley. I finished my speech and took a seat in the front row to listen to the next speaker. It was Frances Sun. She was petite and had to adjust the microphone downward. She wore a bright red dress, and her hair was tinted slightly and cut short above her shoulders.

After thanking the organizers and making a few remarks in English, she switched smoothly to her native language. She flipped through charts and graphs, presenting opportunities and making projections about foreign investment flows, then landed on a slide that made me sit up in my chair. The heading over the bullet points read: "DON'T DO THIS!!!"

"When you arrive in America, don't expect the CEO of the company you are meeting with to come to the airport to greet you. Americans don't do that."

During my speech I could see people in the audience poking at their phones and shuffling papers. For Frances, they were on the edge of their chairs and writing down notes.

"Also, don't expect them to take you out to dinner." She spoke plainly with confidence, and I could tell she was speaking from experience as she went on. "If they don't take you out, it doesn't mean they don't care about you. American CEOs are busy and they want to spend time with their families."

"Exactly!" I thought to myself. I felt like I was reading a guidebook about my own hometown, and learning about it for the first time. Frances Sun was a *hai gui*. She had left China in the mid-1980s. After graduating from the prestigious Fudan University in Shanghai, she studied at Harvard before returning to China. She was an expert in cross-cultural communications, and was the managing director of the APCO consultancy in Shanghai. I learned later that Ms Sun had worked with the Chinese Mayors Association to conduct training for more than three hundred mayors across China.

"And whatever you do, you must not try to force them to drink! Americans don't like that." I liked the speaker from the outset, but now I wanted to jump up and hug the woman. Chinese drinking culture takes many forms, but in one version it's a power play where a supplicant is forced to drink to demonstrate subordination. It's a vile tradition.

"When you go to the United States, don't brag about your

ability to get things done by going around the regulations. Americans don't do that. They value fair play. If you talk about bending the rules they won't respect you." I had never heard anyone describe American business culture this way, but I realized she was right. It may not always seem that way, but Americans place high value on the rule of law.

In hindsight, these were the seeds that grew into the tension that exists between the US and China today, and within China itself. Like Americans, ordinary Chinese citizens also want to live in a predictable rules-based system, and appreciate many of the benefits they see in open societies. Their goal is prosperity and a peaceful life. The party's goal, meanwhile, is control; it recognizes the importance of prosperity as it influences stability and strives for self-sufficiency to avoid having to rely on anyone else.

People in China hold a range of views on America, and opinions have changed over the decades. In just a few years, America went from enemy to friend, then from teacher to competitor as China developed its own capabilities and technology. But in general there has always been a deep reservoir of goodwill and respect for America and our way of life. America's strength and stability are widely admired in China, even among nationalists who resent how the US throws its weight around. That stability is rooted in the rule of law and the consistency with which it is applied.

My Chinese friends might not articulate it in quite the same way that Frances Sun did, but they appreciate the fairness inherent in America's legal foundation, and the fact that our courts are, in general, independent of political pressures. The ideal of "all men being created equal" resonates anywhere, including in China. I learned a lot from Frances, not just about how Chinese managers view the cultural gap, but about America and what makes our country special.

Inside the party, China's officials in those years generally followed the playbook established by Deng and continued by Jiang. They tended to be enthusiastic about collaboration with the outside world, but of course still wary. Party school dogma trained officials to never fully trust foreigners, and to see capitalists as the means to an end. That end was a strong and prosperous party-controlled China. "To get rich is glorious," Deng supposedly said. Later, it would become clear to China watchers like myself that we had misunderstood the desire to become *modern* as being synonymous with a desire to become *Western*. The clues were there; we just didn't want to read them.

To be fair, Chinese society was changing so rapidly in the 1990s, nobody could have mapped a clear direction for where it was headed. Young Chinese were not only learning how to run modern businesses, they were also discovering jazz and rock & roll, as described in Andrew Field's book *Rocking China*. American pop culture was the rage, and baggy blue Mao suits were dropped in favor of miniskirts and makeup.

Looking back, it was extraordinary that rock and roll, which is so much about freedom and rebellion and closely associated with the West, was allowed to prosper. Clubs popped up and young people began experimenting with this new form of music. Chinese society tends to absorb things, turn them around a bit, then make them into something new, which is exactly what happened.

Field's book describes a time when China's system seemed less afraid of outside influences and "Western values." The 1990s and 2000s in China were fun and exciting, as Chinese people were discovering all kinds of new phenomena. The main characters in his book are Chinese musicians and bands, but another important figure described in the book is Michael Pettis, who incubated many of the bands. As Pettis describes the scene in the early 2000s, "There's sort of a lack of self-confidence. China's been out of the world for so long, that there's a sense that foreign things are better than local things, that foreign bands get a much bigger draw than good Chinese bands." Pettis' goal was to create a space for Chinese musicians to experiment and develop that confidence, which he did.

Pettis was right about that, but in another sense, the China of the 2000s was more confident than it is today because people were truly experimenting and they weren't afraid of trying new ideas. In comparison, China's society and system today are actually more closed and inward-looking than they were 20 years ago. The generation that built modern China believed it had, to a significant extent, escaped the political constraints of the Mao era. They now find themselves again working within the system.

In the early days of the Deng era, party elders made little effort to stop these trends, but there were always signs that they were concerned about drifting too far from a Chinese way of doing things. Deng Xiaoping set China on a path he called "socialism with Chinese characteristics." In the West we chose to interpret this as a name change, and Deng's way of finessing the question of communism versus capitalism. But in hindsight, it might have been a clue that China's system was determined to always do things in its own way.

Today China's party leaders assiduously add "...with Chinese characteristics" to nearly every policy announcement, so much so that it's become a joke among China watchers. This terminology came into play as Deng's sly maneuver, placing his own policies next to Mao's. Even as Deng embraced certain elements of capitalism and released market forces in a deliberate way, politically he didn't abandon Marxism-Leninism and the ultimate authority of the party. Therefore Deng's brand of "capitalism" became socialism with Chinese characteristics.

Scholars still debate Deng's legacy and true intentions, especially in the context of China's current direction. Some argue that Deng was a pragmatist who saw the inevitability and value of cooperating with the rest of the world, while others say Deng's reforms were only meant to be interim measures enabling China to catch up quickly to the West, and that his market-oriented policies were temporary tools to accelerate development while preserving the Communist Party's control over the state and economy.

Foreigners who live and work in China tend to have come to terms with this contradiction and place it alongside all the other contradictions that make up daily life in China. True, Chinese consumers sip lattes from Starbucks, and wear Nike sneakers, but the system at its heart is still remarkably similar to what it was when I first arrived in China.

"Your problem, Mr. Gibbs, is you spend all your time in Shanghai." I had been living in Shanghai for a while, and became friendly with government officials in the nearby city of Suzhou. I had just come from a groundbreaking ceremony for a new facility that would create hundreds of jobs.

Local tax authorities told me that jobs with American companies tend to require higher skill levels and pay on average about 10 to 15 percent more in wages than local firms, which is helpful for the tax base. With the ceremony over and formal discussions concluded, officials from the Foreign Affairs Office insisted that I join them for lunch. The ranking member was Mr. Li, a deputy director. He wore wire-rimmed glasses and kept his suit jacket on, despite the heat. He spoke English well, but slowly and deliberately.

"If you leave Shanghai and go to the countryside then you will see that China is still a developing country," said Mr. Li, gently waving his chopsticks at me for emphasis. Mr. Li would not have known, nor did he ask, but over the years I've traveled to nearly every province of China and have seen great wealth and abject poverty, often side by side. Even without leaving Shanghai there was plenty of evidence that China was a work in progress.

China entered the WTO in 2001, but it never fully embraced the rules. The WTO sets norms for global trade, but it made specific provisions for developing countries. Although the basic principle of free trade is fundamental to the organization, member countries have agreed that developing countries should be allowed to protect certain industries from outside competition. If global companies, with the advantage of scale, are allowed to dominate the market then local firms will never gain a foothold. China has been accused of manipulating this rule, since the WTO allows countries to decide for themselves if they are developing countries. No definition has been agreed to.

Therefore Beijing claimed developing country benefits, even while bragging about its space program and having the world's fastest passenger train, among other accomplishments. It was an untenable stance (one that it only recently abandoned), inviting pushback from trading partners. The WTO set guidelines for China's entry, to be reviewed in fifteen years based on its commitments. Both the US and the EU decided that China had failed to meet those commitments, which related to market access and the dominance of SOEs in the economy.

With China's government officials like Mr. Li, I learned to pick my battles. Our conversations generally stuck close to our respective talking points, but once in a while I managed to engage with them in meaningful dialogues. Meals, at times lubricated with alcohol like *baijiu* or some other local poison, were helpful in this regard.

While Mr. Li had a point, I chose to take a different direction. I picked up my own chopsticks and poked them playfully in his direction. "Your problem, Mr. Li, is when you visit the United States you only see New York or Washington. I can show you parts of America where there are no jobs, poor schools, and the people live in poverty. Mr. Li, *every* country is a developing country. You're right—it's a question of where you look!"

America's rustbelt would then have looked a lot like a developing country, with idle workers, empty streets, and vacant factories. Industrial offshoring has fueled political frustration that has shaped the anti-trade sentiment that now defines US electoral politics, and feelings about China.

Economic development is one of those tasks that is never complete. The party takes credit for guiding the nation out of poverty and mapping China's route toward what Xi Jinping calls a "moderately prosperous society," echoing a phrase from Deng Xiaoping in the early 1980s. The industriousness, creativity, and entrepreneurial spirit of the Chinese people have provided the most important ingredients in the recipe of "reform and opening up," and it could be said that the party's key contribution was taking its hands off in the 1990s and 2000s, and providing space for private entrepreneurs and foreign companies to expand, thereby creating the China of today. It's also true that the Chinese economy benefited from the global trading system and international markets, as well as technology, capital, and managerial know-how from the United States. It's an undeniable fact that Bob Ching, Frances Sun, and countless other "outsiders" became bridges between China and the outside world that brought all kinds of benefits to China's developing economy.

Edward Tse worked at the Boston Consulting Group in Shanghai shortly after I did, later becoming something of a management guru. He still advises corporate executives, investors, and government officials in China. In a recent publication for his advisory firm, Gao Feng, he wrote:

> "In retrospect, the period between 1993 and China's entry into the World Trade Organization in 2001 was a critical period. Those were the first years of meaningful exchanges between the West and China. It was a time of adjustment as the two very different systems and cultures came into close contact. As their footholds expanded in China, multinational corporations brought with them new management concepts and practices. They hired local staff and provided training and career development opportunities. The introduction of Western concepts and practices helped many Chinese, especially the younger generation, open up their horizons. New tiers of local managers emerged, trained not only in Western management techniques but also in corporate governance, which typically transcends national borders. In the 1990s, probably the most commonly mentioned phrase I heard from Chinese business people was 'getting aligned with the international tracks.' This epitomized the Chinese mindset of wanting to be a part of the rest of the world, especially from a business and trade perspective."[4]

4 Edward Tse, "The Symbiotic Relationship Between China and Multinational Corporations." November 14, 2023.

In the 1990s and early 2000s, nobody in China seemed to object to America's leadership, or to a global trading system that seemed to be set up using rules established and enforced under the auspices of the United States. The success of the Chinese economy is no doubt primarily the result of the industriousness of the Chinese people, and their government's wisdom in some periods to get out of the way, but foreigners and Americans in particular also played an important role.

Americans who interacted with Chinese people in these early days—the 1980s and 1990s—were generally not in China with the hope of getting rich. I certainly wasn't. For me, it was a mix of curiosity, adventure, and being where the action was, but the optimism was infectious. The sleeping giant was waking up and beginning to consider how it would fit into the world. Foreigners were eager to help the Chinese people with that process, offering a helping hand and a leg up.

People like BCG's Bob Ching were eager to contribute what they had—in Bob's case, management methodologies. Many others from a wide range of professions brought master classes to China in the fields of accounting, finance, law, and medicine. The idea was to bring China into the fold, and set up systems and processes to help the emerging nation and to ensure that it would become compatible with the West. Many foreigners talk about the 1990s as a time when Chinese people were eager to engage and cooperate, unfettered by the pride, nationalism, or mistrust that today, once again, seems to now characterize the relationship of China's system with the West.

Foreigners working in China during those years saw the obvious potential in a hard-working population. That era was filled with lessons, as well as frustration and tears, but it was also a glorious time because of the growth, the changes, and the potential for the future. For their part, the Chinese people were eager to learn and open to adopting new methods and ways of doing things. It was a magical time, and in hindsight very much a golden age of US-China relations. None of the Chinese friends I made during that time resented the West or accused America of "making the rules" that others had to follow. The *"lao bai xing,"* or ordinary Chinese people, were eager to join a system that would bring them prosperity and opportunities.

As things turned out, the economic integration that began in the 1990s only moved in one direction. US firms like BCG and others transferred technology, management expertise, and manufacturing know-how, while China absorbed it all without committing to reciprocity or opening its markets.

Moreover, China's manufacturing was changing. The people we trained left the SOEs to form private enterprises that went from producing low-quality consumer goods to dominating global supply chains for vital products—batteries, electronics, and legacy semiconductors. The US became dependent on China for essential products and inputs, contributing to the tension being experienced today.

The *lao bai xing* didn't spend a lot of time criticizing Marxism either. People were too busy learning how to get rich, or at least improve their lot in life. We all thought the reforms put China on a one-way path toward greater integration with the global economy, and the country would never go back to the days when ideology trumped economic pragmatism and state-owned enterprises played a dominant role. Entrepreneurs mostly believed the "new" new China was one in which they could enjoy the benefits of their own labor without having to look over their shoulders. We were all, to a considerable extent, wrong.

In today's China, Xi Jinping has reinvigorated state control, clarifying the role of private entrepreneurs within the system and restoring state-owned enterprises (SOEs) to a central role in the economy. The result is declining dynamism, reduced foreign investment, and growing inefficiency across key sectors.

China's integration into the global economy that began in the 1990s brought incredible benefits to the Chinese people and set the course for where the country finds itself today. American firms like BCG and countless others played a central role—bringing capital, technology, and management practices that helped build modern manufacturing capacity and connected China to global markets. This model delivered extraordinary growth, while embedding Chinese companies into supply chains. The same openness that once fueled progress created interdependence: China's prosperity benefited from the goodwill of foreign investors, continued access to advanced technology, and stable trade relations with the West.

As geopolitical tensions have risen, those interdependencies have turned into structural weaknesses. Trade frictions, export controls, and investment restrictions have exposed China's reliance on global markets for both demand and technology inputs, and that reliance makes the system feel uncomfortable. The ensuing American and European restrictions on China's access to technology have constrained its ability to climb the value chain, while shifts in investor sentiment both at home and abroad have underscored its sensitivity to confidence. Despite still commanding a major market share in manufactured goods, China faces narrowing access in strategic sectors and growing skepticism among many trading partners after years of unbalanced trade.

China's model is still export-led despite efforts to stimulate consumer spending, and therefore remains tied to US and global markets. As relations have soured, this dependence has become viewed by the party as a strategic liability leading to a desire for self-sufficiency. Beijing's efforts to shift toward domestic consumption have been slow and uneven. As covered in later chapters, the party's own actions have contributed to the loss in confidence that undermines efforts to boost consumption.

The country that once drew strength from global integration has decided that that very integration has become a source of fragility—a reality its entrepreneurs must now confront as they seek new growth engines under more uncertain global conditions. Growth, once the party's primary source of legitimacy, is slowing. Economic stagnation, youth unemployment, and demographic decline threaten social stability. China's economic future will likely be characterized by slower growth and weaker profits, despite impressive achievements in some industries. But the bigger problem is a widening gap in goals. China's people want prosperity, fairness, and connection to the world, while the party wants control above all else. The divergence of those goals exposes an underlying weakness of the Chinese system.

CHAPTER 6
A Sand Foundation

I met Hurst Lin in Silicon Valley in the mid-1990s, during the first "dot com" boom. He was an American-born Chinese, and would go on to become one of the most admired investors in China, with huge successes like Kuaishou and VIP Shop, all of which went public in American capital markets, making himself and his partners fabulously wealthy. I'm not sure if he considered me a member of the American-born Chinese tribe, but we worked for similar companies and got along well. Some people like Hurst felt they hit a glass ceiling in America, getting passed up for promotions or missing opportunities despite having impeccable academic credentials, as Hurst did.

That frustration became a powerful push factor just as China was generating an equally strong pull: a fast-growing economy hungry for talent, offering opportunity, autonomy, and a sense of national purpose unavailable in the US. The result was a wave of returnees who became the backbone of China's early digital transformation, bringing technical expertise, global experience, and entrepreneurial energy that helped drive the rise of companies like Alibaba, Tencent, and Baidu. That pipeline of talent is no longer available to China in the new phase of AI development, due to political tensions and the breakdown in trust on both sides.

Hurst worked for a company called Sinanet.com, which copied the Yahoo business model to create a portal catering to Chinese speaking people in the United States. When the company was founded in the late 1990s, the number of people using the Internet in China was less than five million. For a media business supported by advertising the market was too small. Hurst and his colleagues had dreams about the market in China, but for the time being Sinanet built a business around the Chinese diaspora, which was larger and infinitely more affluent.

I worked down the street from Hurst at a company called Infoseek. Infoseek also competed in the shadow of Yahoo, which was far and away the market leader in the late 1990s. Google hadn't yet come on the scene, but several other competitors were chasing Yahoo for market share.

One of my colleagues, a China-born engineer, was also dreaming about the China market. Infoseek went public in 1999, but many of us had lockups that prevented us from selling our stock. We would need to wait years before we could cash in our shares. Nevertheless, that engineer thought it was a good idea to quit his job, move to China, and start an Internet search company.

Our colleagues at Infoseek thought he was crazy. In 2000, nobody was funding Internet companies in China, in fact the venture capital industry was almost non-existent at that time. Where would he get the money to build a company in China? How would he find workers who knew how the search business worked? Most importantly, how was he going to compete with Yahoo, which already had a dominant market share in the developed markets and was using economies of scale to reach every corner of a borderless cyber world? The engineer ignored our advice and went on to build a company that was valued at over $100 billion at its peak, a company called Baidu. The engineer was Robin Li, who is now considered one of the most successful tech entrepreneurs in China, and an influential figure shaping development in AI, autonomous driving, and cloud computing.

Hurst was less reckless than Robin, but he and his colleagues had similar thoughts about China. They arranged a merger with a China based company, keeping the existing revenue streams from the United States but achieving a toehold in a market that would soon experience exponential growth. Sina, known in Chinese as *xinlang*, or "new wave," became the first China based internet company to go public in New York. Chinese law prohibited foreign ownership in media companies, so the bankers created an unusual structure for the IPO that allowed global investors to benefit from Sina's business growth without actually owning shares in the company. It is the Variable Interest Entity (VIE) structure under which the owners of a Chinese company set up an offshore shell company (usually in the Cayman Islands) which signs contracts with the China operating company through which the offshore entity gains some measure of control and associated economic benefits, without owning equity. More than a hundred Chinese companies have gone public in the US using this structure and they currently have a market value of close to a trillion US dollars. The legality of the VIE structure under both US and Chinese law is questionable, but has never been challenged. Too much is at stake to do so. But it all started with Robin and Sina.

It always surprised me that American regulators allowed this structure, which was an obvious end-run around Chinese regulations. Even more shocking was that Beijing also went along with it. In retrospect, Chinese regulators demonstrated remarkable foresight by taking a relatively hands-off approach in those days, allowing entrepreneurs like Robin Li and Hurst Lin to bring what they learned in the West and more or less let local technology industries develop with minimal constraints.

That early openness enabled the explosive growth of China's tech companies, but it has been replaced by control and suspicion. Today, Beijing has become more circumspect, reining in China's previously un-checked tech entrepreneurs and regarding Western ideas and people with increasing suspicion, but it began with an open, hands-across-the-Pacific effort by both sides which allowed Western funds and technology into China, kick-starting the powerful tech sector it has today.

It was about that time, in the mid-2000s, that Hurst Lin showed up in my apartment in Shanghai, excited about a new business idea. We sat in the living room of my apartment in the former French Concession district of Shanghai. The height of buildings in the historic district were restricted, so we had a commanding view of the city from the seventh floor, just above the tree tops. The French planners from the previous century had lined the narrow roads with plane trees that grew out like umbrellas, providing plenty of shade from the hot sun.

Hurst pointed out the window as he explained his investment thesis: "There are already plenty of five-star hotels in the market. China also has a lot of crappy hotels at the low end. Chinese travelers have money now. They want something better, but there's nothing in the middle."

Hurst was right. China's economic growth and corresponding personal income expansion created demand for all sorts of products and services. High-end hotel brands like Hyatt and Marriott had already staked out locations with properties that catered to the well-heeled international travelers on expense accounts. They were equipped with gyms and swimming pools, fine dining restaurants, and ice sculptures in the lobby. At the low end of the market, rooms could be found for as little as ten dollars a night. These were dimly lit, rarely cleaned, and were so bad they would need vast improvements to become even fleabag hotels. Almost nothing existed in the middle for the independent traveler who just needed a clean room and a fast internet connection.

Over time, Hurst Lin would become known for making large bets based on instincts and his feel for people and teams, and even said the success of his investments was due to "luck." In the earlier years he was more methodical. He calmly went through the business proposition, pointing to China's growing middle class and the increasing number of business travelers, concluding that there was a large unmet market. Hurst leaned heavily on the lessons he learned at Dartmouth, and from business school at Stanford.

His concept was to develop a chain of "limited service" hotels, copying businesses like Motel 6—which offered "clean, comfortable rooms, and we'll keep the light on for you." Hurst, with his Brooklyn accent and street-savvy demeanor, was the perfect advocate for a business that focused on basic accommodations. "If you need an ice sculpture in the lobby then you'll go to Hyatt anyway," Hurst explained, dismissing any objections.

Hurst wasn't pitching me or asking for advice, since I didn't know any more than he did about running a hotel. He was setting out on a new adventure and wanted to know if I wanted to come along, which I did.

A small group of us put together some money and formed a company. As founders we invested just enough to open three hotels. That turned out to be our first mistake—underestimating our initial capital needs— one of several we had to overcome to survive.

Our model was to acquire a long-term lease on a building, which we would then renovate as a hotel with a 100 to 120 rooms, which people in the business call the number of "keys."

Our target room price was 350-400 yuan, or about 50 dollars a night. For that, guests got no room service, no laundry, no gym, and certainly no ice sculpture. The locations were key. The cost of the lease had to be low enough to meet our target price, putting prime locations out of our price range. We scoured the city to find buildings that were just off a main road, but close enough for guests to find the two things they needed—food and transportation. We needed to be close to a subway entrance, and it turned out that our target customers were happy enough with a quick bite at McDonald's or Starbucks, so those became points on the map around which we would hunt for locations.

Hurst and I both had full-time jobs, and neither of us had grown up in China. This would be a purely local business that needed local management. We needed someone who understood our target customer, could negotiate with building owners, hire room cleaning and front desk staff, and manage all the other aspects of a fast-growing business. Hurst found our man.

Wu Hai was working at Ctrip (now renamed as Trip.com), which was already China's premier travel booking site. Wu Hai was a consummate entrepreneur and was only working for Ctrip as part of an earn-out connected to a company he had sold. Ctrip was in the business of booking hotel rooms, but Wu Hai's experience was in information technology; he had never managed a hotel himself. Fortunately for him, neither Hurst nor I had that experience either, so we didn't know what questions to ask. Born in 1969, Wu Hai entered the working world when traditional businesses like hotels were less appealing, and his mind was optimized for challenges in the digital world. Contrary to traditional business doctrine, people like Wu Hai don't believe industry experience is important because their goal is to disrupt and change the industry completely. His way of thinking fit comfortably with Hurst, and Wu Hai became a co-investor and CEO of Orange Hotels.

As it turned out, Wu Hai possessed or developed exactly the set of skills that were required to build the business. He also represented a class of Chinese managers who learned quickly from their foreign counterparts and adapted lessons for the local market. Much of their learning was by trial and error, failing fast, or what Deng Xiaoping called "crossing the river by feeling the stones."

Our first crisis came after we had leased a building and the renovation work came in forty percent over budget. Investors hate that, and tend to lose confidence in management if the business feels like it's out of control. Among the small group that met in my living room, one person in particular believed something sinister was happening.

China is a place that always seems to be in transition, but that time in the 2000s was special. Among investors, China was known as a "low-trust society." This sounds offensive, but locals and foreigners alike acknowledged the gold rush mentality that shaped behavior, especially during this period. Later, after 2012, Xi Jinping's anti-corruption campaign would become one of his signature initiatives but throughout the 2000s, huge amounts of money sloshed around in the economy tempting all manner of thieves to grab what they could. Corrupt government officials were the worst, and they set the standard for others. One investor told me, "When you hire your chief financial officer, go find someone you can trust like you trust your own mother. And if you can't find that person, hire your mother!"

Wu Hai seemed trustworthy, but there were irregularities in

the books, and our fellow investor—also a Chinese American—felt sure that we were being ripped off. He used his position on the board to take control of the chop, which is what companies in China generally use to authorize payments. The company was paralyzed. A decision had to be made. If we didn't make a management change our investor would leave, but finding a new CEO would set us back months. It had to be one or the other.

I suppose we could have conducted an independent investigation or forensic analysis, all of which would cost money and time, but Hurst did what Hurst does best. His instincts told him that Wu Hai may have been playing fast and loose, but China was a messy place and we needed a guy who could take us where we needed to go even if rules occasionally got in the way.

We backed Wu Hai. This meant buying out our co-investor, leaving us with less capital to work with and a shorter runway to get to profit. Looking back, both sides could have been right. There were irregularities, but Wu Hai was simply doing what he needed to do for the company to survive.

Since then, Wu Hai and I have had good laughs over the idea that some of our early investment dollars could have been pilfered, or that he would take something for himself instead of giving it to the company, which became like his baby. As our CEO, Wu Hai was indispensable; every decision he made put the company first and himself last, just like our own mothers would do. Reflecting on the incident, Wu Hai told me: "There are two extremes for foreigners in China—blind trust from the start, or don't trust any Chinese at all. Both are wrong."

Regarding the conflict with the investor, Wu Hai was introspective: "The first lesson I learned is when there is a bomb, alert everyone. Don't try to defuse the bomb before doing that. Our first project went over budget. I worked hard to cut costs but

I should have known there was no way to cut while still getting a better facility and design. Everything costs money. If I had kept all investors informed from the moment I realized it was a bomb, the trust crisis might not have become so extreme."

Chinese entrepreneurs are a special breed, tenacious to the point of insanity, and desperate to succeed no matter the cost or consequence. Younger people in China today are more conscious about lifestyle and work-life balance and care about other things like the environment, their community, and overall quality of life, but Wu Hai was driven. As investors we liked the results, but we were often concerned about him—for his family and his health. He pushed his team ferociously and led by example, working harder and longer than anyone, demanding answers in the middle of the night if an idea or question occurred to him.

Business culture was a different matter. In the West, actual business practices cover a wide range of behaviors but the idealized boss plays by the rules and does the right thing. We despise the guy who cheats and gets caught, or worse yet, the one who cheats and gets away with it. Our movies portray the sheriff wearing a white hat who drives bandits from the town, ridding it of lawlessness and chaos. Chinese movies have heroes like that too, but business culture tends to also value the boss who gets it done, especially if some trick or clever ruse is employed. Chinese people praise the boss, pointing to him or her with reverence, saying *ta hen you banfa*, meaning "he knows how to get things done."

Our project in Tianjin, a port city not far from Beijing, had slowed. The approvals from local government agencies weren't coming through, pushing our schedule out and our costs up. In those days it was common practice to pay a "professional service" company to speed things along, fixing problems here and there, and finding ways to get approvals for things that weren't quite right. As foreign investors, we would have had no idea how to do such things, which is why we needed local management. The construction team provided the financial analysis for how we could use this method to finish the project and stay within our budget. By making a few small payments—in cash, naturally—we could get away with installing fewer fire escapes than required by law and actually save time and money. This is the kind of question that could not even be considered.

Chinese entrepreneurs are huge risk-takers, and will often do whatever they think they can get away with. It would be wrong, however, to conclude that Chinese managers have low regard for safety or human life. The issue is the mindset that regulations are to be avoided and that all options can be considered as long as retribution is unlikely. This way of thinking is embodied in the Chinese expression, *tiangao, huangdi yuan*, meaning "the sky is high and the emperor is far away." What the emperor can't see doesn't matter.

It took some time, with East and West learning from each other, but eventually Wu Hai was able to change the management culture and bring his construction crews into line. With lives at stake, there could be no bending of rules or cutting corners. In fact, compliance with fire regulations was only the starting point. To build a sustainable business, we had to make the safety and well-being of our guests our highest priority.

The Tianjin revelation seemed to focus Wu Hai on people, and the guests who would stay in our hotels. Some of his ideas drew on his IT background, like combining the loyalty program with the booking system. Repeat customers would simply keep their room key, which became their loyalty card. They could book their next stay directly and use the loyalty card to open their room. This allowed guests to bypass the front desk and go straight to their rooms. The system also bypassed Ctrip, which took a flat fee for bookings. The fee amounted to a significant percentage of our room rate, cutting deep into our margins, so this innovation gave a much-needed boost to our financial situation.

Fortunately for us, demand was strong and our occupancy rates were excellent. Some locations even boasted more than 100 percent occupancy, which confused us at first. We soon discovered that a nicely designed budget hotel was a good option for couples who live in small apartments, often with in-laws and small children. A few hours of comfort and privacy was all they needed, leaving a room available for a second booking in a single night.

Wu Hai's focus on the customer led him to other clever schemes, like using lighting and music to create an emotional connection. Again, he devised an IT system that tied the reservation system to the room. According to Wu Hai, "The system knows the age and gender of the guest, so when he or she opens the door, the music will come on automatically. The tricky part is to match the music with the light."

He also experimented with whimsy, putting a live fish—his favorite was the Siamese fighting fish—in each room, even giving the fish a name. The idea was to create an emotional connection, which I thought was silly at first, but it seemed to work. The idea for the fish actually came from where we started the company, in my apartment where I have a fish tank. Wu Hai recalls the fish, but also the minimalist style of my apartment. My wife was an architect and studied the great Japanese designers like Tadao Ando and Kazuyo Sejima in her courses at UC Berkeley. They emphasized simplicity, clean lines, and open spaces, which is the exact opposite of Chinese aesthetics, especially in the 1990s and 2000s. At the high end, Chinese apartments would typically be crammed with Louis XIV couches and stuffed armchairs, lots of gold objects, and ostentatious symbols of wealth. In contrast, Wu Hai found none of these things in my apartment, leading him to assume that I was either poor, or I hadn't yet fully moved in.

We needed someone to design our hotels, but hiring a firm would be costly and we hadn't budgeted for it. My wife Amy said she was willing to do it, but our investor group was skeptical that she could design the hotels. Somebody asked how many hotels she had designed herself, which of course was zero. She also hadn't designed anything that was actually built in China, so she had nothing to point to. But somebody said our apartment was nice, and she designed that. So she was hired as the architect.

Our first three hotels opened in 2007, and we filled the rooms as expected. The business was profitable, but we needed to grow quickly to stay ahead of the competition. Beijing was gearing up to host the 2008 Summer Olympics, and we saw our big opportunity. We put all our capital behind a plan to open nine new hotels in the city of Beijing just in time for the games.

Beijing would spend billions on venues and infrastructure in anticipation of hosting the largest and most successful Olympic Games in history. This would be a crowning achievement for China, having developed into a prosperous nation that could deliver the biggest, the fastest, and the best of just about everything.

Mark Fischer, then the head of the NBA China, said: "The Games were in many ways China's coming-out party. China had accomplished tremendous economic and political reform after decades of isolation and poverty, and the Games were Beijing's chance to show the world how far it had come. In addition to the shiny new Olympic venues, the capital city completed many new buildings designed by top international architects, along with new transport systems and other facelifts throughout the city, all just in time to host visitors from around the world."

To us, that meant hotel rooms would be fully booked at premium prices, filling our coffers and accelerating our growth.

In March of 2008, some months before the Games would start, a bomb exploded killing three people on a bus in Shanghai. Xinjiang separatists were blamed for the attack, which also coincided with anti-Chinese protests in Tibet and violent clashes between Han Chinese and Tibetans. This was deeply troubling to the government, which was counting on a successful Olympics to validate China's political system along with its economic achievements.

Just weeks before the games began, authorities in Beijing stopped issuing visas and restricted the selling of tickets. They had cleaned up the air by shutting down local industries and eliminated traffic by moving thousands of people out of the city, but they would take no chances with the possibility of an incident embarrassing the government. The authorities cared deeply about hosting the Games and making sure television audiences saw them, but people in the stands mattered less and presented too much of a risk. Many seats in the stands were left empty, and so were our hotel rooms.

I was already living in Shanghai so I didn't need a visa. I bought a ticket from a *huang niu*—a scalper—a few days before the games and took a train to Beijing. I sat in the main "Bird's Nest" stadium behind a group of Jamaicans and watched Usain Bolt become the fastest man on the planet, breaking the world record for both the 100 meter and 200 meter sprint.

For Orange Hotels, the 2008 Beijing Olympics was a big disappointment and put us in a bad financial position as we headed into the global financial crisis. With the stock markets in turmoil, business travel budgets collapsed and room bookings evaporated. We were forced to raise money at the worst possible time both for our business and the capital markets. By the time we sold Orange Hotels in 2017, institutional investors owned a majority and the initial investors had very little control.

It was a long hard road, but for me, the Orange experience was a window into what Chinese managers could do on their own, after taking lessons drawn from many sources. It also exposed a number of weaknesses in the Chinese economy. The tension between expediency and accountability continues to be a problem in China. The ambiguity surrounding Wu Hai's financial irregularities is symptomatic of a broader low-trust society, where even basic business relationships require familial bonds to function reliably. While China has made remarkable strides in physical infrastructure and digital innovation, its persistent corruption and weak rule of law undermine the very foundations needed for sustainable growth.

Nowhere is this more evident than in intellectual property protections, which remain inadequate despite repeated promises of reform and some progress. Enforcement of intellectual property remains a major weakness in China, affecting both domestic and foreign companies. When entrepreneurs know their innovations can be copied with impunity and contracts enforced only selectively, the incentives to take risks and invest in genuine breakthroughs are fundamentally compromised. The system that once excused cutting corners as necessary for survival now finds itself trapped: the same institutional fragility that enabled rapid catch-up growth has become a ceiling limiting China's ability to lead in industries where trust, transparency, and reliable property rights matter most. The country's gleaming towers and seamless payment systems cannot fully mask the uncomfortable reality that its economic model remains built on a weak institutional foundation.

I arrived in China when it was backward and messy, the source of cheap labor and low-quality products. Now, China is ultra-competitive. It is a source of incredible innovation, world-class infrastructure, and a digital economy that is simply dazzling. But the foundations of that success are in some ways more sand than stone. The web economy flourished because Beijing briefly tolerated regulatory gray zones and welcomed a flow of talent from Silicon Valley. Control has replaced openness as the default; suspicion has to some extent replaced collaboration. The improvisational system that once allowed entrepreneurs to cut corners and race ahead can now trap them, limiting China's ability to lead in sectors that depend on trust, transparency, and secure rights. Persistent corruption, weak rule of law, and a political culture aimed at control still shape how business is done and will put a drag on China's race to compete.

PART 3

IN CHINA FOR CHINA

CHAPTER 7

The Fragile Hand of Power

"What you need to understand is that China is horizontal!" Bob Theleen was holding court, almost literally. We were in the courtyard of his office compound, sipping wine on a cool evening in October of 2014, shortly after Xi Jinping began his first term.

The period from 2001, when China joined the World Trade Organization, was a phase of liberalization, global integration, and enormous opportunity for foreign investors. The country was still to some extent guided by Deng Xiaoping's "reform and opening-up" policies, emphasizing pragmatism over ideology, although that was changing. The Chinese economy was still more decentralized than it had been and would be again, with provincial and municipal governments enjoying relatively broad autonomy to pursue growth, attract foreign investment, and experiment with policy innovations. The system was remarkably effective—but it also contained the seeds of future vulnerability, as local competition encouraged waste, corruption, and uneven development.

By the time Xi Jinping took power in 2012, the weaknesses in the Dengist model, and its long-term implications for party control, were becoming impossible to ignore. Years of breakneck growth had produced widespread corruption, environmental degradation, and industrial overcapacity. Rising inequality and regional disparities were eroding public trust. For decades, the party's legitimacy had rested on its ability to deliver rapid growth, but by the mid-2010s that growth was slowing. And integration with the world and a rising private sector had implications for the party's position that could not be ignored or countenanced. Confronted with the issues, Xi moved to tighten control—politically, ideologically, and institutionally—seeking to reinforce the party's authority and contain the vulnerabilities that had emerged in the era of decentralization.

None of us could have seen this coming. In hindsight, it also marked the end of a long period of engagement—and a kind of golden age—for people like Bob. His company, ChinaVest, had taken over an elegant Western-style mansion in Shanghai's former French Concession. The grand entrance featured tall columns and a stone portico, opening into a magnificent lobby. An ornate wooden staircase led to the second floor offices for the staff of thirty or so professionals. Outside, a narrow stone bridge crossed a *koi* pond, leading to an octagonal pavilion with red columns and a green tiled roof. The property was perfect for entertaining clients.

Bob and his wife, Jenny Hsui, had started the company in the 1980s to finance businesses and arrange deals, and over the years ChinaVest quietly became the trusted advisor to numerous Fortune 500 clients. Bob was standing at the center of a small circle of people listening to him bend the ear of a client. By the time I met him, Bob was already in his late sixties. He was solidly built, with white hair and blue eyes that seemed to cut through the clutter to find nuggets of truth. Bob was a legend in China and had been part of the fabric of the foreign business community since the 1970s. He was a gentle man with a soft handshake, which belied his years in the military. He had served in Vietnam, and many of us believed he had been a spook. We could never be sure of that, but he seemed to have the trust of the Chinese government, and lectured regularly at the party school in Beijing.[1]

At that moment, in the courtyard of his office, he was lecturing his client, a large American fellow who had been to China a dozen times and thought he pretty much had the measure of things. The visitor was asking about a recent business delegation led by Stephen Orlins from the National Committee on US-China Relations. Orlins had half a dozen foreign CEOs in tow who came away with coveted photos of themselves in the Great Hall of the People. "I need you to get me meetings in Beijing—that's where everything happens," Bob's visitor told the group, in a loud voice with an air of authority.

"Ah…that's what they *want* you to believe!" Bob said, grinning like a gambler putting down aces. "The CCP wants you to think that everything comes from the center, and that Xi Jinping is all-powerful, like the Wizard of Oz. That's why they are so secretive in Beijing. They don't want us to know that the *real* power in China is in the provinces and municipalities. That's where business gets done!"

He was exaggerating, of course. Bob knew that policy direction came from Beijing. His point was that China's governance was complex and opaque, and that understanding the local dimension was also essential. His approach was pragmatic: it was often easier to work with provincial leaders who could move quickly, rather than attracting attention from central authorities.

Bob was also speaking near the beginning of Xi's first term, before power became so thoroughly recentralized and the norms

1 As a banker and venture capitalist, Bob Theleen was one of the first foreigners to serve on the board of a major Chinese state-owned company, Beijing Enterprises.

of collective leadership began to erode. He was describing an era, the Deng era, that had actually already ended.

Xi soon sought to rein in the excesses of local competition, where provinces often overinvested in favored sectors, creating inefficiencies and overcapacity. Ironically, China's system of central planning had encouraged this very behavior. Once Beijing designated a sector as "strategic"—whether solar panels, semiconductors, or electric vehicles—local officials raced to pour money into it, each hoping to win favor and secure subsidies. The result was waves of redundant investment and mounting supply gluts, problems that Beijing now struggles to contain.

Xi used these failures as justification for tightening political control, arguing that only stronger central oversight and party discipline could ensure coordination, efficiency, and what he called "high-quality development." The consequences are now global: as China exports its surplus production abroad, it has triggered mounting trade tensions and revived concerns about the country's economic model.

The US Trade Representative's 2023 Report to Congress sums up the situation as it describes China's WTO compliance:

> "China continues to pursue an extensive number of industrial plans and supporting policies and practices that target industries for domination by Chinese companies, both in China and globally. Pursuant to these industrial plans, the Chinese state offers substantial government guidance, resources and regulatory support to Chinese companies while actively seeking to limit market access for imported goods, foreign manufacturers and foreign services suppliers. The beneficiaries of these non-market policies and practices, which are constantly evolving,

> include not only China's state-owned enterprises but also other domestic Chinese companies."[2]

Companies in market-based economies are competing not just against Chinese companies but also against the Chinese state itself. Backed by state-owned banks, generous subsidies, and industrial policies that direct investment toward priority sectors, Chinese enterprises enjoy advantages that blur the line between market competition and government intervention.

Bob's comment about China being horizontal was not meant literally. We all understood that China is very much hierarchical. And he often traveled to Beijing and served on the board of Beijing Enterprises, a large state-owned company that operated utilities among other things. He was also a member of a Chinese law-making task force that advised on financial reforms under the auspices of the powerful National Development and Reform Commission (NDRC).

Bob was a Republican. He was a Reagan Republican, and believed in the power of free enterprise and the efficiency of markets. I did too, as I had seen firsthand the unintended consequences of businesses run by government diktat and understood the pitfalls of top-down planning, but we argued about industrial policy. It was hard to ignore that China's state-directed system was delivering years of double-digit GDP growth. What, after all, is wrong with having a plan and aligning industries for the common good? The problem lies in the closed-door process through which those plans are made—and in who ultimately benefits from them.

Bob believed that China's economic miracle occurred despite the plans, not because of them. The real dynamism, he argued,

2 2023 USTR Report to Congress on China's WTO Compliance

came from entrepreneurs and officials at the provincial level who found creative ways to work around central directives. He may have been right, but so was I. Both views can be true.

China's Five-Year Plans are delivered top-down from Beijing, with policies and goals set by the Central Committee. But the targets cascade down to the provinces, which are expected to fold them into plans at the local level. China's system is unique and in many ways incompatible with the West, but putting too much emphasis on the central government in Beijing misses a big part of the picture. Government officials at the subnational level have tremendous power and interact with foreign companies in a very different way than at the national level. China's power structure has been described as top-down and vertical, which it is, but in many ways that are important to foreign businesses, it is also flat.

The CCP controls the country at every level, but government officials at the subnational level can be remarkably cooperative and strategically aligned with foreign enterprises. Officials at the provincial and municipal levels show none of the attitude that China's wolf-warrior diplomats have become famous for, primarily because they are measured based on jobs, tax revenue, and overall economic performance. But they still toe the line that is drawn in Beijing, especially now that the environment has become more circumspect and centralized. Provinces often compete against each other, and savvy foreigners like Bob could get better deals by shopping around. This degree of autonomy could also lead to inefficiencies, as the leaders in each province built empires with their own steel industry, automotive companies, and high-tech parks. Many of these industries—especially electronics manufacturing—are dependent on a robust ecosystem, amplifying the redundancies across provinces. Xi Jinping has sought to rein in the excesses of local competition—

even giving it a peculiar term "involution"—which includes provinces overinvesting in favored sectors.

National level regulators and ministries have long been aware of the problem, leading them to focus on limiting, not expanding, foreign investment. It would never be wrong to get support for projects at the highest level possible, but foreign companies could get caught up in the dynamic interplay between national regulators and local governments, which often have conflicting goals. At the national level, the regulators and ministries are primarily concerned with national security, stability, and control. They are conservative, leaning toward preventing problems and avoiding blame rather than developing solutions.

Jenny, who was Bob's business partner and advisor as well as his wife, explained it this way: "The provinces generate the tax money that supports central government expenditures," she said. "Most foreigners have trepidation about dealing with the government, as they tend to avoid government organizations when they are at home. But here, local government entities are strategically aligned with business because they have a profit motive. China's different in that way."

Local government officials are implementers with a bias toward action and see less risk in working with foreign companies, which tend to be easier to control. Local officials have financial and economic development goals and often hide projects from national authorities for as long as possible to prevent them from being taken away and moved to another province.

Foreign companies need to be aware of this dynamic, as Bob explained. "Watch out for red eye disease!" Bob exhorted. The Chinese system revolves around signing ceremonies, group photos, and banquets, but getting too much attention from a jealous official in a neighboring province could lead to trouble.

I took Bob's advice and leaned heavily on local government officials to generate business. Toward the end of the 2000s I moved from operating businesses in China to financing them. One of my investments was sold to the Shanghai Media Group, a state-owned company. Any SOE transaction was complicated, requiring approvals from the SASAC—the State-owned Assets Supervision and Administration Commission of the State Council—and other regulatory bodies, so bringing a bank into the deal was helpful. Once the deal was completed I was invited to join the bank, and I ended up working for HSBC.

As a coverage banker, which is basically a salesperson for the various services of the firm, I was expected to find deals. The IPOs paid the highest fees, but we would also do mergers, divestitures, or almost any kind of corporate transaction. Most of the big deals originated in one of the main financial and business centers—Shanghai, Beijing, or Shenzhen—so I spent a lot of time traveling between these cities, but Morgan Stanley and Goldman Sachs were already dominant in those markets, forcing me to fish in smaller ponds.

Nanjing is a second-tier city about 200 miles west of Shanghai, and I went there often. The high-speed train to Nanjing would cut the trip down to an hour, but in 2010 the trip still took me a good two hours or more. I liked the city, which was smaller and less intense than Shanghai, but rich in history and culture, having been the seat of the nation's capital under multiple governments, including Chiang Kai-shek's administration when he ruled China.

China's government ranks its cities in tiers by GDP, population, and other measures. The first-tier cities—including Shanghai and Beijing—are the most popular for foreign investment, but there are good opportunities in other cities for foreigners who are prepared to work a bit harder and don't expect to use English.

Deputy Director Zhang was in the Commerce Bureau, tasked with bringing foreign investment to Nanjing, despite having no obvious skills with which to accomplish that. He spoke no English, had never been overseas, and seemed to spend most of his time drinking and eating. We had met at an investment conference and struck up enough of a friendship to help each other. Mr. Zhang's face was red and puffy from drinking and his teeth were stained from years of smoking. His eyes were watery but his mind was sharp, and he knew every company and CEO in his district, which is what mattered to me.

I needed access to decision-makers, generally the CEO or CFO, or investors with controlling shares. I also needed to know which companies were good, which were bad, who would sell, and who was looking to make acquisitions for which the bank could earn fees for arranging and financing. In addition to access I needed to establish trust, as these are not questions that CEOs are eager to discuss with just anyone, especially not foreigners. I needed Mr. Zhang to walk me in.

From the Nanjing South train station, I took a taxi to meet Mr. Zhang. The car pulled up in front of a modern steel and glass office building, but the glass was splattered with mud and I had to step over rubble to get to the main entrance, but I was careful not to scuff my shoes. Inside, the building was already showing signs of age, with cracks in the marble floor and plaster peeling from the walls. There was no reception on the ground floor, just a wall listing the many businesses on the floors above. They were mostly consulting businesses and others that sounded too small to be of interest to a large foreign bank. Finding no place to sit, I walked back outside just as Mr. Zhang's black Buick sedan rounded the corner and pulled up to the entrance. The rear passenger door flew open and the large figure emerged, using all his strength to pull himself from the car.

We greeted each other warmly. "Director Zhang, thank you for bringing me to this company. Are you sure they are okay talking to an international bank?"

"Mr. Ji," Zhang said, using my Chinese name, "you asked me to find you good companies, and this is a good company. They'll talk to you because I told them to." Zhang puffed out his chest as he spoke. "I can't say if they will work with you or not, that's up to you."

"I understand, I just hope they are open to the idea. This is a software outsourcing firm, correct? Do you have any idea of what their financing needs are?"

"Ah, they can tell you all about that. These are my good friends. They needed a zoning law changed so they could build a dormitory next to their call center. They are grateful to me. They have six thousand employees now." Zhang pushed his face closer to mine and repeated, "*Six thousand*. College graduates, highly skilled." I smelled the stink of nicotine on his breath but tried not to show it. "Mr. Ji, you think China only makes cheap stuff like shoes and umbrellas? Not true anymore! We have advanced technology."

That particular company in the end was able to get financing from local banks at much better rates than we were able to provide, but it was an excellent acquisition target for the many foreign companies that were looking to buy their way into the market. Mr. Zhang made a number of such introductions that helped us both achieve our goals. With his help we arranged several fund raisings and at least one capital market transaction, but he was old school and retired soon after working with me, and I never saw him again. The new crop of China's government officials is nothing like Mr. Zhang. They are highly educated, well-traveled, and in some cases fluent in at least one foreign language. Like Mr. Zhang, they work long hours but the heavy drinking is thankfully no longer part of the job description.

In the 1990s and 2000s, China's young people wanted to start businesses or work for big companies, but government positions are now considered more desirable because they are more secure—the iron rice bowl. One of my colleagues left banking to go into government. He was not in my group and I didn't know him well, but I was shocked. He had to pass a rigorous civil service exam and undergo a background check, all in order to take a massive pay cut. I didn't know what his government salary would be, but it couldn't have been anywhere near what he earned at the bank.

It's hard to pinpoint exactly when this shift took place, but it broadly coincided with China's years of rapid GDP growth and the rise of domestic enterprises in the early to mid-2010s. What's easier to identify is when that momentum came to a halt, as we'll see in the chapter on Covid. China's strict zero-Covid policy revealed the fragility of a system built around extreme centralized control. Lockdowns disrupted production, crushed consumer spending, and sent youth unemployment to record levels. Growth stalled, private investment dried up, and reports emerged of delayed or reduced pay even for government employees and workers in state-owned enterprises.

Foreign companies generally pay higher salaries and are notoriously obedient and willing to be controlled in China. They have little reason not to be. While the party's internal workings are mysterious and opaque, once decisions are made China's state-led economy is quite transparent about what they expect companies to do—both domestic and foreign. The Five-Year plans clearly explain what sectors are available for foreign investment and which industries will be difficult to penetrate. In many ways, China's unique system of government has worked well for businesses, including foreign enterprises, as long as they pay attention, adapt when they need to, and above all, obey the directives of the party.

Still, the role of government in China is one of its most contentious issues with the United States and other Western nations. Beijing manages the economy using very different tools than those employed in the United States. China's state-owned enterprises and industrial subsidies are vital levers of control that its leaders are unlikely to give up—even if they violate the rules of the World Trade Organization or might keep China out of major multilateral trade agreements like the Comprehensive and Progressive Agreement for Trans-Pacific Partnership as a result. As we will see in later chapters, such agreements anyway lost much of their meaning once Donald Trump entered the scene and turned trade policy into a series of transactional deals.

Chapter 8

Walled Out

Bob Theleen, the ChinaVest investment banker, stepped into the room with the unhurried confidence of a lion on the Serengeti. He was a few minutes late, and our guests from Washington DC were already milling about the large conference room at the American Chamber, exchanging business cards with the dozen or so members who were invited to attend. The spotlight always seemed to follow Bob, and people turned slightly in his direction as he crossed the room.

In 2014 Bob was in his second term as chairman of the American Chamber of Commerce in Shanghai. His white hair was cut short, and his blue eyes flashed around the room looking for the sources of power and influence. His sly smile made everyone believe he knew something that they didn't.

That Bob was late was not a problem, as the Chamber's professional staff handled protocol matters. The elected chairman of the Board of Governors was the head of the chamber, but the president, a full-time paid executive, managed the organization.

The chamber's president, Ken Jarrett, met the delegation in front of our building and walked them up to our offices. Ken, a former US diplomat, was meticulous about managing protocol, both with American and Chinese government officials. If we hosted a meeting with the Chinese, the American flag was placed to the right of both speakers. If China was hosting, their flag would take that position. Since our meetings were often held in hotels or other neutral locations, it was necessary to specify who was hosting and place the flags appropriately.

I learned a lot from Ken—and from Bob—and would later succeed him as president of the chamber, but at the time I had just been elected to the board and this was my first experience with a Congressional delegation, or "CoDel." Members of Congress used to travel frequently to China, but as the relationship deteriorated and American voters became skeptical of China, politicians avoided trips that they would need to explain to their constituents.

Congressman Ed Royce, a Republican from California, was the ranking member of the delegation, but Paul Ryan seemed to occupy center stage. Shortly after our meeting he would be elected Speaker of the House, then later he would join Mitt Romney's ticket as the vice presidential candidate in their unsuccessful bid for the White House. As Congressman Ryan took his turn to speak, he explained "I may be a member of Congress in the United States, but here in Shanghai I'm known as Stan's brother!" Stan Ryan was an AmCham member and a senior executive at Cargill, based in Shanghai. He had helped the Chamber staff set up the meeting and would arrange others as his brother's career progressed.

Ryan and Royce were at the head of the table, seated next to the AmCham chairman and our president, Ken Jarrett. Ken skillfully guided the conversation and allocated airtime as we went around the room. Executives from 3M, Dow Chemical, and other large companies each took a turn explaining their business in China and mentioning one or two issues. The conversation turned to intellectual property (IP). Denis Simon had recently taken up a position as head of Duke University's new joint venture campus just outside the city of Shanghai in Kunshan. "IP theft, though not zero, is actually much less of an issue, now that Chinese companies are fast developing their own IP," the executive vice chancellor explained. "Local authorities are much more eager to enforce violations. We even got a visit from authorities on our campus asking about our own IP situation."

Ken offered, with a sly grin: "Well, maybe they just want to know if Duke University actually has a real Duke?" Everyone laughed, but the delegation was skeptical. For years they had been told that China stole IP, and that American companies would come over and sell one unit, which would be quickly reverse-engineered and copied.

Enforcement of intellectual property is still a major weakness for China, affecting domestic as well as foreign companies. Enforcement is inconsistent, transparency is partial, trade secret protection and deterrent penalties are often inadequate. Foreign companies face significant risks, especially in cross-border contexts. The legal environment is better than it was, but it is not yet fully predictable, transparent, or equal for all stakeholders.

I had only recently been elected to the AmCham board, so as a junior member of our group I was seated furthest away from the head of the table, placing me next to a lower-ranking member of the Washington delegation, a first-term Congressman named Ami Bera.

As it turned out, Bera was coming from a side trip to India, where his parents were born. "I was treated like a rock star," he told me. We would later meet frequently in Washington DC and in his district in Sacramento. Congressman Bera was elevated to the powerful House Foreign Affairs Committee and served as chair of the subcommittee on Asia.

Bera and our other guests were eager to know what we thought of Xi Jinping, who was still relatively new in his role as the supreme leader of China, and what direction the country was headed. What did China's continued growth portend for America's economy, and for jobs in their voting districts?

Were US companies making deals in China that yielded short term profits in exchange for technology? Were they simply enabling their domestic competitors, to whom the enormous market would ultimately belong, and would others eventually be shown the door? China is complicated and constantly changing, such that these questions have more than one answer.

Today, there is no doubt that domestic firms dominate, and that the state plays a significant role in keeping it that way, whether by directing cheap capital, government procurement rules, or outright restrictions, but it's also true that over a period of perhaps two decades from the mid-1990s, foreign companies operated very successfully in China, earning significant profits.

Bob was an optimist, and spoke only about the companies that were allowed into China in the post-WTO, pre-mid 2010s period. Firms in restricted industries had no presence in China and were never members of AmCham. For those allowed in, the government welcomed investments. The market was growing at a good clip, Chinese consumers were snapping up foreign brands, and circa 2014, most foreign company CEOs believed the future was bright.

"Gentlemen, if you want to know what's going on in China today then you need to look inside Mrs. Wang's purse." Bob Theleen loved telling stories, which sometimes took a long way around to arrive at his point. The Mrs. Wang character was a favorite of his, but not everyone immediately grasped that she was a metaphor for China's consumer economy and not a real person.

"What's in her purse?" Bob asked the room, rhetorically, then answered his own question. "The keys to her Cadillac, an Apple iPhone, and beauty products from Estée Lauder. She shops at Ralph Lauren and takes her kids to KFC and McDonald's."

Some people incorrectly assumed Mrs. Wang referred to Bob's wife, but I knew better. Bob's wife was Jenny Hsui, the other rainmaker in the company they co-founded, ChinaVest. It was a boutique investment bank and venture capital firm that was financing companies in China as early as the 1980s. Jenny was a highly educated globe-trotting woman, as much at home in Beijing as she was in Singapore, Paris, or San Francisco. Jenny was anything but average or typical. Bob's fictional character also represented a wealthy middle-class consumer, which Bob believed was key to the success of American companies in the fast-growing China market.

The group of American legislators listened intently as Bob expounded on his story. They were expecting to hear tales of woe, about how American companies couldn't get access to the market, failed to turn a profit because of unfair business practices, and that we were robbed blind by intellectual property thieves. The narrative in Washington was that China cheated, enjoying the benefits of open markets in the West while keeping its own markets closed. The state subsidized its businesses, forcing non-Chinese companies to compete not just against domestic competitors but against the state itself. These practices were distorting markets and damaging the global trading system, the politicians believed.

The US lawmakers had a point, and as things turned out they were more right than wrong. China's markets were open to foreign companies in some industries, but essentially closed or highly restricted in many other areas including cloud computing, financial services, and health insurance, among others. But Bob was an eternal optimist. "If you give me a glass that's half empty then I'll add whisky and make it Irish!" he quipped. His jokes were often about ethnic groups, making younger members of the chamber cringe. His story did not fit the narrative the members of Congress had come to hear, although they knew quite well that China's consumer economy was exploding with growth. And throughout the 2000s and most of the 2010s, it was. Bob's mistake was assuming this trend would continue. It did not.

"I know you hear a lot of noise about China, and I'm sure you get complaints," Bob continued. "The CEO from GM probably tells you they are forced into joint ventures over here with state-owned companies, which is true. You hear a lot about China, but GM never complains about Japan, right? That's because GM doesn't sell any cars in Japan!" GM entered China in the late 1990s and by the early 2010s, was selling more cars in China than in the United States.

I looked around the room and saw heads turned to the side and eyes squinting skeptically, which only spurred Bob to press on. "The CEO of McDonald's in China was planning to be here today, but I'm sorry she couldn't make it…she's too busy opening her two thousandth restaurant!"

In 2014, while McDonald's, GM, and other American brands were doing very well, the market was already starting to shift. Foreign brands were facing a growing list of problems, both market and regulatory, and consumers were turning more toward local brands, some of which had ambitions to go global themselves. Starbucks, Apple, Nike, and Coca-Cola all had local competitors nipping at their heels. McDonald's sold all its China and Hong Kong outlets to local investors in 2017. At the super luxury level, global brands still occupied a layer that ignored national boundaries, but for everyday items Chinese consumers were turning toward local brands that offered similar capabilities at a cheaper price. In the mid-2010s, the shift was just beginning to take place, and by 2024, the keys in Mrs. Wang's purse would more likely fit a vehicle made by a Chinese brand like NIO, XPeng, or BYD instead of a Cadillac or BMW.

Buoyed by the optimism of Bob and others like him, American companies invested heavily in China, confident that scale and early entry would translate into lasting advantage. But the strategies they pursued—and the foundations on which those investments rested—were not designed to deliver durable returns. What the system wanted from foreign companies was access to technology, management know-how, and, above all, time to build its own capabilities. From General Motors to Starbucks, the foreign companies obliged.

In the automotive sector, foreign companies largely accepted 49–51 joint venture structures, ceding effective control of the Chinese operations they were financing and building. These arrangements facilitated market entry and rapid expansion, but they also ensured that critical knowledge, talent, and leverage ultimately resided on the Chinese side—laying the groundwork for domestic competitors to emerge and, eventually, to eclipse their foreign partners.

"How many injuries do you have in a plant like this?" I asked, recalling the factories I toured as a BCG consultant in the 1990s. The Chinese factories of that period were messy, loud, and unsafe; this facility, which I visited some two decades later, was nothing like that. A large foreign auto manufacturer had invited me to tour their assembly plant on the outskirts of Shanghai. We were on the catwalk about thirty feet above the factory floor. My guide had been sent to China from Detroit three years earlier, a move he said worked out well for him both professionally and personally. His family loved living in China.

"Injuries? Yes, I think we had a worker who got hurt two, maybe three years ago. He slipped in the break room and sprained his wrist." As we continued the tour, I noted that neither of us had ear protection. We didn't need it. There was noise, but we could easily converse above the sounds of humming machines, whirring conveyors, and an occasional buzzer.

The assembly line was a marvel of coordination between humans and machines, with a network of systems monitoring for defects and tracking inventory. Parts were stacked in the correct order as car frames moved slowly down the line, a mix of minivans, sedans, and other models. A sensor would immediately detect any wrong part in the stack, which would be whisked away and replaced with the correct one.

I asked if it was difficult to find workers, and how productivity compared to what he had experienced back home. "Fantastic," my guide answered. "Workers here are super motivated and learn quickly. But they aren't tall enough!" That was an answer I wasn't expecting. Apparently, the company built the assembly line to the exact specifications developed in the United States.

Products were tailored for the China market, but the business model of the multinational corporation was to take advantage of economies of scale, and for that, the giant car companies needed to standardize parts, tools, and processes. This was the genius of Henry Ford when his first Model T rolled out of his factory in 1908. Some people think he invented the automobile, but he didn't. He invented the moving assembly line that made cars affordable. "We built the line down there to our exact specifications. The worker at that station needs to be a certain height to reach the controls."

When Ford and GM entered the China market in the 1990s, Beijing forced them into joint ventures and insisted they develop infrastructure and local capabilities that in the end enabled China to develop it's own industry. For a while, the car companies enjoyed incredible growth and profits and by the mid-2010s, China was GM's largest market, hitting a peak of four million units in 2017. China during that time was fantastic for foreign car companies, and for careers.

My guide, who was originally from Europe, had been an auto executive for his entire career. He has traveled the world, following the growth of the industry and taking on bigger and bigger challenges, eventually landing in China in the early 2000s, where he oversaw operations throughout the country. He immediately began learning the local language, and became proficient enough to write messages back and forth with his staff in Chinese.

"This is the only place to be," said my guide. "I'm in China for the rest of my career, full stop." The executive, who declined to be named (and who is no longer in China), explained that it was not just the growth and size of the market that made China important. "It's the innovation. We have to be here. This is where the future of cars is headed, and if we're not here, we're going to miss that. It's a question of our global competitiveness."

Bill Russo, the founder and CEO of Automobility, a strategy and investment advisory firm, agreed. "China is where the growth is, and it's where the innovation happens. I don't want to be anywhere but here." Bill went on to say: "Global automotive companies and their suppliers almost universally seek to deepen their participation in the China market as it represents the key battleground for dominance of the global auto industry."

But Bill, who does still live in China and works with both foreign and Chinese auto companies, was talking about an environment that was changing rapidly. While Ford and GM were ramping up in the 2000s and early 2010s, mesmerized by the increasing volumes, the market was already shifting. Beijing had been signaling for years that the environment had become a priority and that clean energy would be China's future. Complaints had been percolating in China, but an inflection point was reached in 2013. The capital was practically shut down—roads were closed and flights were canceled—by the toxic air that was literally off the charts, impossible to measure by some of the instruments used to monitor the air. Internet users dubbed it the "airpocalypse," and it marked a turning point in people's tolerance for the poisons that damaged their health.

A Chinese journalist, Chai Jing, produced a stunning documentary called "Under the Dome" that detailed the extent of the problem and its causes, laying the blame squarely at the feet of Beijing's policymakers. The film, which has been compared to Al Gore's "An Inconvenient Truth," was viewed 150 million times before it was taken down, four days after its release. To their credit, China's policymakers can be swift and effective once they align on a goal. The government shifted its attention to the quality of the air, water, and soil, putting measures in place that caused enormous disruption to industries but achieved the desired results. Today, China is a leader in battery-powered cars and in renewable energy, generating about a third of the world's solar, wind, and hydropower. It also produces the majority of world's solar panels, wind turbines and other clean-tech equipment. Yet it also remains the largest consumer of coal—a reminder that China's transformation, like its power, rests on a fragile foundation.

According to Russo, the shift to new energy vehicles began even before the revelations about the environment. Policymakers in Beijing understood the strategic value of having a strong vehicle manufacturing industry and were uncomfortable having so little control. Companies from the West had developed the underlying technology for propulsion—the internal combustion engine—and still had a grip on innovation, despite the joint ventures and technology transfers. Moreover, China depended on imports for oil, exposing the country to price shocks or worse, an embargo if the situation came to that. Whether it began as a defense strategy or quality of life decision, electrification was a long-term deliberate effort on the part of the government, accelerated by innovative companies.

Ford and GM claimed the government showed favoritism when they learned of the mandates to sell a certain percentage of their vehicles with zero emissions. Somehow the local companies knew the change was coming and made the necessary adjustments to their capital budgets. It takes at least five years to bring a new vehicle from initial design to market, so planning takes place long in advance. The car makers should have seen this coming, but as Ford and GM continued increasing capacity they missed the transition from ICE to electric. ICE, or internal combustion energy vehicles, had sold well and contributed significantly to the foreign automakers' global revenues, but Chinese upstarts weren't burdened with decades of success, and were anyway part of the China system in a way Ford and GM were not.

One such company wasn't in the business of making cars at all. An innovative local company called BYD made batteries, and got pretty good at it. BYD began making nickel-cadmium batteries but switched to lithium-ion and became a leader in rechargeable batteries. The company began making vehicles in 2003, looking for an opening at the low end of the market, but struggled to make headway against entrenched state-owned players like the joint ventures involving Ford and GM, many of which were already beginning to sell vehicles under their own brands at much lower prices. The shift to electrification changed the game completely and BYD, as a battery maker, was perfectly positioned to succeed.

The company did well, and its electric vehicles (EVs) gained even more momentum after the global market leader, Tesla, entered the market. Beijing allowed Tesla to set up as a wholly foreign-owned entity, not in the clutches of a JV, and built what it called a "Giga factory" in the Lingang district just outside Shanghai. According to Russo, "Tesla's entry into the EV market in China sparked retail consumer interest in electric vehicles, which helped increase retail consumer demand across the entire sector."[3]

The Tesla models were sleek and cool, and early adopters snapped them up quickly. The flashy colors and high prices only added to their appeal as instant status symbols. Demand for electric vehicles had been sluggish up to that point, confined mainly to taxi fleets and other areas where the government had a hand in guiding purchases. The government had been giving the market a boost by offering a subsidy to EV purchasers, but Tesla's validation of the market changed the shape of the demand curve. Traditional ICE vehicle sales went into decline leaving most foreign brands including Ford and GM with unneeded factory capacity ill-equipped to meet the new type of demand.

BYD, now the global market leader by volume, is just one of hundreds of Chinese electric vehicle makers, all competing to out-innovate each other. NIO might be the closest competitor to Tesla in terms of style and the "cool factor." The NIO showroom is in Taikoo Place, a swish new development in central Shanghai. The Starbucks Reserve Roastery, the largest in the world, is on one corner, and luxury brands grace the ground floor of the retail mall. The Tesla showroom also occupies a prime position in the

3 Ker D. Gibbs: *Selling to China.* Palgrave Macmillan (2023) page 109.

same location, and the Chinese automotive upstart picked the site next to it in a not-so-subtle shot across the bow.

NIO was planning to enter the American market and began showing up at AmCham's events, most of which are open to the general public. The managers were eager to learn whatever they could before making a move, and invited me to their showroom for a chat. I was happy to give them whatever advice I could, but I also wanted to drive one of their cars.

A young manager took me out and showed me the features, most of which I was familiar with from driving the Tesla, then invited me to get behind the wheel. Just near the showroom there is a stretch of road with no pedestrian traffic, no intersections, and—most importantly—no traffic cameras. With the manager's permission I stepped hard on the accelerator and felt my head press against the seat for the few seconds it took to travel the quarter mile of safe road. The ride, the interface, and overall driving experience felt to me like the equivalent of a Tesla.

Before returning to the showroom, the manager brought me to the parking garage where he demonstrated NIO's "battery as a service." Customers own the car but borrow the battery. The garage was equipped with what looked like a miniature car wash that lifted out the old battery and within minutes replaced it with a new one, fully charged. China's new carmakers, many of which are backed by tech companies, continue to innovate by integrating smartphone features into the vehicle interface and utilizing AI.

China's capacity for car production—both ICE and EV—and including local and foreign companies—far exceeds the needs of the domestic market, and China has been exporting cars like crazy, and is now the world's largest exporter of vehicles.

Despite the challenges and fierce competition, foreign carmakers still—for now—view China as a necessary place to be. Bill Russo explains: "...maintaining a presence in the world's largest EV market may be the only option if companies are to remain competitive in an electric-powered global automotive industry. Losing the China market will ultimately cede a competitive advantage to ambitious Chinese companies that are rapidly expanding internationally." Holding on in the ultra-competitive Chinese market is the challenge: Ford's sales, for instance, have shrunk dramatically in the past few years and it now has far less than one percent of total China auto sales, compared to four percent at its peak in 2016. An interesting but unanswerable question is what would have been the approach of Ford and other foreign auto makers to the state-mandated shift to EVs if they had actually had full control of their operations, as opposed to being locked inside JVs?

The story of the auto industry was mirrored in ridesharing. Again, an American competitor, Uber, helped establish the market before being pushed aside. In Shanghai, consumers were fatigued with rattletrap taxis driven by unkempt drivers who smoked and chatted on the phone while barrelling around the city. Uber changed that. The cars were new—many of them Teslas—and the drivers were well-groomed and polite, eager to keep their coveted five-star ratings. Local competitors naturally jumped into the market, fueled by venture capital and backed by China's internet giants, Tencent and Alibaba. In the early stages of the new business model, the rideshare companies were all losing money, but the other issue was local regulation, which one way or another favored the local firms which seemed to navigate through the uncertainties more smoothly, while Uber continually faced closures and fines, especially as the company tried to expand beyond the coastal cities.

After struggling for a few years, Uber sold its China business to Didi Chuxing, the local market leader and the chosen "national champion." My guide at the Shanghai factory, the European auto executive who had staked is career on the China market, lost his job as his company's market share collapsed. Foreign brand car sales have plummeted since 2020. China used to be the place where executives were sent, as a way station on their way to the C-suite or the boardroom. Today, it's a graveyard. Those same executives struggle to form strategies in an intensely competitive market that isn't growing.

Local brands now dominate the China market in almost every category. Did they benefit from the presence of foreign firms? Undoubtedly. Could the future have turned out differently for US companies, had they not been forced into JVs, or would the more nimble local entrepreneurs have found a way to persevere anyway? Some answers are unknowable, but the questions have to be asked as foreign companies make decisions and map out their strategies in China. The competitive dynamics have fundamentally changed. Chinese companies in many sectors are no longer catching up—they are innovating, setting standards, and competing globally from positions of strength.

In global markets, China's companies are subject to one of their country's great weaknesses: poor trading relationships. China's reputation for unfair trading practices, flooding the market with state-subsidized products and buying little in return, has caused Europe and the United States to raise barriers and tariffs on Chinese EVs. Policy makers in the US and Europe are also concerned about shaping who controls or influences EV supply chains, battery technology, and charging infrastructure, as matters of strategic importance. China is setting global standards and norms in EV technology, which could entrench its competitive advantages. Ironically, these are the same concerns that led policymakers in Beijing to make the shift from ICE to EVs.

China's rise once seemed inseparable from its integration into global markets, but today in many ways it seems walled off, either by its own system or the global reaction to it. The US opened the door to China's rise through WTO entry in 2001, but Beijing has fundamentally used that access to build the national champions, not to liberalize its system. Foreign companies that once benefited from China's expansion now face a maturing market dominated by agile local competitors, political headwinds, and a weakened appetite among consumers for foreign brands.

Companies entering the China market today need to consider the experience of both GM and Uber: a joint venture will benefit from the local knowledge and expertise of a partner, but often affords little control. A wholly owned subsidiary, like Tesla in China, will face formidable local competition and a system that is designed to prevent foreign brands from achieving a significant share of the market.

China's global push—especially in EVs and advanced manufacturing—is colliding with a world increasingly unwilling to tolerate its state-driven system. Europe and the United States are erecting or at least discussing defensive barriers, linking market access to reciprocity as well as concerns about over-reliance on Chinese industries and supply chains. In confronting China's economic model, they have exposed not only the limits of Beijing's ambitions abroad, but also the fragility beneath its outward appearance of strength.

CHAPTER 9

Precarious at the Top

eBay entered the China market in 2002 with an investment in a local company, EachNet, which had over 80% share of the nascent e-commerce market, according to reports. After paying $180 million for the initial stake, eBay poured money and resources into the market, with the company's star CEO, Meg Whitman, determined to win.

But after spending as much as a billion dollars in China, eBay was still making losses, and its market share had plummeted in favor of Taobao, a division of Alibaba. eBay still has a cross-border business matching Chinese sellers to overseas buyers, but as a consumer-facing business in China it failed spectacularly and shut down local operations in 2006.

Taobao also lost money for much of the 2000s but it grew users and transaction volume quickly and by the time its parent company, Alibaba, went public in 2014 Taobao was an enormous success. HSBC was lending to the parent company using the Taobao asset as collateral, and I was one of the bankers assigned to calculate the actual value of Taobao. The company was still unprofitable at the time, so without earnings, the price-to-earnings ratio was meaningless as a method for valuing the company. We therefore used discounted cash flow models and compared its user metrics to publicly traded e-commerce businesses as a proxy for what it was worth, which was many billions.

What led to eBay's demise in China, and what does it say about America's technology champions and their ability to succeed in global markets? Could this have been avoided?

eBay was not alone. Many foreign companies, especially technology companies, have tried and failed in China, each with its own excuses and tales of woe. Some companies, like Facebook and Twitter, have been blocked from the outset, while others made deliberate, principled decisions to leave. Yahoo, Google, and later LinkedIn were unable to reconcile their corporate values with the local market conditions and regulatory environment, which required them to censor content and share user data with the government. These companies—America's tech champions—aren't prohibited from operating in China; they simply need to comply with local laws if they do, which is true of every business everywhere. China, with its tightly censored Internet and strict laws governing data, is a difficult place for businesses based on the free flow of information and ideas. eBay was different. It was also a content company in some ways, but it was basically an online marketplace. So what was the problem?

My friend Jiang Wei arrived in China in the early 2000s to work for eBay, or rather he *returned* to China. Wei was born in Beijing and graduated from the prestigious Peking University, then joined the early group of Chinese students who came to the United States for an advanced degree, and to work in Silicon Valley, which is where we met. He was enjoying a successful career with start-ups and well-established companies, but in the early 2000s, he saw China climbing up the post-WTO growth curve and could no longer stay on the sidelines. He knew that his business and entrepreneurial skills would rate a high value in his native country.

Alibaba's Taobao business was years behind eBay with a primitive technology platform and little understanding of how to run an auction business. Wei was an expert in category management, which is the core of the business. Silicon Valley was known for its fast-moving culture, but Wei and his colleagues were about to find out how quickly local companies in China could learn what they needed to know to turn things around.

Some of the challenges that eBay had to overcome were endemic to China—online payment systems hadn't yet developed, and delivery logistics were weak. The number of internet users was growing quickly, but there was skepticism about online commerce, and for good reason. Customers often never received the goods they ordered, and the legal system offered little recourse.

In the years following, all that would change. Taobao's brilliant solution was to require all vendors to offer a seven-day no-questions-asked right of return on all purchases. In China's hyper-competitive e-commerce market deliveries are now tracked precisely, and wrong items are swiftly replaced. I recently ordered a pair of shoelaces from my home in Shanghai, just to see if it was possible for something so cheap to be delivered. I paid fifteen renminbi, about two dollars; the shoelaces showed up on my doorstep the next day.

Some people said part of eBay's failure was that the company couldn't adjust to the street fight, restrained by rules that didn't apply to local companies. eBay had a global reputation to protect, and as a publicly traded company, it had SEC and other regulators monitoring everything it did. As Wei puts it, "It's not that we brought a knife to a gunfight—we brought a *jet* to a street fight. Everything we did involved massive resources, endless meetings and PowerPoint presentations. That much firepower wasn't necessary. We really just needed to execute at the ground level."

Wei, speaking from his home in Silicon Valley, went on to explain the legal environment in China in the 2000s. "In America the law is black and white—something is legal or it's not. It was different in China. The laws were vague, and changing all the time. Everyone was guilty of something, so nobody worried about it. The question was more if you were doing something that the authorities didn't like—something political, for instance. Whether it was legal or not didn't matter."

eBay's PayPal unit—the system that processes payments on eBay and other websites—ran into exactly that kind of situation. Alan Tien, a senior executive at PayPal who was sent to China to get things started, explains: "The business was new, with no regulations to govern it yet. We were in a holding pattern until we got the go-ahead." But Alibaba's reaction to the regulatory vacuum was the exact opposite, forging ahead with the AliPay service to facilitate online payments because they hadn't been told *not* to.

"TaoBao was successful because AliPay was successful," said Alan, "whereas eBay failed (in China) because PayPal didn't make it. The two go together." Could PayPal have gone ahead in China? The answer is that the system would not have allowed it. Moreover, could PayPal have engaged in a non-legal business in China, given the oversight of American regulators and public shareholders?

China became strategically important for eBay, but it was nothing but a drain on the bottom line. "It was hard for us to take risks or make demands back at headquarters," says Alan, now back in Silicon Valley after finishing his expat assignment in China. "Even if we needed something urgently, a change or feature for the China business wasn't important to the engineering team at headquarters."

Speed is a key factor, and a major issue impacting the competitiveness of multinational companies in China. For senior managers like Wei and Alan it wasn't a question of authority to make decisions—it was often a matter of how the business was structured. "We needed a simple change to the landing page, but it was connected to our global platform." Wei and his team couldn't make a change in China without affecting the eBay site in Germany and the dozens of other countries where eBay does business. "Our changes had to fit into a nine-month schedule. For our local competitor those changes would take nine days, maybe even nine hours."

China's entrepreneurial environment is famous for speed, even compared to Silicon Valley. Everything in China happens fast—buildings go up fast, and they can fall apart pretty fast too. Decisions are made quickly, but so are mistakes. China's entrepreneurs take incredible risks, often repeatedly, undaunted by failure. Jiang Wei, now a venture capitalist, explains it this way: "Many of China's entrepreneurs come from humble backgrounds, so suffering as a result of a temporary failure isn't a big deal. They can handle it."

The success of China's entrepreneurs needs to be seen in the context of the enormous scrap heap of failures. Every problem or opportunity has thousands of smart, motivated people looking to solve it, almost all of whom will fail. We only see the one who succeeds. The formula of talent mixed with an appetite for risk in a fast-moving environment creates a potent cocktail. With capital to work with and an enlightened government willing to get out of the way—as China had in the decades from Deng onward before Xi Jinping—the phenomenal growth and success of China's local technology giants like Alibaba and Tencent cannot be a surprise.

Joerg Wuttke, my counterpart as president of the European Chamber of Commerce, offers the analogy of a "fitness center" to explain the success of Chinese entrepreneurs. Chinese firms train, improve, and perfect their techniques in contests with fixed rules, and the winners move up in the market. He's right about the intense competition, but the Chinese system could also be described as a Roman coliseum—a ruthless, high-stakes arena where the competition is not just intense but existential. In this coliseum, the winner takes all, and the game is not always fair. Success means domination; failure often means extinction. Companies are not merely trying to improve their form or efficiency—they are fighting for survival in front of a powerful and often interventionist state, much like gladiators battling before the Roman emperor. The party, like the Roman authorities, sets the rules—and can change them at any moment. What is permissible today may be restricted tomorrow. What is punished today may be rewarded next quarter. This unpredictability forces competitors to become both exceptionally agile and fiercely innovative.

In such a system, the firms that survive are the most adaptable and resilient, and are also considered by the system to be useful and compliant. Chinese tech giants like Tencent, Huawei, ByteDance, and DJI are not just the result of market competition—they are products of relentless pressure, rapid iteration, brutal contestation, and solid integration with the system. Each generation of champions is stronger, faster, and more strategically aware than the last because the system relentlessly weeds out the weak. The coliseum, unlike the fitness center, doesn't reward slow and steady improvement—it demands transformation under fire.

Ironically, the rise of companies like Alibaba and Tencent could be seen as revealing the weakness and insecurity of the state, and the leaders in Beijing came to believe its tech CEOs were becoming too powerful. Since its founding, the party has viewed businesspeople and entrepreneurs with suspicion, but Jack Ma, the founder of Alibaba, pushed that suspicion too far. He was preparing to list Ant Financial (the name was later changed to Ant Group) on the stock market and for some reason felt that was the time to make a speech critical of China's state-owned banks and financial regulators, who he felt hadn't kept pace with innovations in the market and consumer demands. Retribution was swift. Ma disappeared from public view, and the Ant IPO, which was to have been the largest in history, was canceled.

Ma had been traveling around the world, where he was treated almost as if he were a head of state, something that the delicate sensibilities of the party could not tolerate. He finally resurfaced, living in Tokyo, but in the meantime Alibaba and Ant went through a huge system-required restructuring. Other tech giants, including Tencent and Didi Chuxing, also came under the microscope, with investigations into violations of antitrust regulations, market manipulation, and data collection. But mainly it was about obedience and subservience to the system.

Private education and health care companies came next, as Xi Jinping pushed ideologies like "common prosperity" and brought China's private sector companies to heal. The goals and ideals were hard to argue against, as the gap between rich and poor grew larger with China's reforms that have taken the country further and further from its Marxist roots. Xi Jinping's speeches have invoked ideas stressing party control not heard for decades, and he has expressed strong views on the role that entrepreneurs, state-owned enterprises and foreign companies, should play in his version of the new China.

The targets of the regulatory assault were mainly local

companies that the party believed had become too powerful, but the data localization law impacted any business that operates across borders, which included most foreign firms. The law was vague, causing firms to often overreact as they searched for the line that they couldn't cross. "I just issued an order for all my China staff," the chief legal officer of a Fortune 500 company told me in 2021, as China's security laws continued to tighten. "If they travel outside China, no matter for business or vacation, they can't take any electronic device. No computer, no phone, nothing. I can't take the risk that Chinese data could be on it."

The regulatory crackdown sent a chill through China's entrepreneur community, with many of those who could leave packing up for Singapore, Japan, or the United States. Or at least massively diversifying. Before the crackdown, China's homegrown companies had become powerful indeed, especially in the tech sector but they also brought innovation to traditional businesses as well.

China's economy produces remarkable successes, but often at the cost of crushing the very dynamism it relies on. The system rewards speed, intensity, and scale, yet punishes independence or influence not sanctioned by the party. The rise of national champions shows what Chinese firms can achieve with state backing and in response to relentless competitive pressure, but the fate of icons like Jack Ma shows how quickly success can turn into vulnerability.

Xi's regulatory measures and tightening controls have drained confidence, driven investors and talent abroad, and left both foreign and domestic companies operating under a cloud of uncertainty. China's growth model continues to generate world-class firms, but it is increasingly shaped by concern—concern about control and about private capital backing that is too powerful. In such an environment, the weak rarely survive, and the strong survive only as long as they remain useful to the system. This fragility at the heart of China's success story is the Dragon's biggest weakness: a system where brilliance is possible, but permanence is never guaranteed.

Chapter 10

The Evolution of "In China for China"

Ken Jarrett huddled with a few AmCham members and staff in a conference room at the Chamber, trying to come up with ways to describe the long arc of American business in China. The year 2015 was the 100th anniversary of the founding of the American Chamber of Commerce in Shanghai, and we had big plans to celebrate what had become the largest foreign non-profit organization in China, and the most influential foreign business association. It was also an opportunity to generate sponsorship revenue for the Chamber, as our member companies eagerly associated their brands with the Chamber's long history and commitment to the market. Over the next twelve months the chamber staff would write stories, produce brochures, and even publish a picture book documenting our colorful past.

In addition to his role as president of AmCham, Ken was our resident historian. He had a life-long passion—some said obsession—for all things Chinese. He had spent four decades in and out of China as a student, teacher, and diplomat. He had a way of offering up weird facts and making obscure references to things like Eunuch advisors from the Ming dynasty, or the origins of the hairstyle favored by the Manchus, the last foreign empire to rule China. (The Manchus forced Chinese men to shave the front of their heads and braid their hair into long strings as a symbol of obedience).

The Chamber's modern history began in the 1980s, soon after the normalization of relations between Beijing and Washington. "Made in China" pretty much summed things up for the country that emerged from years of struggles. China was a source of cheap labor and low cost goods and that was pretty much it, until Deng's policies of "Reform and Opening Up" began to take hold. When China entered the WTO in 2001, access to global markets and foreign capital threw fuel on the fire, and China became the world's factory. Productivity skyrocketed, and China's workers began earning better than just a living wage, and a middle class emerged and gave rise to a consumer economy. In the 1980s and 1990s, Chinese consumers were already acquiring refrigerators and televisions, but in the 2000s they began buying pet food, designer clothes, cars, and even luxury items. Lifestyles had changed.

As China became more wealthy, foreign businesses began paying more attention to China as a market. Instead of investing in factories producing goods for export, they began producing goods—and later, services—in China for sale in China, giving rise to the short-hand description, "in China for China." That phrase described the goal of many foreign businesses in China in the late 2000s and 2010s. But even then the economy was changing quickly, as was the political landscape and the future was getting murky.

"That's not the right term anymore." Dan Krassenstein was on the AmCham board and had made trips to Washington representing the chamber. "People in DC will get the wrong idea. 'In China for China' sounds like we changed teams." Dan was right. In 2015, the wind was also shifting in the United States with people finally beginning to understand that China was not only a market but also a competitor.

"Well, according to the 2013-2014 survey, fifty-nine percent of companies reported that they were primarily in China to compete in the domestic market." Ken had an encyclopedic knowledge of the numbers. "A significant number reported developing unique products and services for domestic consumption." Our annual survey—the longest-running survey of its kind in China—captured members' sentiments by asking detailed questions, which were then assembled into a report. For years, Ken had been presenting the numbers to the media in interviews with the business papers and television and he knew them inside and out.

For years foreign companies complained about being forced into joint ventures, often with bloated state-owned enterprises with sclerotic corporate cultures that added little value. As China developed, both in terms of managerial skills and the capabilities of local companies, and the market became more complex and competitive, foreign companies began partnering rather than entering the market alone.

"In China *with* China should be our new bumper sticker," Ken declared, and this idea was folded into the narrative we used to explain how American businesses were operating in China. At the time, we had no idea how right Ken would prove to be. In August 2016, shortly after we began using Ken's new phrase, Uber announced it would merge its China business with a local company in exchange for a 20 percent stake, and agreed to exit the market. Was Uber in China *with* China, or would some say *out of* China?

The year 2016 also marked a change in my own career. I had left banking and began making private equity investments, at times with a fund but also on my own. Orange Hotels had done well, giving me confidence and capital to work with. The working hours also gave me the flexibility to spend more time with the Chamber.

I had been serving on AmCham's board of governors since 2014, and developed a reputation among members for being outspoken, but balanced with my views on China. I decided to run for chair.

The board elections had become a bit of a dogfight. The Chamber had grown to almost 3,000 members, with a paid staff of 50 professionals and an annual budget of five million dollars. In recent years, under the leadership of Bob Theleen and Ken Jarrett, the organization had risen in stature and developed an influential voice both in Washington and Beijing. Board members were unpaid, but enjoyed the privilege of sharing their views with policymakers, prompting more and more members to vie for the eleven elected seats.

Candidates from lesser known companies began handing out fliers and seeking endorsements, bringing democracy and retail politics to the People's Republic of China, or at least the foreign segment of it. The Chamber had long since moved to electronic voting, which was audited by one of the Big Four accounting firms. Despite the fierce competition, at times followed by tears when the results were announced, we never had a problem with credibility of the results.

I was elected chairman, succeeding Bob Theleen, and served for two years. When Ken Jarrett finished his term as president, the board chose me to take his place, and I managed the Chamber as the full-time executive for the next three years.

As chairman, I oversaw a staff reduction and cut in budget, ending years of operating deficits. In the 1990s and early 2000s the Chamber experienced frenetic growth and expanded the staff and programs accordingly. By the late 2000s, and accelerating into the 2010s, the Chinese economy was becoming more localized. In the early days, expat managers were sent from headquarters to manage subsidiaries in China, but as the economy matured and local staff developed more skills—or brought skills from overseas as *haigui*—the foreigners were replaced. For expatriates, joining the American Chamber was almost automatic. Local professionals, however, had more options for networking and information-sharing, and sometimes viewed the Chamber's role in advocacy as stirring up trouble as opposed to solving problems.

The Chamber was made up of foreign companies, but the people representing the firms could be of any nationality. By 2016, the year I took over as chairman, the majority of the members of the American Chamber of Commerce were Chinese. The culture and the mission remained the same, but the needs were different. Adding to the issues, the Chinese economy had matured. Fewer new companies were entering the market, using the American Chamber as a landing pad. Despite efforts to adapt and cater more to a changing market, our membership—and revenues—had peaked.

Ken and I spent countless hours on the budget and mapped out a more sustainable future, bringing the chamber back to profitablity. In my years as the chief executive, the chamber was consistently profitable and I never had to go to the board to explain a net operating loss. As an organization, we extended our reach into adjacent markets, redefining "Shanghai" to include not just the neighboring city of Suzhou, but Nanjing and Hangzhou as well. But the biggest change that Ken suggested I consider, as he handed the keys over to me, was moving the office itself.

The American Chamber had been in the Shanghai Centre

for two decades. It was a mixed-use complex designed by the renowned architect John Portman. It was developed to serve foreign businesses, with two office towers, serviced apartments, and a hotel. The retail base had shops, restaurants, and a supermarket, initially catering to foreigners, making Shanghai Centre the ideal hub for business and social activities for Europeans, Japanese, Americans, and others.

The twin office towers were the tallest in Shanghai when they opened in 1990. The city's iconic Oriental Pearl TV Tower on the other side of the Huangpu River would not be completed for a number of years, and the financial center around it was still in the planning stages, as was the entire "new area" of Pudong. The skyscrapers that would rise over the following decades, such as the 128-story Shanghai Tower, which twists as it rises through the clouds to a height of over 2,000 feet, have transformed the skyline and dwarfed the old Shanghai Centre.

It was said that from above, the profile of the complex was shaped like an American eagle, but that required some imagination. From that angle an eagle would have flown directly over the Sino-Soviet Friendship Building,[4] a Stalinist neoclassical structure that was gifted to the city in 1955 as a symbol of cooperation. Today it stands as a relic of that period, just as the Shanghai Centre may someday become.

Some people appreciate the design of the Shanghai Centre—also called the Portman— but others say the entrance feels like a freeway underpass, with its enormous columns and closed interior that fills with exhaust fumes when diesel-powered tour buses come through. As fewer foreign companies entered the market and those already established became more integrated into the local environment, the Portman lost its appeal and began

4 The name of the building was later changed to the "Shanghai Exhibition Center."

to seem tired and hollowed out. Some people reported that the complex, once vibrant and bustling, felt like death, while others said it was symbolic of a time long past.

Either way, it was time for the Chamber to move. The board was reluctant but finally agreed to take up a new space in Xintiandi, a dynamic, modern district with new office towers and an energy that spoke to the future, whatever that future might be. The centerpiece of Xintiandi, meaning "new heaven and earth" in Chinese, was a retail center that was redeveloped by Shui On Land and the architect Ben Wood. The rebuilt brick structures gave it an old-world charm, harkening back to Shanghai's heyday of the 1930s. It was said that young people liked Xintiandi because it was old, but old people liked it because it was new. Westerners liked it because it was Chinese, and Chinese people liked it because it was foreign. Somehow, that seemed fitting for AmCham's new home.

The "In China for China" strategy has evolved and now means something different than it once did: what began as a strategy for market access has become a struggle for survival. Foreign firms once entered China to shape its market and fuel global growth, but today they operate within a system that expects compliance, rewards localization, and narrows the space for foreign influence. The party leadership's emphasis on self-reliance, political discipline, and security has pushed multinationals into deeper isolation, with China operations increasingly siloed from global headquarters and constrained by rising regulatory and political risk.

AmCham's changing membership—more local, less focused on expansion, and with fewer new foreign entrants—reflects a market no longer defined by fresh opportunity but by cautious maintenance. Most foreign companies are staying, but they are no longer betting big. The era when global firms helped integrate

China into the world economy is to a large extent over; the new reality is a China more self-contained, more suspicious, and far less receptive to the kind of foreign participation that once fueled its rise.

Stephen White, an AmCham member who ran a local design firm, arranged our new space with open offices and a large community area for members. "It's time to move," he said, as he helped prepare my presentation to the Board. "Members are thinking about their future here in China, and the old office at the Portman makes them feel stuck in the past." By 2020, in the middle of the Covid lockdown, when the Chamber finally moved to the new space, expats had already been leaving China for a while, and the slick new offices weren't going to change that. Shortly after the move, Stephen White left China himself, after some thirty years. "It was time to move on," he said.

PART 4

THE END OF ENGAGEMENT

Chapter 11

The Fragility of Power

The conference room in the old offices of the American Chamber of Commerce faced an inside courtyard, providing natural light but not much of a view. Winter was coming, but that was not the cause of our dark mood. In 2008 the Lehman Brothers bank had just collapsed, the stock market was in turmoil, and a recession was coming—or worse. The crisis originated in America but the ripple effects were already hitting China, with major implications for US-China relations as well as our businesses.

"I hope they don't actually speak to Chinese government officials like that," said Ben Kinnas, jerking his head toward the conference room door through which a group of US officials had just left. Ben was the head of Wells Fargo in China, and chair of the committee. His thinning hair and stocky frame gave him an air of authority, but everyone in the room also knew he had paid his dues with decades of experience as a banker in Shanghai, Hong Kong, and earlier in Japan. He laughed about having worked for five banks without ever changing jobs; banks are constantly getting merged or acquired, resulting in management shuffles that leave some people out of a job, but not Ben. He was a survivor, and we looked to him to read the landscape. "They won't get far trying to tell the Chinese what to do."

A group of US Treasury officials had just left our meeting, and several of us lingered to discuss their visit. Treasury had a number of staffers based in the embassy in Beijing, where they could be close to the People's Bank of China (PBOC), which serves the same function as our Federal Reserve, and other national government offices. They visited us regularly, Shanghai being the financial and commercial center of China. In the wake of the crisis that was unfolding, the Beijing based officials were joined by colleagues from Washington who brought with them a long list of measures they expected the authorities in Beijing to implement. It sounded like a lecture.

The tables in our conference room were set up in a horseshoe so all the members of the chamber's financial services committee could see each other. Two flags—one for the People's Republic of China, the other for America—were placed at the open end of the horseshoe. Ben, the chair of our committee, sat at the bottom of the horseshoe facing the flags.

The financial services committee was one of about twenty industry committees in the chamber and included members from large companies like Bank of America, AIG, and Wells Fargo as well as smaller firms. In accordance with Chinese law and the chamber's own rules, only foreign firms were allowed to join, but they did not necessarily need to be American. European bankers to join our meetings. Japanese financial institutions were invited but rarely attended, perhaps because of language difficulties.

The industry committees formed the core of the chamber. The roughly 3,000 members grouped themselves by industry or function to form committees to share best practices, exchange information, and organize events to address issues of common interest. I would later succeed Ben as chair of the financial services committee, but at the time I was still a junior member.

I worked for a boutique investment bank some years before moving to HSBC.

Throughout the 1990s and 2000s the committee heads were still in the habit of inviting US government officials to attend meetings as observers. The Consulate appointed two non-voting members to our Board of Governors. Their presence was mutually beneficial, as it gave us an informal channel to communicate with the US government and provided officials with access to practitioners' on-the-ground views.

All that changed after Edward Snowden leaked thousands of classified government documents. We were not in the habit of discussing sensitive security matters, but our committee meetings were closed to the public and everything discussed was understood to be confidential. The last thing we wanted was for our private comments—especially about China's government policies and personnel—to become exposed to the public. American government officials, especially State Department staff, take meticulous notes from their meetings, which they put into cables sent to Washington. We had no issue with that until the Snowden incident revealed how vulnerable the information could be. Our members, especially those from the larger companies, were very sensitive about what they said in public, especially about the Chinese government.

Ben's criticism of the officials hung in the air. None of us wanted to say out loud what we were all thinking: US government officials had a habit of talking when they should be listening. Given that the crisis originated in their jurisdiction and resulted from financial mismanagement and inadequate regulation, a certain degree of humility would have been appropriate. These were, after all, the same Treasury officials who had failed to understand the risks associated with securitizing mortgages and allowing banks to create what some have characterized as a "financial time bomb."

As one of the most senior executives managing a major foreign financial services firm in China, Ben Kinnas had regular meetings with Chinese officials at the highest levels. He was close to people like Fang Xinghai, who was Director-General of the Shanghai Municipal Financial Service Office at the time and would go on to become a top official with the China Securities Regulatory Commission. With a degree from Tsinghua and a PhD from Stanford, Fang did not need to be schooled by people from Washington.

Han Zheng was another of China's capable bureaucrats in whom foreign businesspeople had a great deal of confidence for his skills as a manager. He served as the mayor of Shanghai from 2003, and in 2006 he served briefly as the acting party secretary for the city, which is above the mayor in the Chinese political system. He served only five months before being replaced by none other than Xi Jinping, who moved from Zhejiang to the top post in Shanghai on his way to becoming the most powerful leader in the country. Han later returned to the role of Shanghai party secretary, serving from 2012 until being elevated to national level as executive vice-premier in 2018.

China's financial technocrats had already managed their way out of a domestic banking crisis, demonstrating a high level of competency. In the 1990s China's banks extended too many loans—mostly to inefficient, unprofitable state-owned enterprises—without adequate risk management. This built up an enormous non-performing loan portfolio, causing China's skeptics to predict a collapse of the banking system. Governance and the regulatory framework were indeed weak, and the lack of transparency deepened concerns. Because the state owned the banks, it was assumed they would continue supporting their state-owned enterprise (SOE) clients regardless of performance.

This created the so-called "moral hazard" that was also a problem for the US regulators as they navigated their own financial crisis.

The widely predicted banking crisis of the 1990s never happened. None of China's major banks collapsed, because they are all state-owned. New regulations were put in place and special asset management companies were formed to contain the bad loans and move them off the books. China's financial system continued to function and support the country's extraordinary growth, which continued in double digits right up to the global financial crisis of 2008. The key here is the movement of bad debts off the books. The way the Chinese system handled the crises in the late 1990s and later in 2008 and 2015 was with massive stimulus and the creation of huge piles of debt, which remain one of the key fragilities of the China system today.

China's issues of the 1990s were different from the problems that brought down the big global banks in 2008. The causes were different, and the fact that the global banks were interconnected across regulatory jurisdictions made the 2008 problem more complex and damaging to the world economy. This is exactly what the regulators were worried about, both in Beijing and Washington. But in the longer term, the US approach involved accepting the consquences of a situation and allowing companies to collapse. The China approach was the opposite.

In the years that followed the 2008 crisis, Ben Kinnas, the Wells Fargo banker, put the pieces together to explain what happened as the crisis unfolded. "We were summoned up to Beijing every few days, usually with a phone call in the afternoon telling us to appear the next day. I was told to come alone," Ben recalls. "I walked into the CBRC[1] (China Banking Regulatory Commission) offices in Beijing, and I saw in the room

1 The CBRC is the China Banking Regulatory Commission, which later merged to become the China Banking and Insurance Regulatory Commission

my counterpart from some of the other foreign banks in China. My heart skipped a beat, and I wondered if we were about to become cellmates. I didn't feel any better when the people we met with didn't identify themselves." Ben and his colleagues interacted regularly with CBRC officials and knew them to be professional and forthcoming, but they were noticeably absent from the meeting.

Apparently, the bankers were summoned by Communist Party officials—as distinct from government—who stepped in to deliver a pointed message. The CBRC, a government body under the State Council, had been moving China cautiously toward liberalizing the financial sector, gradually opening up the capital account and planning to internationalize the renminbi. All that was about to change.

China's economy in the mid-2000s was already deeply enmeshed in global trade and supply chains, but its financial system would remain cordoned off, tightly controlled by the state. Foreign banks were permitted to operate, but despite WTO pledges, only within carefully defined limits. China—guided by the party—had no intention of exposing itself to the discipline or the volatility of the global financial system.

This impulse was less about confidence than about fear. To the officials delivering the message, financial integration represented not opportunity but fragility. Xi Jinping would later give voice to this instinct, embedding the idea that control equals security at the heart of China's political economy. The global financial crisis of 2008 seemed to confirm their caution, reinforcing the belief that openness is weakness and that China's stability depends on insulation from the outside world. Yet that same insulation—the refusal to liberalize, the reliance on administrative control—has become one of China's enduring vulnerabilities, a constraint that limits both innovation and trust in the system itself.

"I think now that the financial crisis gave the party the excuse to do what they wanted to do anyway, which was separate from the West," Ben explained, in a recent conversation from his home on Hilton Head Island in South Carolina. "That meeting sent a message not just to us, but to their own people in the CBRC who were heading in the other direction." Party officials would have known that Ben and his counterparts from other foreign banks would discuss what they heard with their CBRC colleagues as well as US government officials. The Snowden leaks made sure of that. We discovered US government notes on WikiLeaks, detailing the conversations we had in 2007 and 2008—mentioning some of us by name—discussing sensitive topics like protectionism, exchange rates, and our understanding of the Chinese government's plans.[2]

Before the crisis, Beijing had announced a plan to transform Shanghai into an international financial center, even setting 2020 as the date by which it should be accomplished. As chair of the financial services committee, Ben led an effort to produce an AmCham study, together with the Brookings Institution, supporting the idea and providing technical guidance on changes that would need to take place for it to work. None of that happened. Shanghai remains a powerful domestic financial center, but its international capabilities fall far behind New York, London, or even tiny Singapore.

It took the United States most of a decade to fully recover from the Global Financial Crisis, and not before millions of people lost their jobs, and countries throughout the world experienced a prolonged decline in economic activity as financial institutions failed to provide liquidity. The US government poured billions into the auto industry, saving GM and Chrysler from an

2 *Scoop News:* "Cablegate: Shanghai Bankers On Rmb, Protectionism and the Future," October 5, 2007.

inevitable collapse that would have sent shock waves through the broader economy. American taxpayers spent $700 billion on the Troubled Asset Relief Program (TARP), making GM and AIG among the largest state-owned companies in the world.

China responded by investing heavily in infrastructure projects and stimulating demand, largely by funneling stimulus funds through the SOEs, rather than through the private sector which was already providing the core of jobs. While economic growth recovered quickly in the years that followed, in the end China was left with a massive debt overhang and a property market weighed down by massive oversupply. Because it was into the property market that much of the stimulus cash went. The Chinese economy continued to expand in GDP terms, but it is also instructive to look at how the respective stock markets have fared since. In mid-2008, the Shanghai stock market was at about 2,650 while the Dow Jones index was around 11,400. In late 2025, the Shanghai index was around 3,800, up around 50 percent, while the DJI was at 48,400, more than FOUR times higher. That raises the question of how much of China's growth over the years has been healthy and organic.

Regardless, the global financial crisis marked a turning point in how China viewed the United States—and itself. For decades, the Communist Party had promoted the idea that China's political and economic model was more stable and resilient than the West's, but after the very visible collapse of major American banks, this narrative began to resonate with ordinary citizens. For the first time, the United States appeared fragile, its authority in global finance shaken. Yet China's newfound confidence masked its own vulnerabilities. The very mechanisms that Beijing portrayed as sources of strength—state power, insulation, and central control—also revealed the system's deepest weakness: a dependence on control itself, a persistent fear of exposure to the forces that make open economies more resilient over time and an unwillingness to face problems publicly and deal with them.

CHAPTER 12

China's Fear of Containment

In 2009, President Obama appointed Hilary Rodham Clinton, his rival Democrat in the presidential primary election, as his Secretary of State. China hated her.

Clinton, a lawyer who would go on to become a New York senator and make a second bid for the presidency, was an early advocate of women's rights and various family issues. She served as first lady when her husband, Bill Clinton, became president in 1993 and she made these issues—human rights in particular—her signature causes. In 1995 she was invited to give a speech at the United Nations Fourth World Congress on Women, which was held in Beijing. This was exactly the platform she needed as she began to establish her own identity, stepping beyond her husband's shadow and becoming a leading politician in her own right.

China's authorities were nervous about her speech from the outset. They should have known this would not end well when the White House demanded that Chinese human rights advocate Harry Wu be released from a Beijing prison as a precondition for its support of the event. Clinton declared in her speech in front of thousands of international delegates that "Human rights are women's rights, and women's rights are human rights." Her speech did not criticize China directly, but she went on to speak about female babies being drowned and girls being sold into slavery and prostitution, all subjects that Beijing did not want to discuss. China has long been criticized for forcing abortions under its one-child policy, now ended, and officials were sensitive about foreigners involving themselves in what they consider to be domestic issues.

From Beijing's perspective, Hilary embodied the strain of American idealism that emboldened moral interventionism. Her public comments about internet freedom and women's rights were not just words of advocacy—they were, in the eyes of China's leaders, challenges to the party's legitimacy. Clinton also played an essential role in an incident involving one of China's most famous dissidents, Chen Guangcheng. Chen, a self-taught lawyer who was blind, spoke out about problems in China's system, and was subjected to harassment and finally detention in 2012. A dramatic escape from house arrest in his village was arranged and he took refuge in the American embassy in Beijing, creating a major diplomatic issue.

Clinton worked closely with Gary Locke, the US ambassador to Beijing, and others to secure Chen's release and departure from China. From Beijing's perspective, there was little affection for Clinton personally, but she may have been even more disliked as the main architect of Obama's signature policy, the "pivot to Asia."

By 2011, China's economy had surpassed Japan as the world's second largest economy, and the debate began about when it would overtake the United States. China also become the most important trading partner for major countries like Germany, Brazil, and India, traditionally aligned with America.

That same year, China launched its first aircraft carrier, the

Liaoning, and unveiled its first stealth fighter jet, the J-12. The ship was originally built for the Soviet navy but it was never completed, allowing China to purchase the unfinished hull from Ukraine and haul it home for reconstruction and retrofit. Such advances signaled China's military modernization and ambition to press various territorial claims.

China's nationalists rejoiced, with some adopting an image of the ship to use on their social media profiles. China's neighbors were less enthusiastic, fearing how the carrier would be used in territorial disputes. America's naval dominance was not being challenged directly, but the aircraft carrier was a powerful demonstration of China's arrival on the world stage, roughly a decade after joining the WTO.

China's advances demanded an American response, and Secretary Clinton made the case for why the United States should focus more attention on Asia. Writing for *Foreign Policy* in an article entitled "America's Pacific Century," Clinton stated: "One of the most important tasks of American statecraft over the next decade will therefore be to lock in a substantially increased investment—diplomatic, economic, strategic, and otherwise—in the Asia-Pacific region."[3]

No matter how often Clinton and other Obama officials emphasized the diplomatic and economic initiatives, the "...and otherwise" part rang most loudly in the halls of Zhongnanhai. The pivot to Asia placed more American military assets in Asia, which Beijing considered its exclusive area of strategic influence. In the event, it did not happen to the extent originally planned, because another threat emerged in the Middle East—ISIS—which occupied an enormous amount of US time and energy that had been earmarked for East Asia.

---

3 *Foreign Policy:* America's Pacific Century, by Hillary Clinton, October 11, 2011.

To Chinese officials already uneasy about their dependence on foreign technology, markets, and the US-dominated global financial system, the Trans-Pacific Partnership (TPP) represented an attempt to rewrite the global order without them. It confirmed to them their fear that China's rise had outpaced its resilience. Beneath the confident posture of a rising power lay a deep vulnerability—the realization that China's integration into the global system had not made it secure, but exposed.

Clinton, during her time as Secretary of State, went on to talk about closer ties not just with Australia, but also with Vietnam, Myanmar, and other countries that border on China. To the officials in Beijing, the message was: "containment."

The TPP was supposed to be the economic leg of the stool, but even that would keep China out, at least initially. The agreement was between 12 nations bordering on the Pacific Ocean, and was intended to establish free trade among them and set rules to govern intellectual property, labor standards, digital trade, and more. The idea was to establish rules and standards that China would eventually be forced to adopt or be forever kept out of the most important trading block in its own region.

Beijing was always cool to the idea, viewing TPP as an example of the United States bullying countries into adopting American standards that would keep the pecking order as it was, while sidelining China and ignoring the unique characteristics of other countries and governing models. Foreign Minister Yang Jiechi said: "It is important for the United States to sincerely welcome and support a stronger, more prosperous China that assumes more international responsibility." Beijing disliked the TPP and detested the entire idea of the pivot. But in fact, this was more a reflection of changes in Beijing than in Washington. In 2001, the US had clearly indicated its desire to see China join the global family with its approval for China to join WTO, a step which opened the whole world up to Chinese exports. But after 2008, the party leaders decided that the shift towards integration with the world was fraught with dangers for China, and for the party itself. The example of the fate of the Soviet Communist Party worried them mightily, and still does.

The TPP was a hard sell to China, and many Americans also had reservations about it. Obama and Clinton did their best to explain to America's voters why the TPP was important and deployed allies like Gary Locke, the US ambassador to China at the time. He had served as commerce secretary previously and was intimately familiar with trade issues and their impact on the US economy, and on jobs. He stepped down as ambassador in 2014 but continued promoting the TPP and visited the American Chamber in Shanghai frequently. "Guys, I don't know what to tell you," Locke said, knowing he was speaking to allies for his cause. "I'm talking to people all over America and people just don't seem to want international trade. I'm talking to people who work on the docks loading ships in my home state of Washington, and they don't want trade! Where do they think those ships are going? They aren't going to Iowa!"[4]

Congressman Mike Kelly, a Republican from Pennsylvania, supported American business in China but had problems with international trade and its impact on jobs. He represented a part of the state with mostly traditional industries, and explained to me from behind his desk in Washington: "My constituents are trying to hold onto jobs that their father and their father's father held." He personally believed they would need to adapt, and that trade with countries like China was good for America, but convincing his voters was difficult. He was eager to learn more about our business in China but non-committal on the Trans-

4 I had several conversations with Locke where he made statements to this effect.

Pacific Partnership.

Ash Carter, who served as secretary of defense from 2015 to 2017, explained the connection between the TPP and America's security interests, saying it was a critical demonstration of America's commitment to Asia and our partners in the region. Speaking at the McCain Institute at Arizona State University in April of 2015, the defense secretary stated: "...passing TPP is as important to me as another aircraft carrier."[5]

After years of negotiation, in February 2016 all twelve countries included in the TPP gathered in New Zealand to formally sign the agreement. Michael Froman, Obama's trade representative, signed on behalf of the United States. But it was never ratified. By the 2016 presidential election, the anti-globalization movement was too strong with voters from both major political parties.

Some years later, I spoke with lawmakers in Washington who admitted privately that withdrawing from TPP was a strategic mistake, especially in light of the competition with China. Forming strong commercial alliances with the countries of Asia was a critical weapon of soft power, but instead America withdrew from its role as an economic leader in the region.

Japan was left to fill the void, as Prime Minister Shinzo Abe reassembled the group—minus the United States—and formed the Comprehensive and Progressive Agreement for Trans-Pacific Partnership (CPTPP). China, not to be undone, created its own free trade agreement, the Regional Comprehensive Economic Partnership (RCEP), leaving the United States out of both blocs. And in the final irony, China has announced its desire to join the CPTPP.

---

5 *The Diplomat*, "TPP as Important as Another Aircraft Carrier," by Prashanth Parameswaran.

Our visitor to AmCham was unusual, and I wasn't sure how to prepare. Regular Congressional visits ("CoDels") had already slowed by 2016, but we still had talking points prepared for staff delegations ("StaffDels"), former ambassadors, or the occasional visitor from some part of the administration, most often Commerce Department or Treasury officials.

Energy Secretary Ernest Moniz had visited us a few months earlier, taking a victory lap after successfully negotiating the JCPOA—the Joint Comprehensive Plan of Action— on behalf of the Obama administration. Implementation had just come into effect after a difficult process to obtain Congressional support. Secretary Moniz mentioned that China played a constructive role, or at least resisted Iran's desire for China to side against the United States. Apparently, the chief negotiator for Iran had attended MIT at about the same time as Moniz, so the two were already well acquainted before the negotiations over the Iran nuclear deal began.

An energy secretary visiting the Chamber wasn't common, but there was a fairly direct link to energy issues and many American businesses operating in China. Moniz demonstrated his remarkable intellect and technical depth as he questioned a select group of AmCham members on all aspects of energy in China from nuclear to wind, geothermal and combustibles. Moniz reported that the United States and China were cooperating on a center for nuclear safety, which we were glad to hear.

On this particular occasion, our visitor had no obvious connection to the American business community in China. For the first time in our history, someone from NASA was going to visit the Chamber.

The weather in August was miserably humid, and most expats had long since cleared out to spend the summer in the south of France, or with grandparents in the United States, or anywhere but Shanghai. Still, I had no trouble pulling together a group of a dozen or so senior executives who were interested in meeting the NASA administrator.

Charles Bolden was appointed by President Obama in 2009. Bolden had flown on four space shuttle missions, twice in the pilot's seat. He was the mission commander on two additional flights, making him one of the most experienced astronauts ever to lead NASA. He was also the first Black man to do so, and one of Obama's few African American appointees.

Space would have had little direct relevance to most of our businesses, but China had been making a lot of noise about its own space program, and the and competition with the United States was inevitable.

A Chinese astronaut successfully completed a walk in space in 2008, something that American astronaut Edward White accomplished in 1965. Still, nobody in the room doubted China's ability or motivation to catch up. We were eager to hear what Commander Bolden thought of China's space program, and what his meetings with his counterparts were like.

"I actually can't meet them," he said. "I'm not allowed to." The room fell silent. As businesspeople we were accustomed to the idea that governments work in different ways. Senior officials were subject to all kinds of restraints, disclosures, and limitations that we would have found impossibly stultifying in the private sector, but there was something about the way he said the words. Bolden almost sounded like a schoolboy being told he couldn't play with the kid down the street anymore. He was clearly irritated by the restriction.

"Congress won't let me." He went on to explain that Congress had passed a law banning NASA from using federal funds to "... collaborate or coordinate bilaterally in any way with China or any Chinese-owned company." Bolden shook his head as if he still couldn't believe China could be singled out like this. "We've been working with the Russians in space for over twenty years!"

American and Russian scientists somehow managed to cooperate even through the Cold War, and the International Space Station has always had at least one Russian and one American on board continuously for the entirety of its existence. Excluding Chinese scientists seemed odd. American scientists had in fact pushed back on the rules, and actually boycotted a scientific conference in 2013.

As our meeting progressed, Bolden explained the broader mission of NASA and why it was important for the United States and China to cooperate on certain issues. While the FAA—the Federal Aviation Administration—governs commercial transportation in the airspace, NASA also plays an important role in keeping things moving above the ground. Airspace is shared by a number of operators and everyone from commercial airliners, private jets, and crop dusters compete for the right to fly through corridors at certain altitudes.

In China, it's quite simple. The military controls all the airspace. Commercial planes are given permission by the military to fly only through certain narrow routes, which it frequently blocks. For this reason, commercial flights are notoriously unreliable, getting delayed almost more frequently than they leave on time.

Mr. Bolden had apparently come to China to discuss airspace and explore ways to improve cooperation and ensure that more flights leave on time. We peppered him with questions, and he explained how important it was to strengthen our capabilities in math and science.

As our meeting came to an end, Norwell Coquillard took the honor of asking the last question. Nor was one of the most senior members of our business community, but he was also an avid sportsman and adventurer. "We want to know if you blew chunks."

"Excuse me?" Charles replied. We could have addressed him by any number of titles, including his military rank of major general, but he asked us to call him Charles.

"Blow chunks. Puke. Vomit. Did you hold down your cookies when you were in space?" Among other things, Nor raced cars on the weekends and had experience with the effects of G-forces. We all laughed. Our visitor assured us that yes, he had held everything together while traveling in space.

The US is diverse, led by people with a range of opinions on globalization, trade, and engagement. Leaders like Lock, Moniz, and Bolden were on their way out of office, soon to be replaced by people who were more skeptical of China's intentions. American businesses felt generally supported by Obama's administration, but many of its policies—human rights pressure, trade pacts excluding China, and new security alignments—added strain to an already brittle relationship.

Beijing's reactions revealed more than just defensiveness; they exposed a deeper anxiety about control, legitimacy, and the limits of China's model in a world still shaped by US rules. For China's leaders, years of diplomatic friction and strategic encirclement hardened a conviction that the country's vulnerabilities were structural, not circumstantial. When Xi Jinping took power in 2012, he inherited not just an economy showing signs of slowdown, but a system deeply dependent on global markets and foreign technology. His answer, no doubt with the fate of the Soviet party in mind, was not liberalization, but control. Xi's policies—tightening the party's grip on private enterprise, pushing for "indigenous innovation," and launching the "Made in China 2025" and "dual circulation" strategies—were all designed to reduce exposure to external dependencies, thereby reducing globalization but increasing China's capacity to face sanctions in the event of whatever developments emerged. Yet the very act of insulating China from the world has created new fragilities: less competition, slower innovation, and growing distrust between the state and the entrepreneurs who once drove its phenomenal economic growth. What began as a strategy of resilience became a symptom of insecurity—a powerful nation striving to appear unshakable, yet still haunted by the vulnerabilities that global integration first revealed.

CHAPTER 13

A Fragile Financial System

By the mid-2010s, the Chinese economy had recovered from the global financial crisis, but a range of systemic issues were festering largely hidden, and it was slowing down after more than a decade of extraordinary double-digit growth. The US economy had also recovered but President Obama was still in the process of unraveling many of the measures that were put in place, like selling off bonds and unwinding equity positions in the so-called systemically important companies like GM and AIG. It was a process that recouped almost all the funds the government had invested in 2008 to save the system, a very different situation from China, where the result was a debt mountain. Looking for a strong leader to join his economic team, Obama made the historic decision to appoint a woman, and in February of 2014 Janet Yellen became the chair of the US Federal Reserve Bank.

Yellen was the first woman ever to hold the post, and she later became Treasury Secretary in the Biden administration. Her appointment to Treasury was somewhat controversial, since she had less political deal-making experience, coming from academia rather than Wall Street. She had spent two decades teaching economics at the Haas School of Business at UC Berkeley, and we had met several times while I was there as a student, although I did not take her class because I had already completed equivalent coursework as an undergraduate at UCLA. Still, everyone knew Professor Yellen, and we liked her; she was like everybody's grandmother—kindly and caring, interested in all aspects of our lives as students—but strict about assignments. With her diminutive stature she also looked the part, and spoke with just a hint of her Brooklyn-Jewish-Polish roots.

In February 2016, now as Chair of the US Federal Reserve, she visited China. The country was attempting a transition—from an investment- and export-led economy toward one driven by services and domestic consumption. Yet the old model and its deep imbalances was resilient. America's exports to China were declining, even as China's trade surplus soared past $500 billion, the largest in history. Yellen's immediate concern was the strength of the dollar, the softening renminbi, and what both meant for U.S. jobs and exports. Her official meetings were with senior policymakers in Beijing, but she also traveled to Shanghai and agreed to a private discussion with a few of us from the foreign business community.

We met in the Shangri-La Hotel in Lujiazui, the gleaming financial district on the eastern bank of the Huangpu River. When I first arrived in China in the 1990s, the area was little more than a mudflat. Now, it rivals Manhattan or Canary Wharf—its skyline a symbol of China's modernity, but also of its overbuilt ambitions. Yellen greeted us warmly, indulging in a few minutes of Berkeley nostalgia before turning serious. "Tell me what you see happening over here," she said.

I had the China heads of Citibank and JP Morgan with me. We sat opposite her at a long table covered with green felt. She was flanked by two staffers who took notes. The three of us looked at each other, unsure where to begin. We were all members of the chamber's financial services committee and knew each other well. When I was chair of the committee I made a habit of hosting a dinner once every six months, so the ten or twelve heads of each of the foreign banks could meet and talk informally. We would sometimes have a guest speaker but the main function was so we would know each other for occasions such as this.

Normally these meetings were well scripted, but this one was not. The two bankers looked at me, so I got things started with remarks on behalf of the Chamber. I thanked Fed Chair Yellen for taking the time to visit us and walked her through the findings of our recent Business Climate Survey that I thought would most interest her.

The majority of our members remained fundamentally optimistic about the five-year outlook for China's economy and reported revenue expansion and strong profit for the year. But cracks were visible. Some expressed apprehension about the Made in China 2025 plan, which had been announced the previous year. The plan laid out specific market share goals for local companies in certain strategic industries—semiconductors, robotics, aerospace—effectively signaling that foreign firms would be pushed aside.

We were nearing the end of Xi's first term, and the initial enthusiasm for him as a reformer was giving way to the realization that he was nothing of the kind. Our members reported that regulations were becoming increasingly opaque, and foreigners were generally feeling less welcome than they had been before.

Our guest listened intently, jotting notes and asking questions to clarify here and there. Brett Krause, the China president of JP Morgan Chase, summarized his business and made some general observations about China's market for financial services, drawing on his previous experience working in Vietnam. Beijing had promised to liberalize the market for financial services as part of its WTO commitments, but so far the market was limited. The foreign banks collectively occupied less than two percent of the total market share for banking services.

Insurance was even more restricted. Licenses were issued province by province, and foreign carriers could apply for only one at a time. Regulators might take up to two years to approve a single license, leaving American insurers like AIG dwarfed by domestic giants such as PingAn and China Life. The rationale was not merely protectionism—Beijing feared that foreign competition could expose weaknesses in its own companies. China's half-open financial system was a façade of strength; underneath lay a pervasive anxiety about losing control over capital, data, and institutional power.

China would not fully lift equity caps for banks and asset managers until 2017—long after its domestic players had secured dominance. These policies didn't just protect local companies; they insulated the system itself from outside influence. To Beijing, financial liberalization wasn't progress—it was exposure.

"That's all very interesting," Yellen said, bringing an end to this part of the discussion. "But what are you hearing about China's consumer sentiment?" America's Fed chair did not need us to quote statistics or cite numbers. She had traveled to Shanghai and met with us because she was looking for insight, something she couldn't get from reports in Washington.

Again, the three of us glanced at each other, hoping someone else would start off. "Well," I began, "my daughter goes to a local school here in Shanghai, and I meet up with the parents of her classmates from time to time. They may not be typical of the middle class but I can tell you what they are saying."

My daughter's school, YK Pao, was registered as a local school by the Ministry of Education, but it was actually a private local school attended by local and foreign passport holders, and tuition was pricey. "Consumers are spending, and the growing middle class supports the market for big-ticket items like cars and refrigerators. But I also see that nine out of ten families are looking to leave China." I went on to explain that this was not a mass exodus, but it was more a cold calculation about the shift in the wind. Middle-class people were seeing trends that made them feel more comfortable moving assets outside China. They were buying property in Australia, Canada, and the United States because they wanted their children to attend foreign schools, but they also sensed that Xi's China was becoming more repressive and less integrated with the West. The parents of YK Pao students, who were typically business owners or executives with large firms, were not so much a cross-section of society as a bellwether. They were well informed with a good sense of what was happening in China; they weren't political dissidents by any means, but they were not Marxist believers either. Deng's policies of reform and opening up, and China's relationship with the West, had been good for them. Xi Jinping's policies were taking China in a different direction, and they recognized that a system built on control, not trust, was not necessarily in their long-term interests.

"No, this is just the same as what's been happening for a long time." Andrew Au, the chairman and CEO of Citibank China, broke in with his own views, capturing the attention of the Fed Chair. He may have thought my conclusion was too negative.

Andrew was a classic banker, right down to his French cuffs and pinstripe suits. He was from Hong Kong, educated in Canada, and worked for Citi in Asia for most of his career. Andrew was a recipient of Shanghai's prestigious Magnolia award, which recognizes foreigners who make significant contributions to the city. Accepting the award, Andrew said: "I am confident about

Shanghai's future and remain dedicated to supporting Shanghai as a major financial center, as we continue to provide innovative and value-added services to our growing customer base here." Andrew was a major proponent of the city's plan to become an international financial center, a plan that would prove difficult to implement with Beijing's increased emphasis on control.

Regarding the movements of people, Andrew was right of course. People had been leaving China since the 1980s, and many of them never came back. But it was also true that something different was happening in the mid-2010s—after the investment boom of the 2000s—and the local elite saw it first. China's policies were shifting inward, and the leadership was becoming more autocratic and ideologically driven.

Opportunities for China's foreign-educated elite were diminishing, with indications that, as a social class, they faced growing mistrust—a sentiment reminiscent of the way the group was treated during the Cultural Revolution in the 1960s. They were still earning high incomes, and owned property in China, but they harbored long-term skepticism about the system, prompting them to consider exit strategies in their best interest.

The parents of my daughter's classmates were mostly in their fifties, so unlike younger people they had some memory of what had happened when one man ruled China. Soon, they would see how this system would react to the Covid-19 pandemic, and the exodus would accelerate. Many of this group of Chinese citizens would not stick around for Xi's third term in office when people like them would be required to spend the first few hours of every day studying "Xi Jinping thought," and their smartphones would be checked to see if they spent sufficient time each week reading the party's latest documents.

China does not publish emigration statistics but in recent years, many people—not just foreigners—have left China. This particular wave may have started in the mid-2010s, accelerating more recently, and mostly included wealthy and high-net-worth individuals, many of whom have become disillusioned with the country's political and economic trajectory.

My narrative and Andrew's represented slightly different views, and hopefully Professor Yellen took away the lesson that China was complicated, with multiple trends happening simultaneously. There were many layers to consumer sentiments, often conflicting. Looking back, however, it is clear that China's elite had at that stage already begun looking to move cash and assets offshore. Whatever it was making them feel uncomfortable with China, perhaps the crackdown on tech entrepreneurs, perhaps something else, this group saw a need to at least diversify away from China. And they are in a financial position to act on their choices.

Shortly after our 2016 meeting with Yellen, Beijing's policymakers tightened capital controls in an attempt to slow overseas transfers and purchases. Annual quotas for foreign currency exchanges were reduced, keeping assets in China. Consumers could still get money out, but only in small amounts at a time, giving rise to the term *"ma yi banjia,"* like an ant moving house. Various loopholes existed, such as using electronic payment systems like Alipay to convert renminbi to dollars, manipulating export invoices to disguise capital outflows, or buying insurance policies in Hong Kong. One scheme used stacks of Chinese ATM cards to pull foreign currency cash from casinos in the Philippines. These schemes and loopholes were mostly shut down, beginning around 2016. The rush to impose capital controls revealed a deep fragility: Beijing trusted its citizens to earn money, but did not want them taking it out of the country.

China's capital controls had an impact on the policy of *"zou chu qu,"* which encouraged domestic industries to "go out" and acquire foreign assets and technology. First announced as part of the 10th Five-Year Plan in 2001. The controls also made Shanghai's plan to become an international financial center practically impossible to achieve. China was becoming more separate and isolated from the global economy, which revealed a system afraid of its own success. China's leaders increasingly showed a distrust of the very openness that had fueled their rise. Policies that once encouraged Chinese companies to acquire assets and technology abroad were quietly curtailed. Shanghai's dream of becoming a global financial hub faded.

I learned an important lesson that day from Professor Yellen, one that I wouldn't fully appreciate until years later. She pressed us on our views of consumer sentiment because she knew how important it was to look beyond the numbers. Business in China depends heavily on consumer sentiment, and the level of optimism people feel about their environment and future prospects.

Central bankers and policy makers have many levers with which to guide the economy, but how people *feel* still shapes outcomes. Through the 1990s, 2000s, and much of the 2010s, the mood in China was optimistic and enthusiastic. Cooperation with the West experienced bumps but was generally high, and Chinese entrepreneurs and investors saw opportunities wherever they looked. Sentiment shifted in the mid-2010s, after Xi Jinping assumed power in 2012. The result of the party's pursuit of control at all cost was fragility disguised as strength. Optimism faded as state control increased, and entrepreneurs found less space to maneuver between the state-owned enterprises that were growing in size and power.

Later, after the global Covid pandemic of 2020 to 2023, that fragility became undeniable. Consumer sentiment again became the driver, confounding the leadership in Beijing.

Analysts predicted a post-Covid economic boom, which is what happened in other countries, but instead, China's recovery stalled. Sentiment matters. Ordinary people had lost confidence and delayed purchases, while investors were reluctant to back projects even when the numbers suggested solid returns. Without optimism, every purchase and every investment felt like a risk.

Janet Yellen continued visiting China, maintaining relationships with people like Fang Xinghai in her role as the Treasury Secretary in the Biden administration.

She had met before with China's economic leaders like Liu He (Vice Premier), Yi Gang (Governor of the People's Bank of China), and Fang Xinghai (Vice Chairman of China Securities Regulatory Commission), but her mission in 2023 was more diplomatic than about the economy, coming at a time when America's relationship with China was at a particularly low point. She would make the case that America's goal was not to contain China, but that further export controls may become necessary because of the potential military conflicts.

Also on that trip, Yellen hosted an informal lunch with a group of female Chinese economists. Knowing that men dominated her profession, she wanted to take the opportunity to build a connection with other women in the field. Sadly, some Chinese of a "nationalistic" bent chose to criticize the meeting, suggesting she had ulterior motives and sought to co-opt these women, who now could no longer be trusted to support China's interests. In a way, that small incident captured the broader truth: a system that fears ideas, people, and money leaving its borders cannot call itself strong.

For those building businesses in China, vulnerability was no longer abstract—it was personal. The very mechanisms that had once enabled rapid growth—openness to foreign investment, integration with global markets, and trust in the flow of talent and capital—were now sources of fragility. Entrepreneurs faced a system that demanded loyalty, discouraged independence, and punished deviation. Confidence, both domestic and foreign, had become the most precious commodity, yet the party's insistence on control made it scarce. In this environment, every deal, every hire, every expansion carried not just business risk but the weight of systemic uncertainty.

PART 5

UNDER PRESSURE TO PICK A SIDE

"Only enemies speak the truth; friends and lovers lie endlessly, caught in the web of duty."
— Stephen King

"Remember not only to say the right thing in the right place but far more difficult still, to leave unsaid the wrong thing at the tempting moment."
— Benjamin Franklin

Chapter 14

Dodging the Uyghur Question

I arrived at the American embassy in Beijing in plenty of time to get through security. A perimeter fence surrounded the square compound, which felt like a fortress. Chinese security guards stationed outside glared at visitors as they walked by, and I wondered why diplomatic missions seemed so undiplomatic. Inside the gate, I approached a window made of thick glass slid my passport and phone through the tray. After a minute or two, the passport came back through the tray, along with a numbered chit that would allow me to retrieve the phone on my way out. Inside the gates, the main building was a glass and steel structure, with large sculptures decorating the grounds.

Beijing-based business people were invited to the embassy from time to time, but living in Shanghai I had little exposure to the diplomatic community before taking up the role of chairman of the Chamber. Once I came to represent the American business community in Shanghai, I made a habit of visiting embassy officials every six months or so to exchange information about the market, discuss challenges our companies were facing, and to get an update on American policies, especially export controls. I sat down across from the commercial attache, and she got straight to her agenda: "Mr. Gibbs, don't you think American companies should take a stand against forced labor?"

She was new in country, an African American woman who had arrived to explain what's what. The two of us were alone in a large conference room, seated at the corner of a square table, but even without an audience she seemed to be putting on a performance.

"Of course they should," I replied. "And I believe they do. Forced labor is something that my members would never want to be involved with."

"Do they have no responsibility to support American values?" Her tone was stern, and I felt a lecture coming.

"On the contrary, we see ourselves as contributing to the improvement of labor and environmental standards here. And in the area of food safety… "

"Then why don't you speak out publicly about the atrocities happening in Xinjiang?"

"Well…" I had no answer.

Some of the stories coming out of Xinjiang were disturbing, but the official position was that there was a serious terrorist threat to be addressed, and any company or organization taking a public stand or criticizing China would have a short future in the China market. The party has little tolerance for criticism, especially from foreigners who are enjoying economic benefits from access to the market. American companies understand the environment and work assiduously to stay clear of issues that will land them in trouble with the government, or local consumers. Moreover, foreign companies generally view their role as separate from that of diplomats representing the government, although they broadly support America's foreign policy.

There may be no issue in China as vexing, or one that places the foreign business community more perfectly in an impossible situation, like that of Xinjiang. There are other human rights questions, of course. China has taken action against lawyers and others who have been working to defend people in trouble for various reasons. This includes advocates for women's rights, LGBTQ rights, or people involved in land disputes and other matters. However, the Uyghur issue is the one getting the most attention in recent years, and it's the one that affecte global business and chamber member companies most directly.

The question of human rights has long been a point of conflict between China and the West, with American presidents taking different views on China's record, and more importantly, what the United States should do about it. President Clinton, as he championed the cause that brought China into the World Trade Organization in 2001, reversed his early approach and separated trade from human rights, neatly sidestepping the issue. In this way, he also avoided complications arising from China's government crackdown on the student uprising of 1989. His logic, shared by many observers at the time, was that deeper engagement would steer China toward a more liberal form of government, once economic reforms took hold. It hasn't quite turned out that way. Or not yet, anyway.

President Trump, in the middle of a trade deal of his own with China during his first term, took a step further and not only declined to criticize China's record on human rights, but, encouraged Xi Jinping. John Bolton, Trump's National Security Advisor at the time, quoted an interpreter who was in the room for the Trump-Xi meeting in Osaka in 2019; according to Bolton Trump said of the Xinjiang situation that building labor camps to address the problem was the right thing to do. President Biden took the opposite position, putting human rights at the center of his agenda with China.

Political pundits have advanced a number of theories about

this, some less kind than others. Those who knew Biden well said that support for human rights was deeply embedded in his worldview; he believed the role of America was to champion the rights of the weak and advance the cause of the oppressed everywhere. Others said he gave up on any trade agenda with China and needed an issue to show that he was continuing to pressure them. He also needed an issue to tie the United States to its European allies, related to shared common values on human rights. Whatever the case, the issue of human rights in China is not going away, and foreign businesses are stuck in the middle.

Public opinion tends to go against the multinationals, with their history of abuse and exploitation in developing countries. In China, American businesspeople have always felt misunderstood in their own country on the question of what they're doing and how they're doing it. Although there was a time when cheap labor was the main attraction, that's no longer the case in China today. Moreover, business leaders bristle at the idea that just because they've left home to work overseas, they somehow leave their values behind. The idea of using forced labor or in any way participating in or supporting the abuse of a group of people because of their ethnicity would be repulsive to anyone. They don't like being painted with a broad brush and take offense at implications that they abandoned their values and sense of ethics in order to work in China.

There will always be one or two people making bad decisions but as a group, American businesspeople operate with high ethical standards in China, maybe even higher than they would in the United States. This is partly because they see themselves as representing our culture, but it's also fear of getting caught, since foreigners in China are under more scrutiny than local people. Again, there will always be someone behaving badly, and that will get a lot of attention, but the overwhelming majority of

American businesses in China pay a great deal of attention to working conditions and they are careful about who they work with and how things get done. Inside China, foreign businesses get a great deal of credit for improving safety standards by introducing specialized equipment and management techniques.

Part of the problem is a lack of information. Chinese authorities are so sensitive about this issue that it's difficult to get accurate first-hand information about what's actually happening in Xinjiang. It is a complicated issue that has been around for a long time.

From my home in Shanghai's former French concession district, Urumqi Road was a short walk down a tree-lined street. It was a hot summer day, and a group of Uyghurs gathered on the street corner cooking skewers of lamb over coal briquets. A dozen or so people were milling around, hunkered on low plastic stools, chit-chatting in a language that sounded nothing like Mandarin Chinese. School age children bent over notebooks, while smaller kids clung to their mothers or slept in their laps. An older man stood near his cart, piled high with small bags of dates, dried apricots, and various types of nuts.

"How much does this cost?" I asked in Chinese, picking up a bag of raisins. The man gave me a puzzled look so I switched to English. He paused, and I could tell he was calculating what price I would pay.

"Twenty yuan!" He finally came up with a number.

I handed over the equivalent of three dollars. It was about twice what I would pay in a grocery store, but I wanted to support a local merchant, plus I got him to throw in a small bag of almonds. I also wanted a reason to chat with the man, and learn more about these people who fit so awkwardly into Chinese society. Unfortunately, he had only a basic grasp of Mandarin, and spoke little English, leaving us without a common language to communicate.

Who are the Uyghurs, where did they come from, and what kind of a place is Xinjiang? The Uyghurs are an ethnically Turkic group from Central and East Asia. Those who find their way to the big cities often engage in tertiary pursuits, like the fellow selling dried fruits and nuts from carts on the street, or exchanging foreign currency, which is illegal in China. Visitors to China would recognize them immediately because Uyghurs look nothing like the rest of the population, which is over ninety percent Han Chinese. If anything, Uyghurs look Western. Mandarin-speaking foreigners are frequently mistaken for Uyghurs, although Uyghurs often don't speak Mandarin, which is a big part of the issue.

Numbering about twelve million, Uyghurs make up roughly half the population of the Chinese region of Xinjiang. The other half are mainly Han Chinese, which is an issue by itself. In 1949 the Han population in the province was only six percent, but for decades Beijing's official policy has encouraged the migration of ethnic Han people to minority regions like Xinjiang and Tibet. The Han migrants are typically better educated and bring skills and capabilities that are lacking in the region. Without a doubt, the Han have contributed to economic development, while enjoying financial incentives to live and work in Xinjiang. There are even cash rewards for Han-Uyghur marriages, suggesting that the goal extends beyond economic development.

As an economy, Xinjiang is important, although not nearly as wealthy as the coastal provinces. The land area is enormous. It is the largest region of China and nearly the size of Mexico. Xinjiang is rich in minerals and oil and is a major source of production, especially for cotton and other agricultural products, but also chemicals, electronics, and other manufactured items. The majority of economic production in Xinjiang is for domestic use, and of the exports, most go to Russia and neighboring Central Asian countries. However, cotton is an important input for textiles that find their way into Western markets, and polysilicon is used in solar panels that ship all over the world.

Some Uyghurs have assimilated, but others not so much. There were reports of various protests in the 1980s, and in the years following, incidents took place in several locations around China, notably in 1992 and 1993. Reported attacks blamed on the Uyghurs took place in department stores, hotels, and markets, and in 1997 the bombing of a bus led to the death of several people. Bombings and violence of any sort in public places are extremely rare in China. Guns are not available, so attackers usually employ knives or cleavers, or use a vehicle to ram a target. This type of attack, though deadly, usually results in casualties on a relatively small scale.

In March of 2014, an incident took place in a train station in China's southern city of Kunming when a group of eight Uyghurs, six men and two women, used knives and cleavers to attack random people. Thirty-one people died in the attack, with many others injured. A black "East Turkistan" flag was found at the scene. Soon after, another attack, this time using explosives, took place at a Xinjiang railway station.[1] Since then, the party has taken a hard line in enforcing security in the region. And also since then, there has been little agreement between China and Western nations regarding the actual situation on the ground in Xinjiang.

In 2017, the Chinese government issued an order to "round up everyone who should be rounded up," which led to the

1 Sup China: "What can we expect from Xinjiang's new Party boss Ma Xingrui?" By Lizzi C. Lee, December 29, 2021.

construction of the camps that have become so controversial. President Xi appointed Chen Quanguo as the party secretary of Xinjiang, moving him from Tibet, where he employed high-tech methods to bring security and stability to the region.[2] Critics of Chen claim his methods accelerated cultural assimilation, which eventually earned him the distinction of being one of the highest-ranking Chinese government officials to be sanctioned by the United States government.

Meanwhile, China's Ministry of Public Security began to construct monitoring systems that could apparently identify people according to their race. Human Rights Watch and other groups have reported the existence of camps, but the government says they are for vocational training and that Muslim extremists need to be dealt with by law enforcement. From Beijing's point of view, its problem with Muslim extremists is no different than it is anywhere else. They are confused about the lack of support and understanding from the global community. After all, when the United States was attacked on 9/11, NATO invoked Article 5, declaring the attack by the Al Qaeda terrorists as an attack on all NATO allies. Why then are attacks on Chinese civilians viewed so differently by the international community?

China's government has explicitly linked its issues in Xinjiang with the 9/11 attack, saying in a 2002 White Paper that "the East Turkistan terrorist organization based in South Asia has the unstinting support of Osama bin Laden, and is an important part of his terrorist forces."[3] The United States government initially accepted this narrative, in an apparent exchange of support for America's war in Iraq. The State Department later distanced itself from this position. The dialogue about the Uyghur issue

---

2 ibid.

3 China.org.cn: "East Turkistan" Terrorist Forces Cannot Get Away With Impunity," January 21, 2002.

became highly contentious, and the party has accused the United States government of hypocrisy, pointing to America's history of slavery and the incidents that led to the Black Lives Matter movement.

The problem with this argument is that it addresses the wrong part of the issue. The controversy isn't so much about the existence of these inequalities as about the government's reaction to them. In America, anyone can investigate the situation, document it, and suggest ways to address problems that are identified. There is, for instance, an active and non-curated discussion about reparations for slavery, policing in our communities, our historic and ongoing abuse of native Americans, and any number of issues. Such topics are not openly discussed in China.

The Xinjiang issue lands foreign companies in the middle of this controversy between China and Western countries. In the 1990s, many of these companies, including Nike and others, endured years of complaints and accusations involving labor in their factories and suppliers, and they paid a price for their relaxed standards. Foreign brands coming from liberal societies have learned that lesson and well understand that their customers, employees, and partners expect them to uphold certain standards, and they are at pains to escape culpability by using third-party suppliers to shield themselves from responsibility for how their products are made. The standards that foreign companies now hold for themselves often exceed legal requirements, such as the UN Guiding Principles on Business and Human Rights.[4]

Ultimately, the issue exposes a certain fragility in China's governance model. The surveillance systems and cultural assimilation programs are not signs of confidence but of a state worried about instability. Western expectations that economic

4 "Guiding Principles on Human Rights," United Nations (2011).

engagement would lead to political opening have been disappointed by the reality of a system that sees control as the main priority, even at the cost of international credibility and economic friction.

Chapter 15

China and a Hard Place

I arrived at the gate of China's Ministry of Foreign Affairs almost a full half hour before my meeting. Security was minimal, but Beijing's traffic could have kept me trapped in a maze of ring roads and roundabouts, and I could not risk being late for my meeting with the vice minister.

Guards on either side of the gate stood at attention. I felt sorry for them in the heat, but at least the umbrellas over their small platforms provided some shade.

I gave my name at the guardhouse, and after about ten minutes a young man slipped through the gate and hurried toward me. He was dressed in a blue suit and white shirt; he was thin, slightly shorter than me, and energetic. He guided me up the ramp that flag cars used when they delivered ambassadors and foreign dignitaries to the main entrance, so they wouldn't have to suffer the indignity of walking through the gate. I didn't mind.

The young man peppered me with questions, practicing his English, carefully avoiding any topic of substance. "Where are you from?" he asked. I thought about the many Chinese people who told me "China" when I posed the same question. It was unfathomable to them that an outsider would be familiar with China's cities, provinces, or regions, so they gave the most generic answer. I offered my young companion a more detailed answer than "America." He asked if I could speak Chinese, and I told a modest fib that I could speak "only a little Chinese," giving him the opportunity to continue demonstrating his English skills.

He led me through the cavernous lobby, and paused to point out the enormous mural above the long row of national flags. "Each group represents one of China's minority groups," he told me, pointing to a cluster of figures wearing ornate hats next to a spinning prayer wheel, identifying them as Tibetans. I gazed at the mural and found Miao women with their distinctive embroidered skirts, and shirtless Dai men enjoying a water-splashing festival.

The young man brought me to a conference room and asked me to wait. I remained standing, but put down my phone and notebook so I could be ready for the handshake.

"Mr. Gibbs, it is wonderful to see you." Vice Minister Xie Feng glided into the room and shook my hand firmly. He spoke English with almost no accent. His pin-striped suit looked expensive. We settled into armchairs and he got straight to the point. I had asked for the meeting and had a list of questions and topics to discuss that were of importance to the American companies I represented, but the vice minister had something on his mind.

"Mr. Gibbs, you have been in China for a long time. You really should understand the true situation in Xinjiang." His tone was friendly, and just a touch patronizing.

"Yes, of course, Mr. Vice Minister," I replied. "I've seen some reports."

"What your government is calling forced labor camps are simply vocational training schools!"

"I see, Mr. Vice Minister."

"China has every right—in fact, we have the responsibility—to care for our ethnic minorities, don't you agree?"

"Yes I do, Mr. Vice Minister."

"So why don't you speak out publicly and tell your government that nothing is happening in Xinjiang for anyone to be concerned about?"

"Well..." This put me in a jam, stuck between two governments trying to get me to pick a side.

"Mr. Vice Minister," I pleaded, "I want to help you, but I'm based in Shanghai, which is far from Xinjiang. To be honest, I don't have any direct knowledge of the labor conditions there."

"Ah, we can arrange that!" My interlocutor was hopeful, but this was clearly an offer I couldn't accept. On this particular issue, the American Chamber was in no position to support either side. For one, auditing supply chains is a highly specialized task. For some types of labor violations, "I know it when I see it" may be an acceptable standard but in other situations, it can be difficult to know what's actually happening. Without the proper training, experience, and a methodical approach, it would be all too easy to visit Xinjiang and observe happy workers in normal factories, yet miss seeing egregious conditions elsewhere. Chinese authorities have hurt their own case by restricting the activities of third-party audit firms, something they have acknowledged when I pointed it out privately.

I rushed through my talking points, and ended our meeting with an invitation for the vice minister to meet with my members, either in Beijing or Shanghai. Mr. Xie took me up on my offer and met several times with groups of AmCham members, and he was eventually promoted to become China's ambassador to the United States.

As Vice Minister Xie walked me out, I turned to him and

asked him why was it not possible for there to be greater transparency, if it was true that there wasn't a problem with forced labor in Xinjiang, and no human rights violations. It was the kind of question that can only be asked *after* a meeting, when a direct reply is not necessary and there is less risk of causing a loss of face. Xie didn't answer, but his expression told me that he understood my point.

The American Chamber of Commerce has no policy-making authority, it makes no laws, and enforces no claims. Our only power derives from information and the influence that flows from investment dollars, tax payments and employment. Before government authorities, whether Chinese or American, my only tool was to explain how businesses react to policy and government actions. Foreign businesspeople in China have no appetite for debates about human rights. In China, any conversation about this topic leads to a lose-lose situation, as many companies have discovered.

The China team at Thermo Fisher saw early signs of the problem they could have in Xinjiang and took proactive action. The company makes medical instruments, measuring devices, and test equipment. One of their products is used to sequence human DNA. It came to the company's attention that the Chinese government was using its technology to identify Uyghurs by their DNA. No matter what the company itself believes about what's happening or not happening in Xinjiang, no good could come of this if their global customers became aware of how their product was being used in Xinjiang. On the other hand, withdrawing the product from the China market would be interpreted as a signal that Thermo Fisher was siding against China on the matter. Retribution for such a move would be swift and severe. So they were stuck.

In order to avoid such circumstances, most of the multinational companies operating in China have sizable and well-paid government relations teams. Keeping abreast of regulatory changes is the core of what they do but in China, the task involves much more. Their responsibilities cut across business development, community relations, and strategy. When needed, they devise clever schemes for self-defense.

Early in 2019, when Xinjiang was in the news almost every day, the ThermoFisher team visited the American Chamber to discuss their predicament. The conversation centered on the export control list maintained by the US Department of Commerce, which generally includes so-called dual-use technologies, meaning products that could have military as well as civilian commercial use. The definitions are vague and subject to interpretation. Although DNA sequencing wasn't normally part of advanced weapons development, who knows? If Thermo Fisher's DNA product was added to the list, that would certainly be a shame from a sales point of view, but it would also give the company just the excuse they needed to quietly withdraw their product from a controversial market.

Fortunately, companies like Thermo Fisher maintain relationships with people in Washington -- as does the American Chamber -- precisely for situations where a subtle and nuanced conversation is necessary. Some weeks after Thermo Fisher visited the American Chamber, the Department of Commerce updated the entity list to include certain DNA testing products, forcing Thermo Fisher to withdraw them from the China market. The company was able to back slowly away from the Xinjiang controversy and escape with minimal damage to its business in China and, more importantly, keep its relationships with the government in Beijing.

The Swedish retailer H&M did not fare as well. A simple, vaguely worded statement on its website landed the company in trouble. Like other companies with European sensibilities, H&M maintains high standards for suppliers and pays close attention to labor practices. Their customer base demands nothing less. In 2020 someone at H&M headquarters added a statement on their website saying the company was "deeply concerned" about "reports of forced labor in Xinjiang."

That was enough to launch a firestorm in China. Sweden's ties with Beijing were strained to begin with, and without the economic heft of a Germany or France, the sparsely populated Nordic country became an easy target. Social media lit up with messages criticizing the retailer. Overnight, the locations of H&M's hundreds of stores disappeared from location-based services like Baidu and Didi, the Chinese versions of Google maps and Uber. Citizen activists dressed in black tee shirts patrolled the stores, urging the few shoppers who managed to find the stores not to buy anything.

The idea of this type of activist consumer seems far-fetched, but in China, it's impossible to know what's real and what's contrived. In some cases, as with the black tee shirts, the timing and organization would lead us to believe there are higher forces in play. It's also true that Chinese consumers understand their buying power and will use it when their sense of national pride is threatened.

China's efforts to manipulate social media have been clumsy but effective. Blocking foreign content and removing messages is only the beginning. There are reports of an army of *"wu mao"* who are paid to post messages that support the party's narrative, on social media networks both at home and abroad. The name *"wu mao"* comes from the amount that is allegedly paid to people per post, roughly half of one renminbi or the equivalent of about ten cents. The main focus of control and manipulation is within China, but the cybersphere outside China is susceptible as well. Twitter (now called X), despite being blocked in China, is a favorite platform for Chinese government officials to promote their side of stories such as Xinjiang. Other platforms like Reddit and Quora are heavily populated by Chinese trolls who push the party line and ridicule and threaten those who take alternative views.

Chinese retailers that compete with H&M saw an opportunity and moved in to take advantage of the situation. Their advertising campaigns immediately shifted to celebrating Xinjiang and products sourced from the region. The banners—in red, naturally—declared, "we love Xinjiang, we love Xinjiang cotton, and we use nothing but Xinjiang cotton."

The American retailer, Walmart, saw what was happening and tried to sidestep the issue by quietly removing all products made in Xinjiang from its shelves. It didn't take long for a zealous Chinese shopper to notice the pattern of missing items and raise the alarm on social media. The consequences were swift and severe. Consumers avoided the store, not wanting to face the wrath of their nationalistic countrymen.

The French retailer, Carrefour, had its own reasons for taking the opposite approach as Walmart, pandering to Chinese consumers and their political tastes. As the Xinjiang issue dominated the news cycle, the company launched a promotion on all its products sourced from Xinjiang. They gathered together grapes, almonds, wine, and clothing made in Xinjiang and launched a special promotion.

Why the difference? Carrefour in China is no longer a French company. It's Chinese. In 2019 the Chinese retailer Suning purchased 80% of the shares in Carrefour China and installed their own vice president as the CEO. Carrefour then operated over 200 stores with annual sales of over 30 billion RMB.[5]

Suning planned to open hundreds of new outlets, running the retailer as a thoroughly Chinese company. The nationalistic response to the Xinjiang issue is just one example of how a retailer can cater to local tastes.

Just as H&M was being punished for its corporate statement of values, Hugo Boss became entangled in the same controversy over its use of cotton. The German fashion house is a major user of cotton, one of Xinjiang's main exports. In Germany, where liberal values are taken seriously, the company put out a statement supporting workers' rights and expressed concern about the accusations of forced labor being used in Xinjiang. At the same time, the Hugo Boss team in China moved quickly to respond to its customer base and put out a statement supporting China's position on Xinjiang. The backlash was immediate, with criticism coming from both sides of the controversy. The sloppy response and apparent contradiction handed Hugo Boss the worst possible combination of outcomes, criticized by human rights groups, government leaders, and its customer base both inside and outside China.

I visited Washington in December of 2021, just as the Uyghur forced labor bill was headed to the Senate for a vote. Normally I would come with a delegation of AmCham members, but China's Covid travel restrictions were still in place. Most of my members weren't traveling.

I waited in the reception area for my meeting with Senator Marco Rubio. It was a large office in the Russell Building, across the street from the Capitol. A few other visitors were seated in

5 PR Newswire, " Suning Completes Acquisition of Carrefour China, Accelerating Full-Scenario Retail Layout." September 27, 2019.

the comfortable couches and armchairs, and members of a Boy Scout troop were horsing around in a corner. Stacks of "Visit Florida" brochures were scattered about, and I flipped through a coffee table book with a pink flamingo on the cover.

After a few minutes, a staffer brought me through an inner door to the conference room. Three men were already seated at the long table that could have accommodated twenty visitors, maybe more.

"Will the senator be joining us?" I had met Senator Rubio before, but I had had a large delegation with me then, including a member with business operations in his state. His staff would know that I voted in California, not Florida.

"He wanted to, but he sent his apologies," offered the youngest of the three men who sat across from me. He looked like an intern, probably in charge of scheduling. Another man wore a coat but no tie and seemed to be the senior person in the group, sitting in the middle. He slid a business card across the table, and I saw that he was the senator's legislative director. The third one had removed his jacket and rolled up his sleeves. His forearms were wiry and he looked a bit menacing. He didn't give me a card or tell me his name.

"Thanks, that's fine," I replied, and moved quickly to my talking points. I never knew how much time I would have in these meetings. "I'm hoping to get your thoughts on President Trump's tariffs. Many of our businesses are paying at both ends. They ship goods made in China back to the United States, where the importer pays the tax. But some of them bring raw materials and machinery into China, where they face a retaliatory tariff imposed by Beijing." I had just come from a meeting with a senator from the Midwest, who told me that China used to buy one out of every five rows of his corn. As a Republican, he supported President Trump, but the trade war had effectively shifted business away from his state, as China was now buying corn and beans from Brazil. "We're caught in the middle," I explained. "I'm wondering if the senator—"

"China's been hurting us on trade for years," said the man with rolled-up sleeves. "Senator Rubio is very focused on that. We want to know how bad the labor camps are, and why you are still doing business there?"

"Ah. You're talking about Xinjiang." At least now I knew why he was glaring at me. "We're aware of the issues. I've read the reports, but you probably have more information about it than I do."

"But you're there on the ground, aren't you? When you set up this meeting your office said you wanted to brief the senator on the current situation in China."

"Yes, we're very concerned about the tension," I replied. "The trade war has created a dynamic in China that is tense and antagonistic, which is bad for business. American firms have operated in China for years, with good profit and revenue growth, but the current environment has turned –" Rolled-up sleeves cut me off again, and his voice was beginning to get louder.

"The senator is co-sponsoring a bill that will put a stop to the forced labor. Any products using forced labor can't come into the United States." Sleeves seemed very proud of himself. He thought he was solving the problem, but the legislation was poorly drafted.

The Uyghur Forced Labor Prevention Act (UFPLA) required companies to prove a negative. Evidence can be found if forced labor has been used or if abuses have taken place, but how is it possible to prove that something has not happened? "If I run a red light then you can prove I did it. But how can anyone prove I have NOT run a red light in the last month? It's impossible."

I tried to explain that the legislation would end up cutting off trade and punishing the entire province of Xinjiang, and do little to help the Uygurs. As I pointed this out, the temperature of the room seemed to go up.

I probably should have just ended the meeting, but I asked, "Is the senator's goal really to help the Uyghurs as an oppressed group, or is he simply sending a message to China, and to American voters?" Sleeves glared at me, but he let me continue. "Look, it's good that the US government wants to promote human rights, but we just think the conversation should be respectful. I mean, it's not like we have a perfect record ourselves. How did we treat native Americans, and don't we have two hundred and fifty years of slavery to explain? Can we approach this issue with some humility?" My question sent Sleaves into a rage.

"That's a false equivalency!" Now he was shouting at me, and for the first time I was glad there was a large table between us. As he waved his arms I could see spit coming out of his mouth. "Does China have transparency on this issue? No! Does it allow investigations? No! Free journalism or independent courts? No! It's not the same thing!"

I hadn't said it was, but the argument was going nowhere. Representing the view of the American business community, I was simply pointing out that Chinese officials wanted to be treated with respect, but often felt that Americans talked down to them.

Of course, the Chinese don't help themselves by being overly sensitive on issues they consider none of anyone's business but theirs, walling off topics as "domestic issues" and quickly resorting to "whataboutism." If critics point to Beijing's suppression of free speech and democracy, China's officials point to the January 6th riots at the Capitol that challenged America's democratic institutions. When someone asks about Chinese navy ships ramming Filipino boats in the South China Sea, they shift the conversation to America's wars in Iraq or Afghanistan.

The other staffers from Marco Rubio's office also seemed shocked by their colleague's outburst, but they said nothing. It was time to leave. I mumbled something more about tariffs, and that the China market was important to our companies and for employment in the United States, then got up and left.

The Uyghur Forced Labor Prevention Act easily passed in the US Congress and was signed into law just before Christmas in 2021.

Al Jazeera, the global television network based in Doha, invited me to come on air to discuss the UFLPA. As the cameras got rolling and the host set up the segment, I learned I would be appearing with Jewher Ilham. She was the daughter of Tohti Ilham, a Uyghur economist. Professor Ilham was jailed in 2014 on charges of separatism and sentenced to life in prison. Her story was tragic and sadly, it's difficult to say whether the Uyghur Forced Labor Prevention Act (UFPLA) will bring any real change for the Uyghurs in China. The law effectively presumes that anything made in Xinjiang is the product of forced labor unless the importer can prove otherwise. This broad approach penalizes the entire region and is unlikely to compel Beijing to alter its policies. Poorly drafted legislation and impassioned finger-wagging lectures from American government officials will do little to influence China or make life any better for the Uyghurs.

China's nationalists are guided by the CCP's deep distrust of America that was pushing the country further down the path of self-sufficiency and independence from the West. Washington's criticism of China's record on human rights stuck in the craw of

Beijing's bureaucrats, causing Yang Jiechi, China's top diplomat to flip the script:

> "We hope that the United States will do better on human rights. China has made steady progress in human rights, and the fact is that there are many problems within the United States regarding human rights, which is admitted by the US itself as well. The United States has also said that countries can't rely on force in today's world to resolve the challenges we face. And it is a failure to use various means to topple the so-called authoritarian states. And the challenges facing the United States in human rights are deep-seated. They did not just emerge over the past four years, such as Black Lives Matter. It did not come up only recently. So we do hope that for our two countries, it's important that we manage our respective affairs well instead of deflecting the blame on somebody else in this world."

Some companies have managed to avoid getting stuck in the middle, as Thermo Fisher did by convincing the US government to restrict sales of certain products in China. The strategy allowed the company to extricate itself from the Xinjiang controversy and escape with minimal damage to its business in China and, most importantly, maintain its relationships with the government in Beijing. Other firms faired not as well, with some landing in a lose-lose by alienating their customers in China while disappointing a global audience that was more sympathetic to the Uyghurs.

Western business leaders need to prioritize geopolitical intelligence throughout the organization and across departments. A company that operates in silos is prone to mistakes, miscommunication, and misalignment. Whatever messaging comes from the China unit must be consistent with global, and vice versa. This is increasingly difficult because operations in China need to be separate due to China's data localization laws and US export controls as both governments push to decouple.

China's treatment of dissent—whether from foreign business leaders, domestic lawyers, or anyone else—reveals a political system that sees vulnerability wherever it cannot exert full control. The polished diplomats and globally minded technocrats who present a cooperative face to the world cannot mask a deeper insecurity at the core of the party's governance: a fear that independent voices, civil society, or competing identities might erode the party's authority. Beijing constantly signals that even limited pluralism is intolerable, and that engagement with the outside world is acceptable only on its own terms. For foreign governments and companies, this creates an environment of chronic uncertainty, where cooperation is conditional. The CCP has trapped itself between a desire for global influence and a political system that has trouble tolerating the openness that real partnership requires.

CHAPTER 16

Beijing to Washington: The Fragile Dialogue

In a tradition going back many years, the American Chamber of Commerce arranged trips to Washington, where we met with administration officials, members of Congress, and various think tanks. We discouraged members from using these visits to push their individual agendas; instead, we focused our discussions on US-China relations generally and broad economic issues. Policymakers wanted to hear from people on the ground about the business environment in China and how policies were affecting us. They were looking for insight into a system that remained opaque and contradictory—fast-growing, yet fragile; open in some ways, but closing in others.

Once our delegation was formed, the Chamber staff would draft talking points. Led by the chair, we would debate which messages to emphasize: our survey data showing business confidence, the expanding role of local competitors, and the uneven enforcement of rules. The same themes returned year after year—that China's market was too big to ignore, but our position was delicate and we had to move carefully.

We would also meet with Washington think tanks like CSIS, Brookings, and Heritage. These groups are highly influential, as they generally house people who rotate in and out of government. We would typically spend at least a day on the Hill meeting with members of Congress, but our main focus was the administrative branch, which the Constitution designates as responsible for foreign policy and trade.

At times, our agenda would clash with the priorities that members of Congress felt were important. Jim McGovern, a senator from Massachusetts, came from a long tradition of supporting liberal causes and progressive issues. He had worked on the Uyghur forced labor legislation with Senator Rubio. I read his comments in the press and knew he also had strong views on Taiwan and Hong Kong.

I glanced up and saw a Tibetan flag on one wall and a Republic of China (Taiwan) flag on the other as the senator turned to me and said: "So, Mr. Gibbs, what would you like to discuss?"

I knew exactly where he wanted the conversation to go—human rights, Hong Kong, or Xinjiang. Those topics were radioactive for our members. Even being seen discussing them could trigger retaliation back in China, where surveillance was pervasive and tolerance for open discussion on these topics was limited. The very fact that we had to be so careful said something about the fragility of China's system—a regime which seemed to view even respectful criticism by foreigners as a threat.

Our delegation was typically composed of fifteen to twenty senior members of the American business community in Shanghai, with each person carefully selected based on what they could bring to the discussion. We needed a cross-section of industries and balance in terms of company size. In many ways the smaller companies were more important as the main drivers of employment, but it was easier to get attention from people in Washington if our group included large companies from the Fortune 500. Members of Congress also pay more attention to a delegation if it includes a company headquartered in their state. We never failed to get meetings with Johnny Atkinson, the senator from Georgia, as long as the China CEO of Coca-Cola was in our group.

Bringing China-born members on our visits was never a requirement, but by the mid-2010s the majority of our member companies were run by Chinese nationals so it was inevitable that a third or more of our delegation was Chinese. People in Washington understood this and we never had an issue, perhaps because America itself is a country of immigrants, but our Chinese colleagues were sometimes shocked that they would be allowed to casually walk the halls of the nation's capital.

"I can't believe it," said Tony Ling, a Chinese entrepreneur who was working for an international company when he joined our delegation. He was an expert in human resource management, and I went to him often for advice and insight on workforce issues, like China's labor laws. "We could never get inside Zhongnanhai or ask questions like we do with American politicians." The term "Zhongnanhai" refers to a compound in Beijing that houses the party leadership and the State Council. It's not an exact equivalent to White House—tours, for example, would be unthinkable in Beijing—but it's often referred to that way.

I encouraged Tony to write about his experiences in Washington and publish something in Chinese about our trips. China will continue to develop its political and economic system according to its own priorities, but knowing more about our system would seem to be a good thing, with so many conflicts arising from misunderstandings. In the mid-2010s an article like Tony's would have been well received in China, but geopolitical tensions would later become higher, with loyalties more likely to be questioned in both countries.

In Washington, some departments had security requirements that precluded non-American citizens, which created some awkwardness as our group moved from meeting to meeting. The Treasury Department was particularly sensitive and only allowed American passport holders to enter the building, leaving our Chinese friends outside. I'm not sure how much it bothered our Chinese colleagues that they were kept out, but the mistrust and suspicion probably troubled me more than it did them.

By 2016, President Obama was nearing the end of his second term and preparing to host a summit with Xi Jinping in Washington. After starting out reasonably well, their relationship had become tense as Obama's "pivot to Asia"—intended to rebalance US attention toward a rapidly growing region—collided with China's increasing assertiveness and Beijing's perception that the policy was aimed at containment. The result was a more openly competitive dynamic, with geopolitical tensions rising across trade, security, and regional influence. We timed our annual trip to Washington to coincide with the summit, when China policy would be squarely at the center of the debate.

An aide led our delegation into a conference room. It was enormous, with a high ceiling, double chandeliers, and an unused fireplace at one end. We gathered along one side of a long, polished mahogany table and took seats in high-backed leather chairs. The room was bright with natural light, despite the heavy drapes that covered at least half the opening of the tall arched windows.

Our host, a senior official from the National Security Council, was punctual. He stepped quickly into the room and took a seat opposite me. "Welcome to the White House." It was more a statement than a greeting, and he paused to let the words sink in. He brought a stack of papers with him, which he placed to one side on the wide table that separated us.

Technically, we were in the EEOB—the Eisenhower Executive Office Building—which is the next building over from the actual White House, but nearly everyone there works for the executive office of the president. Historically, the president's staff was small, consisting of an appointment secretary and a few trusted advisors. The founding fathers insisted on a relatively weak chief executive who would never behave like the autocratic king they had fought a war to break free from. Before Franklin Roosevelt's presidency fewer than fifty people worked on the White House staff, but since then it has ballooned to more than 6,000, including the National Security Council.[6]

The introductions went quickly, as we were all eager to get to the point of our meeting. Before we could launch into talking points our host surprised us with an admonishment. "Gee guys, the president is trying to get something done here. Who's side are you on?" He pulled a copy of that day's *Wall Street Journal* from the stack of papers in front of him and pushed it across the table. I glanced at the article it was opened to, then handed the paper around to my colleagues. We knew what he was referring to.

In preparation for the summit, President Xi went on a major charm offensive, trying to bring the American business community onto his side. On his way to Washington he stopped in Seattle to meet with Bill Gates and the leaders of other companies with big operations in China, including GM, Disney, JP Morgan, and others. They were all AmCham members, and some were represented on our Board.

6 The White House Historical Association, "Under This Roof," by Bradley H. Patterson, Fall 2009.

Ahead of the meeting, President Xi granted a rare interview to the *Wall Street Journal* in which he cited the results from our annual survey. Xi had cited our Chamber's survey, proudly pointing out that most US companies were thriving in China. We had seen the article that morning, and Chamber staff had congratulated themselves on achieving such a high level of visibility for the survey, which had taken months of tedious work to prepare. The Chamber had accurately reported that most of our members were profitable and growing in China, which was still true in 2016. The squeeze on profits and decline in growth came later but in Washington, our messages landed badly. The White House wanted leverage, not reassurance.

"We're trying to get a deal on intellectual property," the official continued. "But are you saying that's not a problem?"

Actually it was, but not in the same way that Obama's people wanted us to present it. By 2016 the business environment in China had changed dramatically. Disputes still occurred, but the rampant theft, bootlegged movies, and fake Rolex watches had largely disappeared. Don Williams, a veteran lawyer with Hogan Lovells, explained that pressure from the US might have been a factor, but in recent years Chinese companies were developing intellectual property themselves that they wanted to protect. "They're protecting their own IP now," he told us, "and that's changing everything."

The legal environment in terms of IP had improved. Our members still complained that settlements and penalties weren't severe enough, but at least there was a process for enforcement. Justice in China, like its growth model, was progress wrapped in fragility.

The National Security Council was concerned about cyberattacks originating in China against companies in the United States, especially state-sponsored attacks. Max Baucus, who took over from Gary Locke as US ambassador to China, had been working on the issue for months with his counterparts in Beijing. Baucus finally got his counterparts to acknowledge the distinction between ordinary criminal behavior and state-sponsored theft of industry secrets, and that it was unacceptable for governments to steal industrial secrets for the benefit of their own companies. Still, the summit concluded without Xi agreeing to make policy changes, which would have required admission of guilt. It was a reminder that the system doesn't easily admit to fault.

Instead, the leaders settled on climate change as an issue they could agree on, and the United States and China would both join the Paris climate accord. It was a win for both sides, especially as China had been making strides toward cleaner air and water. Beijing initially resisted making firm commitments and refused to submit to monitoring, but in the end came up with a plan that sought to outdo America with its ambitious goals, in a win for China and for the planet. The US under President Trump would later withdraw from the Paris accord, but China remained a party to the agreement and has since taken on a leadership role.

China's portrayal of itself as a global leader on the environment and its ambitions to effect a transition to clean energy have exposed the same paradox that defines its rise: a drive to appear strong masking deep insecurity. A confident power would welcome scrutiny. A fragile one fears it.

Companies today no longer believe they can influence China's trajectory; the old confidence that engagement could shape Beijing's behavior has collapsed, removing any incentive to speak up when political pressures mount. Instead, firms see a landscape where criticism can only trigger retaliation—from regulatory investigations and license delays to orchestrated online shaming or surprise police visits—

reinforcing the message that challenging the party carries real costs. Growing political risk, tightening data and security rules, and unpredictable enforcement have further chilled corporate willingness to say anything that might be construed as political. As China increasingly links market access to political alignment, companies feel compelled to avoid crossing opaque redlines simply to maintain the ability to operate.

At the same time, US domestic politics under the second Trump administration has shifted even further, and firms face an environment in which deference, if not outright obedience, is expected to navigate trade restrictions, tariffs, and export controls, adding an additional layer of pressure. The resulting silence from American business leaders is not neutrality but a measure of discomfort—a reflection of how coercion, political risk, and fear of retaliation from both Beijing and Washington have reshaped the business environment and exposed a more profound vulnerability in China's ability to retain the confidence of foreign companies and investors.

The dialogue between Beijing and Washington has become fragile because neither side trusts the other's intentions, and both increasingly doubt the value of engagement itself. Washington sees a China that demands political deference from foreign companies, suppressing open discussion at home, and refusing accountability on issues like cybertheft—all signals of a system that fears exposure more than competition.

Beijing, for its part, no longer looks to the United States for validation or guidance, convinced that American politics have turned hostile and that China must chart its own course, even if that means abandoning the cooperative frameworks that once anchored the relationship. American businesses now speak cautiously, trapped between Washington's strategic expectations and Beijing's coercive demands, a silence that underscores how risky China has become for those who operate there. Human rights, Xinjiang, Hong Kong, and the climate agenda have been reduced to symbols in a wider struggle rather than foundations for dialogue, reflecting not only deep structural flaws in China's governance but also the collapse of the old assumption that engagement could shape China's evolution. The result is a relationship defined by mistrust, misreading, and mutual insecurity—a reminder that China's strength and fragility are inseparable, and that the United States must navigate both simultaneously.

CHAPTER 17

Going "Renegade" in Taiwan

Taiwan is home to people whose prosperity has been built on pragmatism and strategic flexibility. Nevertheless, the people who live there find themselves at the center of a contest between China and a US-led coalition of nations. Taiwan has become the flashpoint for competing ideologies, diplomatic wrangling, and the target of practice invasions and threats from one of the most powerful militaries on earth.

Taiwan today is self-governed, with its own military, legal system, currency, and democratically elected government, yet Beijing continues to say that the island is an inseparable part of China. From the PRC's narrative, the Chinese Civil War of the late 1940s never formally ended, and Taiwan's separate political existence reflects not self-determination but the lingering legacy of foreign interference—especially from the United States. But the other side of this narrative is less often acknowledged: Taiwan's success in many ways draws attention to Beijing's vulnerabilities. As a prosperous, orderly, diverse, and ethnically Chinese society, Taiwan demonstrates that political pluralism and Chinese culture are not necessarily incompatible. Its existence quietly undermines the argument that only one-party rule can deliver stability and effective governance for Chinese people.

The island is at the center of a conflict and in many ways the victim of its own success, as well as the accident of its strategically important geography. And the industriousness and creativity of its people have led to the development of a specific industry that could contribute to a sudden change in its circumstances.

Beijing has consistently stated that a formal declaration of Taiwan independence would trigger military action. More recently, Chinese officials have indicated that even Taiwan's rejection of a Chinese identity constitutes an unacceptable challenge to mainland interests.

How did all this happen? What continues to keep the two sides apart? Why is Taiwanese identity an issue, and what is the island actually like?

As described at the beginning of this book, after I graduated from college, my mother insisted that I go to mainland China and meet her sister, but at the same time she also encouraged me to visit Taiwan. She had been a schoolgirl in Taiwan and had a happy life there. She became a teacher and was popular among her students, who were mostly male. Many of the local men were fascinated by this pretty young woman from the mainland, and she had her pick of suitors. Eventually she met my father, who was also a teacher at her school. After Korea, he used the GI Bill to finish college and set off on an academic career, starting with an appointment to teach in Taiwan.

Throughout my business career in management consulting and banking I would continue to return to Taiwan, but I initially landed on the island as a fresh college graduate.

I arrived in the summer of 1985, and stepped off the plane

into a wall of humidity. It was like breathing water. It didn't help that the air was filled with blue smoke from thousands of motorcycles, the kind with cheap two-stroke engines that let out a roar as they blasted through intersections. As a kid growing up in California I rode motorcycles myself, and later became an honorary member of the Harley Owners Group (the HOGs) in China. Still, I wasn't ready to brave the roads of Taiwan on a bike, so I borrowed a car from one of my mother's friends for my tour around the island.

I set out for the south of Taiwan, which is covered with lush forests and rich farmlands. Tea plantations blanket the foothills, and a mountain range down the center divides the island from east to west. Yu Shan, or Jade Mountain, is its highest peak at almost thirteen thousand feet, just a bit higher than Japan's Mount Fuji.

As a subtropical island, Taiwan gets plenty of rain and almost any plant will thrive there, but it is known for the delicate beauty of its orchids, of which there are some 400 native varieties. Pineapples, mangos, and melons of all shapes and sizes can be found in abundance, but in Taiwan I discovered something called a *lianwu,* a waxy apple shaped more like a pear. The *lianwu* is as beautiful as it is tasty and refreshing.

I drove down the east coast, taking the Su-hua highway that links the village of Su-ao ("su") in the north with the city of Hualian ("hua") to the south. The east coast of the island is rugged, with mountains that plunge directly into the ocean. It is reminiscent of California's Pacific Coast Highway, which is also a two lane road that wraps like a ribbon high above the rocks below.

The views were breathtaking, with mountains to one side and the ocean on the other, but I was worried about falling rocks and needed to pay full attention to the winding road. Other drivers, finding themselves stuck behind slow-moving vehicles, decided to try their luck around blind curves. The Su-hua highway continues to claim lives every year.

I stopped in the village of Su-ao to stretch my legs and get a bite to eat. I walked along the dock, where fishing trawlers were bringing in their catch. As a village, it was not much more than a cluster of seafood restaurants that took advantage of fresh supplies and served tourists on their way to and from Taiwan's southern retreats. The laid-back atmosphere of the village belied its historical significance.

During World War II, the Japanese used Su-ao as a base to launch submarines that hunted American warships in the Pacific. Taiwan had been under Japanese control since the war of 1895, when Qing Dynasty China was defeated and ceded the island under the Treaty of Shimonoseki. Taiwan became integrated with Japan's war machinery, and many Taiwanese served in the emperor's army. Taiwanese men either volunteered or were drafted into the Japanese imperial army. The brother of Taiwan's first democratically elected president, Lee Denghui, served in the Japanese military. This legacy, and Japan's ongoing relationship with Taiwan, is an important point that will become clear in the next chapter.

My mother arrived in Taiwan just as Japan's occupation was ending. In August 1945, Emperor Hirohito surrendered unconditionally to the United States and allied forces, and China's KMT-led government took control of Taiwan. The new government needed administrators and my uncle, Li Lin, was asked to go and help establish a legal system on the island. He left behind a successful law practice in Shanghai to pack up and move to Taiwan, which I'm sure he thought was a temporary assignment. The civil war between the KMT and CCP had been put on hold during World War II, and it was not yet clear which side would prevail.

For me, the important aspect of my uncle's position was that it enabled him to bring my mother out of China, escaping the civil war between the KMT and the communists. The rest of her family, including her sister, stayed on the mainland.

Li Lin arrived in Taiwan around 1948 and became the head of the Taipei Bar Association. I was never told much more about my uncle's work, or how deeply he was involved with the KMT, but when the communists took full control of the mainland in 1949 he decided to stay in Taiwan and his temporary assignment became permanent.

KMT soldiers retreated to the island of Taiwan beaten and resentful, with little respect for the local culture. Taiwan wasn't even their first choice. General Chiang originally planned to retreat to the island of Hainan, off the southern coast of the mainland, and even began moving his stockpiles of gold and American weapons toward the south. In the end he decided that Hainan, located much closer to the mainland, would be too difficult to defend. Taiwan, separated by a ninety-mile strait, was the better choice. It was a fateful decision for the Taiwanese people.

For the next thirty-five years the KMT ruled Taiwan under martial law, based on the view that the civil war was not yet over. The CCP could attack Taiwan at any moment, or the KMT could launch a counter-offensive to retake the mainland. The Americans kept a military presence in Taiwan as much to prevent the KMT from provoking a fight with the mainland as to defend against an attack from the CCP. American ships and soldiers maintained the delicate peace.

Under martial law, the Taiwanese who lived on the island

had no right to govern themselves and lost many other freedoms they might otherwise have enjoyed. The schools, which the KMT controlled, imposed the use of Mandarin instead of the local Chinese dialect and inculcated students with the idea that Taiwan was not just part of the mainland, but that the Republic of China government would one day once again rule over all of China.

The occupation was often brutal. The Taiwanese suffered at least one massacre at the hands of the KMT, when trigger-happy troops from the mainland gunned down some 20,000 Taiwanese civilians. The incident, known as "2-2-8" from the date, February 28, 1947, started as an argument involving an old woman selling contraband cigarettes, but tension had been building up for months between the native Taiwanese and the mainland KMT, which was viewed from the outset as an occupying force. Under KMT rule, this history was repressed, but as Taiwanese society shifted, the politics changed. In a deeply symbolic gesture, the park near the presidential palace in Taipei, originally established during the Qing dynasty (later renamed by the Japanese and again by the KMT), is now called 228 Peace Memorial Park. The nearby Chiang Kai-shek memorial is also a center for the current and ongoing debate over who the heroes and villains of Taiwan's history are. Taiwan's history—Japanese rule, KMT takeover, martial law, and democratic reform—has produced a society with its own political arc that, in many ways, challenges the CCP's view that Taiwan "has always been part of China." Just how Chinese is Taiwan, and how true are the CCP's claims? Why has Taiwanese identity become such a big part of the debate? Who are the Taiwanese, and how do they see themselves and the situation they face?

The answers are complicated, and depend on how far back you want to go. In order to find people who are truly indigenous to the island of Taiwan it's necessary to go back quite far. The indigenous people, closely related to the Polynesians of the Pacific islands, arrived in Taiwan around 3000 BC and still made up the majority of the population in the late 17th Century. Beginning around the 1660s, a growing number of Chinese farmers and fishermen crossed the strait, pushing local people into the mountains and establishing farms and homes. Today, those indigenous people, who go by tribal names such as Tsou, Amis (ah mei), and Kavalan, make up about two percent of Taiwan's overall population and are referred to as *yuanzhumin*, meaning "aboriginal people." [7]

Confusingly, the term "native Taiwanese" now usually refers not to the *yuanzhumin* but to the majority of the island's population, who are from the racial group that originated in Fujian province, across the Taiwan Strait on the mainland. The ancestors of most of these people would have migrated from the mainland sometime between the 17th and 19th centuries.

The Taiwanese speak a language known as *min'nanyu*, or southern Min, which refers to the southern part of Fujian province, around the port city of Xiamen. People from that region in those years—the early period of the Qing dynasty—migrated not only to Taiwan, but to various points in Southeast Asia, notably Malaysia and Singapore. Of the 23 million people living in Taiwan today, over 90 percent are in this group of "native Taiwanese," as opposed to the *yuanzhumin* or the more recent arrivals from the mainland—people like my mother and my uncle.

7 Taiwan's first female president, Cai Yingwen, supposedly has a small amount of Polynesian blood, and has used it to her advantage. Taiwan, the Republic of China, has desperately tried to hang onto the few countries that are willing to defy the PRC and recognize Taiwan as a country. When visiting the micronesian states of Tuvalu, Marshall Islands, and Palau, President Cai has tried to play up her Polynesian ancestry and make the case that Taiwan is more Micronesian, thus weakening China's claim to the island.

As China's civil war drew to a close in 1949, roughly two million soldiers and civilians fled the mainland for Taiwan, together with Chiang Kai-shek and the KMT. These mainlanders are referred to in Taiwan as *"waishengren"*—people from other provinces. The term carries a slight pejorative connotation, the way Americans might say someone is from "out of state" and therefore not familiar with local customs and norms. In Taiwan the term *waishengren* emphasizes that the person is not a native of the island.

In the days after the 1949 communist victory, and early in the KMT's occupation of Taiwan, this distinction was important. People like my uncle occupied privileged positions, not just because they were well educated but because political power was held entirely by the KMT. Today there has been so much intermarriage and blending of native Taiwanese and *waishengren*, the distinction is far less important.

Taiwan's transition from authoritarian one-party rule under the KMT was not easy, or sudden. Demands for liberalization and democratic reforms began in the 1970s, led by students, intellectuals, and civil society groups. The government of Chiang Kai-shek instinctively wished to suppress the trend, but he died in 1975 and his son, Chiang Ching-kuo, took over as leader.

The younger Chiang, the general's only biological son and heir, had spent years in the Soviet Union, some voluntarily and some not. In the early days, the KMT struggled as a new party and looked to Moscow for support. In 1925, Chiang Ching-kuo was sent to Russia to study and bolster support for his father's party, but as the conflict between the KMT and the communists in China turned increasingly violent, the relationship fell apart. Chiang Ching-kuo became a hostage in the Soviet Union. He was eventually released in 1937, but not before taking a wife, a Russian-speaking ethnic Belarusian.

In Taiwan, Chiang Ching-kuo ended martial law in 1987 and put a stop to any idea of a family dynasty, solidifying the role of the constitution. He brought more Taiwanese into the government, appointing Lee Teng-hui as his vice president and eventual successor. Lee continued the reforms, legalizing opposition parties and implementing democratic elections. In 1996 Lee Teng-hui became Taiwan's first directly elected leader.[8] The process took time and commitment from many leaders in a society determined to shape its own path to democracy. Taiwan's unique form of democracy has been messy at times, marked by occasional fistfights on the floor of the legislature, but the people of Taiwan have been choosing their own leaders in elections that are reasonably free and fair since the 1990s. Taiwan's successful transition from authoritarian rule to a vibrant democracy poses an ideological threat to the CCP, and exposes a fundamental weakness in its governance system: the lack of political pluralism and diversity of opinion.

Today, it would be hard to imagine that the people of Taiwan would have any interest in giving up that which they've worked so hard to attain, making voluntary unification implausible. Taiwan demonstrates that a Chinese society can be both orderly and democratic, undermining the CCP's central justification for one-party rule and highlighting the fragility of a system that depends on controlling narratives rather than competing for public consent.

As Taiwan has developed into an open, rights-based society, it has set a precedent Beijing views as problematic: a demonstration that Chinese societies can succeed under democratic governance. Given Taiwan's shared cultural and historical foundations with the mainland, its political model may serve as a reference point

8 Lee became president in 1988 after Chiang Ching-kuo died in office. He was elected in his own right by popular vote on March 23rd, 1996. He was a member of the KMT.

that calls into question the CCP's assertion that its system is uniquely suited to Chinese conditions. Taiwan's successes therefore represent both an external diplomatic challenge and a potential domestic legitimacy concern for the CCP.

CHAPTER 18

Ties with Japan

By the time I arrived and began working in Taiwan in the late 1980s, my uncle had long since passed away. Li Lin's name, however, was still held in high regard within the legal profession in Taiwan, and I was able to leverage my uncle's reputation to my advantage.

Mr. Dai, a lawyer who had worked with my uncle, helped me get set up in a small apartment on the west side of the city off a main drag called *luosifu lu*, the transliteration of "Roosevelt Road." The thoroughfare was named after Franklin D. Roosevelt, a reminder of the close relationship between the KMT and the United States. To call it an apartment was in fact generous. The truth is I was bunking in a *xiuxi shi*, or a "resting room" attached to Mr. Dai's law office. The Taiwanese are accustomed to taking short naps after the midday meal. This is generally accomplished by reclining in a chair or resting on a desk, but more privileged people have a dedicated room for this purpose.

Mr. Dai was retired and rarely needed the office. I didn't pay rent, but I did observe the Chinese tradition of symbolically handing over my first paycheck once I began working. Normally that tribute would go to my parents, but in this case it seemed appropriate to give the money to lawyer Dai. It wasn't much.

I found work with a small trading firm called the Taiwan Transportation Machinery Corporation, run by Mr. RT Peng. He was an older gentleman, thin and energetic, with the air of a man who could get things done. His white hair was thinning but his mind was sharp, and he listened intently, always looking for openings and advantages. The idea for the business was to leverage his connections and expertise to represent foreign machinery and equipment providers, mostly from Japan and the United States. Mr. Peng spoke Japanese with native fluency, but his English was rough, which was perhaps why he hired me.

Mr. Peng's office was enormous, which it needed to be, not just to give his small company stature but also to serve as his conference room. I sat at a desk just outside the boss's office, separated by paper-thin walls so I could generally hear the proceedings, except when voices were lowered. Mr. Peng knew how to hold confidences. He had a habit of shouting "kaaa!!!" whenever he needed me. The first time he did this I didn't realize he was calling my name. The meetings we attended together were in Chinese, using my Chinese name, Ji Kaiwen, so I was unfamiliar with how he pronounced my English name. He had to leave his meeting to poke his head outside and beckon me to come in. I didn't make that mistake again.

My tasks were simple. I explained English terms to him and the other staff, drafted correspondence, and focused on clients from America. About the time I came along in the late 1980s, and as democracy gave ordinary people a larger voice in how budgets were allocated, Taipei's city government finally got around to planning its first subway line and created the Department of Rapid Transit System, or DORTS.

Until then, Taiwan's government had not invested in major infrastructure projects on the assumption that a return to the mainland was imminent. This had been going on since 1949, but Mr. Peng saw the shift taking place, with Taiwanese demanding more from their government, and knew that big money was about to be spent on infrastructure projects. He made it his business to become a familiar face in the hallways and conference rooms at DORTS.

Japan's Kawasaki Heavy Industries was a major player in transportation and infrastructure, but Motorola and a few other large American companies banded together to compete for projects. We made every attempt to pressure DORTS to favor us, arguing that American exports of technology and equipment would help reduce Taiwan's trade surplus, which had become embarrassingly large. We visited the de facto American embassy in Taipei—called the "American Institute in Taiwan," as a diplomatic smokescreen—to get the commercial officers on our side to apply pressure on DORTS to lean in our favor. They made a few introductions but that was about the extent of their influence on actual deals. The US government, despite its support for the island and diplomatic commitment to help Taiwan defend itself, was reluctant to exert influence in domestic affairs.

Mr. Peng used his influence to guide DORTS and navigate Taiwan's bureaucracy and bidding process, with some success. Mr. Peng won several contracts to build components of the Taipei mass rapid transit system, but not the entire project, which was worth hundreds of millions of dollars. I learned later that DORTS had developed a strategy early on to break the project into smaller parts so that no one bidder could have too much control. Looking back, I suspect Mr. Peng knew that would happen, which is why he assigned me to look after the American clients while he tended to more important matters.

Mr. Peng's business tracked Taiwan's economic development

model almost exactly. Following the civil war, Taiwan relied on financial aid from the United States as it transitioned from agriculture to manufacturing, producing products such as toys, shoes, and clothing. Labor was cheap, and Taiwan developed mainly through exports.

Taiwan's trade benefited from a close relationship with two of the world's largest markets for its products—the United States and Japan—and by the 1980s the export model had transformed Taiwan into the well-developed economy that it is today. Taiwan quickly moved up the value chain into heavy industry, chemicals, and infrastructure, with Mr. Peng's business perfectly positioned to facilitate large deals.

The factories that Taiwan was building needed more and more power, which meant huge contracts for plant and equipment, much of which came from Japan. Mr. Peng had all the right connections and worked the halls of Taiwan's power company, known as TaiPower, learning the specifications for the next large deal and, in some cases, helping to write them. Time and again he delivered bids that fit perfectly with TaiPower's needs and budget while competitors continued to take shots in the dark. Taiwan consumed more and more power as the economy shifted from low-end manufactured goods to advanced electronics, and eventually semiconductors.

After some time, I left Taiwan and Mr. Peng's company, but I returned after graduate school in a new role as a management consultant. Like most people, I knew little about semiconductors and had never actually seen one, but my job at the Boston Consulting Group was to identify efficiencies in the factories I was assigned to, which often meant learning about new products and manufacturing processes.

In the early 1990s, Taiwan couldn't have been more different from mainland China. Across the Taiwan Strait in Shanghai, I cleared debris out of workshops so metal stamping machines didn't clog, and had to wake up the man holding the keys to the cabinets so I could access spare parts and inventory. In Taiwan, manufacturing was decades ahead of the mainland in terms of sophistication and quality controls, but it was about to become even more advanced, and geopolitically important.

Over the centuries of human evolution, the value of different commodities has changed. There was a time when salt was more valuable than gold because it could be used to flavor and preserve food, which could then be traded across large distances. With the Industrial Revolution and the advent of the automobile, oil became a valuable commodity and an important influence in geopolitics. Today, in the age of information, data, and quantum computing, the product we all depend on is the tiny semiconductor. Semiconductors are the new oil. It's worth noting that America's embargo on oil to Japan was the trigger that led to the bombing of Pearl Harbor.

I reported for work in a low, white colored building in Xindian, a suburb of Taipei. As always in the summer, it was a blazing hot day but the interior was carefully temperature controlled. The cool air was comfortable for workers, but it was also filtered and free of particulates that could interfere with the precise manufacturing process for silicon wafers. As in mainland China, my task was to follow the process steps and identify improvements that could lead to greater efficiency, fewer errors, and higher profits. The project was for General Instrument, which was testing semiconductors that would be used in televisions, clock radios, and other consumer products. Taiwan was no longer the source of cheap goods, having made the shift to higher-value electronics.

I walked the factory floor holding a notebook and stood behind workers who pulled one out of every hundred pieces off the line, carefully placing it into a device to see if a light would come on, indicating proper function. If it did, the piece was placed back on the line. If the light did not come on, the line would be stopped until the source of the problem was found. With a single error, entire batches of product would be discarded or sent for rework.

The testing facility where I worked was part of a process called "packaging," the last step for an integrated circuit before it is placed in an electronic device. The steps involved in making semiconductors are performed by different companies in various locations. The integrated circuit could be designed in California, printed on a wafer in Japan using tools from Europe, and then placed in a package in Malaysia or Taiwan before being shipped to China to be placed into a toy. Or a car, or a guided missile system.

Semiconductors have been important for military applications since the earliest days of the industry's development. US Defense Department contracts were crucial sources of capital for companies like Fairchild and National Semiconductor, helping them develop capabilities and scale up in the early days before commercial uses for microchips emerged. But semiconductors were used from the outset by the military for everything from guiding missiles to landing airplanes. At the time, the CEO of my client, General Instrument, was none other than Donald Rumsfeld, who would later become the Secretary of Defense under George W. Bush.

Before semiconductors, most bombs fell only approximately near an intended target. Accuracy was typically measured against a goal of 1,000 feet from a target, with scores in the low teens considered good. Due to this low accuracy, bombs would frequently be used to destroy an entire area instead of a precise military target, vastly increasing collateral damage and wasting large amounts of ordinance. Semiconductors, and the guidance systems they go into, have changed everything about military hardware, from communications satellites to HIMARS and shoulder-launched Stinger missiles. These systems all depend on semiconductors, especially the most advanced types. Military hardware typically uses the most advanced semiconductors, currently those between about three and five nanometers in size. Remarkably, given the strategic importance of this tiny input, the United States lacks any substantial capability to produce them. Almost all of the advanced chips are made on the island of Taiwan.

Taiwan produces over 60 percent of the world's semiconductors and over 90 percent of the most advanced ones. The "fabs," or fabrication facilities where the chips are made, cost billions of dollars and are delicate and impossible to move. Highly trained engineers make adjustments to machines that are so precise they can be thrown off by a passing train, a weather event, or trace levels of contaminants.

If we suddenly lost our supply of semiconductors from Taiwan, our lives would be transformed dramatically. The semiconductor is the essential input without which we can't make any of the products that we depend on in our daily lives. We wake up in the morning and brush our teeth with an electric toothbrush, maybe while listening to music playing on a speaker. All these devices have microchips in them, as does our coffee maker, thermostat, and almost everything else we touch even before getting to work in the morning, which we might do in a car that could have as many as 3,000 semiconductors in it.

Taiwan—and continued access to the chips it produces—is vital to the global economy. The US military establishment is also concerned about the continued reliability of its supply of chips, and losing control of the source of new semiconductors. It is even more concerned that this supply chain could fall into the hands of an adversary that will use these same chips in the weapons it uses against the United States.

How did Taiwan become the world's dominant supplier of semiconductors, and how did its flagship company, Taiwan Semiconductor Manufacturing Company (TSMC) become the main supplier for some of the most technologically advanced companies like Apple, Qualcomm, and NVidia?

Taiwan has a dominant position, but only in one segment of the supply chain in an industry that is geographically dispersed and highly integrated. The life cycle of a chip begins with the design. The United States leads in design, but this function is done in many other parts of the world as well. The design is then etched onto a silicon wafer, which is done in Taiwan, but also Japan, South Korea, and other countries. Testing and packaging are done mostly in lower-wage countries like the Philippines and Malaysia. Sophisticated tools are used throughout this process, which come from several countries, most notably the Netherlands. The final step is to place the microchip into the device for which it was designed. This takes place wherever that particular product is made, and in most cases that country is China, giving Beijing a keen interest in how this industry is organized and controlled.

The story of Taiwan's semiconductor industry begins with the story of one man: Morris Chang. Chang is a brilliant engineer and visionary, but the industry itself is the way it is—with Taiwan at the center of it—as a result of his failure to become the CEO of Texas Instruments (TI). Or, looking at it the other way, it was TI's failure to grasp what Chang saw as the inevitable evolution of the semiconductor industry. Economic planners in Taiwan did not make this mistake.

Although Morris Chang is a household name in Taiwan—at least as famous as Warren Buffet or Elon Musk in America—he is not from Taiwan at all. Chang was born in mainland China in the city of Ningbo, not far from Shanghai. During the revolution, Ningbo was a KMT stronghold as the birthplace of the KMT general, Chiang Kai-shek, and many of his loyalists. As a result of China's conflicts with Japan, and between the KMT and the Communists, Chang's family moved around and eventually found refuge in Hong Kong. In 1949 he made his way to the United States, where he briefly attended Harvard University before transferring to MIT, where he studied mechanical engineering.

As an engineer, Chang joined Texas Instruments and rose quickly through the ranks. Eventually, Chang saw that semiconductors are one of those products that can cost up to a billion dollars to make the first one, then per unit cost becomes very low once they can be made in high volumes. He pioneered the concept of pricing "ahead of the cost curve," meaning he would lose money selling chips in order to secure market share. The business would become profitable once the chips were produced at high volume.

The cost of designing the semiconductor was less the problem than manufacturing, or fabricating, the wafer that the design is printed on. The tools required to make wafers with the precision necessary to fabricate extremely small chips can cost hundreds of millions of dollars.

The equipment also requires very specific expertise to set up, run, and maintain. The level of precision required to manufacture something so small that it's measured in nanometers (a human hair is about 100,000 nanometers in width) is hard to imagine. Even the smallest speck of dust could disrupt the process, which is why "clean rooms" need to be built. Every aspect of the environment must be carefully controlled, from dust to humidity, temperature, and vibration.

Chang recognized that if each company that designed chips also manufactured them, then each company would need to build its own semiconductor fabrication plant, or "fab." Each fab can cost ten billion dollars or more to build.

Chang's proposal to TI was to separate the design from the fabrication of microchips. He wanted TI to abandon designing chips, which TI at the time considered to be its core competency, and open its fab to build the chips that other companies designed—companies TI considered its competitors. The design firms would become "fabless" semiconductor companies because they would no longer need to own their manufacturing facility. This was a huge leap that the TI board was unprepared to make, so Morris Chang was passed over to lead the company.

Instead, Chang became president of General Instrument and eventually moved to Taiwan, where he met Li Kwoh-ting and Sun Yun-suan. Their partnership changed everything. Together, they shaped the global semiconductor supply chain and transformed Taiwan's economy, but they also inadvertently pushed the island closer to peril on the geopolitical chessboard.

Li and Sun were Taiwan officials in charge of the economy and held various ministerial-level positions in the government. They knew that Taiwan's labor force could do better than assembling simple toys, shoes, and Christmas tree ornaments. They wanted to move Taiwan's economy up the value chain, much like mainland China is doing today, away from low-margin products and toward high-tech industries and jobs that required a higher level of knowledge and training.

Sun established Taiwan's Industrial Technology Research Institute, which produced a number of companies that formed an ecosystem around the semiconductor industry. He also founded the industrial park in Hsinchu, now known as Taiwan's Silicon Valley. Li was the planner who moved the economy toward high-tech industries and electronics and promoted entrepreneurs, which Taiwan is now famous for. Most importantly, Li and Sun were responsible for funding Morris Chang to start TSMC. Starting in 1987, Taiwan's government poured billions of dollars into getting TSMC started, but they also fostered the ecosystem that would provide TSMC with the materials, suppliers, and most importantly, the workers that Chang would need.

TSMC was formed using the business model that Chang had proposed to TI, manufacturing chips designed by other companies. Key to Chang's strategy was that TSMC would never design its own chips, which was a major concern for the fabless semiconductor firms that did not want to see their designs stolen. Instead, TSMC was dedicated to manufacturing, and maintained a process that kept each design separate and protected from competitors. This enabled the company to build enormous volume and spread the cost of building the fab and buying the equipment across many lines of business. Machine utilization and efficiency were high, costs were low, and design firms were satisfied, all of which helped TSMC grow into the world's largest and most advanced maker of semiconductor chips.

Taiwan is also home to the ecosystem on which the industry depends. Suppliers of everything from materials to equipment are all located in Taiwan, as is the most critical element of all: people. By now, generations of engineers have learned to use sophisticated equipment and follow the complex processes involved in manufacturing these tiny, precision components. TSMC is still building capacity in Taiwan, but partly due to geopolitical tensions, it is also building new fabs in Arizona and Japan, which will require hundreds of highly trained Taiwanese workers to operate.

Beijing, meanwhile, has poured billions of dollars into building up its own semiconductor industry on the mainland, with limited success. Companies like SMIC (Semiconductor Manufacturing International Corporation) and YMTC (Yangtze Memory Technologies Corporation) have used public funds—and talent drawn from Taiwan—to try and close the gap, but they still lag at the cutting edge, particularly after US export controls restricted access to advanced tools. Taiwan, meanwhile, accounts for roughly 60 percent of global foundry production and more than 90 percent of the most advanced chips—a dependence that undermines Beijing's narrative of technological self-reliance and highlights its reliance on an island it claims as its own territory. For China, reducing that dependence can happen only through years of costly industrial upgrading—or, as some in Beijing imply, by bringing Taiwan under its control.

Some analysts have argued that Taiwan's semiconductor industry creates a "silicon shield," protecting the island from a Russia-style attack that would devastate the island, destroy the chip fabs, and alienate or kill the people who are needed to continue operating the industry. Others say Taiwan's possession of this strategically important industry that is so closely aligned with the West is an additional thorn in the side of party officials in Beijing who are already determined to bring Taiwan to heel, using military means if necessary. Taiwan's possession of this strategically important industry, according to this narrative, contributes to Beijing's desire to control Taiwan. The government in mainland China has long identified semiconductors as a vital industry and has poured billions into an attempt to develop domestic capabilities that could keep pace with the West. Capturing Taiwan—and its semiconductor industry along with it—would accelerate this process.

Companies like TSMC are now under intense pressure to

choose a side. TSMC's global centrality—and its exposure to both the US and China—creates pressure Beijing cannot easily manage, revealing its limited leverage over critical technology. China is TSMC's single largest market, accounting for about a fourth of global revenues. The company has invested billions in mainland China, a matter of great concern to Taiwan's officials, who would prefer to see that capacity stay at home.

Taiwanese people working in the semiconductor industry now face pressure to pick a side, as they are offered attractive compensation packages to work for Chinese fabs, often just before retirement. Stopping them from going to China and taking valuable skills—and sensitive intellectual property—with them has proven to be extremely difficult.

Taiwan's relationship with Japan, however deep it goes, exposes a strategic vulnerability for Beijing, encompassing two of its greatest geopolitical anxieties: a separate Chinese polity on its periphery and persistent competition with its principal regional rival. Any sense of cooperation between Taipei and Tokyo narrows China's strategic space in the East China Sea and enhances regional capacity to resist Chinese pressure—an outcome Beijing views with growing concern.

The semiconductor industry sits at the intersection of this conflict. Japan supplies critical equipment, materials, and precision components that Taiwan's chipmakers—especially TSMC—depend on. As Tokyo and Taipei coordinate more closely on economic security and jointly work to diversify supply chains outside China, Beijing sees itself increasingly excluded from the technologies that underpin the strength of modern economies. The relationship between Taiwan and Japan therefore becomes not only a diplomatic challenge but a structural one, reinforcing a network of relatively open societies whose cooperation weakens China's leverage in both security and high-tech industries.

Chapter 19

Taiwanese Identity

Taiwan has established itself in important global industries, like semiconductors, and plays a role that far exceeds its actual size, in part because of the nature of its people. They are accommodating and adaptable, absorbing outside influences in a way that has had a significant impact on the nature of Taiwan as a society, and in opinion polls most people on the island nowadays identify as "Taiwanese." A poll in June 2025 by the Election Study Center of the National Chengchi University (NCCU), reported 62.9% identifying as Taiwanese, 2.3% as Chinese and 30.5% as both. Other polls generally have similar results. Taiwanese society has been drifting further from the mainland. This is a matter of deep concern in Beijing, which many pundits fear could accelerate any timetable for "reunification".

Beijing has been abundantly clear that Taipei declaring independence would provoke an invasion, but the party has also set a more vague condition, saying it would use force to take over the island if the "possibilities for a peaceful reunification are completely exhausted." What that means exactly is impossible to know, but there is widespread speculation among analysts that Taiwan's identity and view of themselves could be a red line, or used as a pretext for invasion.

In the year 2000, Taiwan's elections put a non-KMT candidate into the presidency for the first time, ending the Kuomintang's many decades of continuous rule. The elected president, Chen Shuibian, came from the Democratic Progressive Party (DPP) and further confirmed the end to the dominance of *waishengren* (mainlander) elites. Chen, like his predecessor, Lee Teng-hui, was a Taiwanese and favored a more neutral path for the island. This appealed to the majority Taiwanese population, but was of course a problem for Beijing.

Chen managed to win two terms as president, but in 2008 voters were swayed by a combination of fear of Beijing and the allure of economic benefits that might come with a more cooperative arrangement with the mainland. China's economy was booming, and people in Taiwan were eager to ride the wave of prosperity by strengthening their economic ties with the mainland. Hotel owners eagerly welcomed tourists and business people from the mainland, while retailers lured buyers from over the Strait into their shops. Momentum in Taiwan shifted toward a more conciliatory relationship with Beijing, and the majority of voters returned to the KMT, which had always supported unification with the mainland. They elected Ma Yingjiu, a handsome and charismatic former mayor of Taipei, as their president.

Ma's family came from China, making him *waishengren*, but from the dais he always insisted that he would not attempt to unite Taiwan with the mainland or accept Beijing's offer of "one country two systems," even though at the time it seemed to be working for Hong Kong. The former British colony was still in its first decade under Chinese sovereignty. The long-term viability of Hong Kong's autonomy framework remained uncertain—a question that particularly concerned observers in Taiwan, where skepticism about Beijing's commitment to such arrangements was widespread. More recent events in Hong Kong have only deepened Taiwan's sense that the formula offers little protection for its way of life.

While some welcomed Ma's election and the warming of cross-strait relations as reducing tensions, the policy shift prompted reassessment in Japan. Japanese strategic planners expressed concern about scenarios in which closer Taiwan-China ties might alter the regional balance of power. Tokyo has a keen interest in the fate of its former colony. Historical ties and cultural affinity are a part of it, but the Japanese are primarily concerned with their own security and the status of security arrangements in East Asia.

For Taiwan, Japan was of critical importance for trade, investment, and geopolitical alignment. President Ma needed a representative who could explain to Japan the nuances of his policies toward China. He needed someone who understood the intricacies of Japanese politics, and could speak to the Japanese in their own language. In 2009, President Ma approached my former boss, RT Peng, and invited him to join his administration as a representative to Japan.[9]

Many people in Taiwan, especially of Mr. Peng's generation, speak Japanese and feel a close affiliation with the country to which it once belonged. It is not uncommon to enter a home in Taiwan and find the television tuned to the Japanese news channel NHK or a Japanese drama. Young people tend to favor Japanese fashion and pop culture (although K-pop has been coming on strong), and Japan is a popular destination for Taiwanese tourists and honeymooners. The holiday resorts in

9 Mr. Peng was appointed on the recommendatition of Lee Denghui, the former president. Peng was never a member of Ma's party, the KMT.

Okinawa can be reached by ferry or a short flight.

Mr. Peng's role was with the "East Asian Relations Association," an arrangement set up in place of an embassy. Like many other countries, Japan switched formal recognition from Taipei to Beijing in 1973, but maintained communication and exchanges through associations instead of diplomatic missions.

Mr. Peng's task was to assure the Japanese government that Taiwan's closer relationship with Beijing presented no threat to Japan's interests, and did not signify a change to the status quo. Ma's administration said it was committed to maintaining Taiwan's close relationship with Japan. Similar political systems and shared values further strengthened the strong economic ties. Japan has its own style of democracy, but there are similarities with other democratic nations in Asia, including Taiwan's vibrant yet relatively new system.

Tokyo had other reasons for concern—any military conflict in the region would of course impact Japan, which has disputes of its own with China over territory and islands. Tokyo is concerned about China's growing military capabilities, and is acutely aware that the compromises made at the conclusion of World War II left it with little to deter a growing power like China, without the aid of the United States.

The war left Japan defeated militarily, but America and its allies understood from experience in Europe that leaving an enemy crushed would lead to resentment, instability, and a resurgence of its military ambitions. The current situation is complicated, but the original deal was simple. Post-imperial Japan agreed not to develop its military capabilities, and the United States agreed to guarantee its security. Japanese strategists understand very well the interlocking pieces that have maintained peace for nearly three-quarters of a century.

In particular, Japan has declined to acquire a nuclear weapon, although it has the economic and technological capabilities to do so. The Japanese people live with the horror of being the world's only victim of a nuclear attack and have no enthusiasm for being involved in any such conflict again. At the same time, Japan lives in a dangerous neighborhood: China's expanding nuclear arsenal, North Korea's repeated missile and nuclear tests, and Russia's increasing military assertiveness all raise the strategic stakes. Tokyo is watching closely for any sign that America's security guarantee may be subject to different interpretations, and is aware that there is little or no margin for error.

Today, however, Tokyo is far less confident about the US security guarantee. Recent statements by Donald Trump—including threats to reduce commitments to allies who do not "pay enough" and implied willingness to let Japan and South Korea consider their own nuclear weapons—have amplified longstanding anxieties about US reliability. Japan now worries that the alliance may be subject to shifting political interpretations in Washington, especially as US domestic politics become more polarized and isolationist.

The American military bases on the island of Okinawa (and elsewhere in Japan) simultaneously protect Japan and put it in harm's way. Any attack on Taiwan that draws the United States into a conflict would immediately put those bases in play. The American assets in Guam and Hawaii would be too far away to provide immediate defense, but American F-35s based in Okinawa could reach Taiwan in a matter of minutes. Therefore, war games often assume that military action against Taiwan could begin with a strike on those bases to pre-empt an American defense of the island. While Japan's constitution would not allow its military to be involved in a foreign conflict, action against Okinawa would be a different matter. If Beijing were to take military action against Taiwan and the United States failed to intervene, Japan's security arrangement with the United States would immediately be called into question, as would the interlocking security arrangements throughout the region.

For decades Taiwan was closed off from travel from mainland China, as both governments were wary of contact between the two. Ironically, when they were completely separated by the "three nos"—no contact, no communication, no trade—Taiwanese identity was much less of an issue. Taiwan—the Republic of China—prohibited its citizens from traveling directly to China, although many did anyway, going through Macao or Hong Kong. I took that route myself in 1985, traveling from Taiwan to Hong Kong, and then walking across the border at Lo Wu into mainland China. In 1987, Taiwan lifted the ban for those with relatives on the mainland. Later, in 2008 Taiwan got rid of the restrictions completely, opening a floodgate of people traveling in both directions for business and tourism.

Around the time travel between Taiwan and the mainland opened up, I was working as a banker for HSBC in China, where I was surrounded by well-heeled Chinese professionals. Some had studied or traveled overseas, and in general this was a fairly elite group. They favored long trips to Europe or Australia, but sometimes a short hop to a destination within Asia was what they needed for a quick getaway or a long weekend.

"You were so right about Taiwan!" My colleague at the bank had just returned from her holiday and was handing out little cakes around the office. She had selected a box of *fenglisu,* or pineapple cakes, a Taiwanese specialty. "It's such a nice place," she told me.

"Well, I'm glad you had a good time. What did you like about Taiwan?" I asked, eager to hear about her trip, but also hoping our Chinese colleagues would pick up her message. Everyone in the office knew about my fondness for the island, although I avoided discussing politics and I was careful to never refer to Taiwan as a country.

Naturally, she turned first to Taiwanese cuisine, since food is of paramount importance to Chinese people of all ages and persuasions. Once that was done, I prodded her further. "What did you think of the people in Taiwan?"

"Oh, they are super nice!" She looked around, then lowered her voice. "People are so free, and unafraid. They don't scold each other like we do!" It was an odd thing to say, but I knew what she meant. People in China can be aggressive and harsh when they don't get what they want, which happens often in a country as populous and resource-constrained as China.

"I'm happy that you liked it," I replied. "I'm curious though. You appreciate Taiwan as it is now—would you want to see that continue?" This drew a puzzled look and I knew I had to be careful, but our colleagues had taken their pineapple cakes back to their desks and were well out of earshot. "You say Taiwan is nice the way it is. How do you think about reunification then?"

From the perspective of the official narrative, which argues that the Taiwanese people have been separated from the mainland against their will, "reunification" would not constitute an attack but rather a restoration of natural unity. This interpretive framework remains influential in mainland China, where some continue to view Taiwan's political evolution as shaped by external manipulation. It's worth noting that Freedom House, a Washington based non-profit, gives Taiwan a high score for civil liberties, even above the United States. China ranks just above North Korea.[10]

10 Freedom House, "Countries and Territories."

My colleague brightened as the meaning of my question became clear. She was absolutely sincere in her answer: "Why would we leave Taiwan the way it is?" she replied. "It's ours." This is a common view amongst mainland people, which is unsurprising given the unequivocal media and education message delivered over so many decades: Taiwan needs to return to the embrace of the motherland. Self-determination may be enshrined in the United Nations charter as a basic human right, but it plays no role in influencing how people in China generally view the issue of Taiwan. However, anecdotal evidence and what polls have been done suggest support for military action is not high. Regardless, Beijing has a clear need to control the narrative on Taiwan. To lose control of it could have domestic implications.

The protests and street rallies in Hong Kong in 2014 and later in 2019 involved similar emotions and issues. For Beijing, this is a control issue of paramount importance. The issues that sparked the demonstrations were Beijing's insistence that the slate of candidates for Chief Executive would be pre-screened, with only candidates acceptable to Beijing being considered, and a proposal to enact an extradition arrangement under which people in Hong Kong could be transferred to the mainland to face detention or trial. Many of us who watched similar events in China in 1989 wondered about the attitudes of younger and Western-educated people. They ranged from puzzlement to opposition. One of my banking colleagues, a young Shanghainese fellow, told me: "If anyone should get to have democracy, we should have it here first."

He was referring to mainland China, as Hong Kong maintained separate governance as a special administrative region. His reasoning revealed a fundamentally different framework from the one held by advocates of a broader defintion of Beijing's formula of *yiguo liangzhi,* "one country, two systems" under which Hong Kong was reunited with the mainland in 1997. Where some saw Hong Kong's political freedoms as a potential catalyst for liberalization, he viewed the divergence as problematic. He didn't dispute that democratic participation, transparency, and expanded civil liberties might be beneficial in principle. Rather, his concern was one of political coherence: if such arrangements were judged unsuitable for the mainland, then maintaining them in one region while denying them elsewhere created what he saw as an untenable contradiction.

Hong Kong's evolving relationship with Beijing is closely watched in Taiwan. Taiwanese people were generally skeptical about the "one country, two systems" arrangement from the outset, and they were closely watching the changes that came at the conclusion of the Hong Kong unrest, with Beijing's involvement in the process of governing the territory becoming much more public, and questions being raised about the changes in the media and the legal system. Still, Taiwan society itself is easily recognizable as Chinese, with all that it entails. Taiwan is very much Confucian, with elders and teachers at the top of the pyramid, and ancestor worship rituals still carefully observed, as they have been for a thousand years.

Taiwan never experienced the Cultural Revolution, when Mao's acolytes wiped away the "four olds"—old ideas, old culture, old customs, and old habits. The damage was far greater than smashing Buddhist statues, burning paintings, and destroying temples. The ideological campaign changed something deep in China's society on the mainland, something that has been preserved in Taiwan today. People like my colleague who traveled from China to Taiwan immediately felt the warm embrace of the original culture that had become bent and difficult to recognize at home.

Bo Shao, a China-born entrepreneur now living in the United States, offers his perspective on China and Taiwan, and the effect of the Cultural Revolution: "From political leader, to business tycoon, to taxi driver in Shanghai, everyone in China today carries the imprint of those few years. The imprint can be found through its absence in Taiwan, which has the same Chinese roots but did not go through the Cultural Revolution. After visiting Taiwan, all of my Chinese friends tend to comment on how incredibly warm, open and trusting people are. Two generations of Chinese people have forgotten that there is another way of being."[11]

Overall, the people of Taiwan enjoy their way of life, and it seems most of them would not be eager to rejoin the mainland unless China evolves in a way that offers an appealing alternative. Today, Taiwanese identity is a unique blend with Chinese culture at its core, but it also with influences from Japan and from the West.

Beijing's approach to Taiwan reflects several strategic calculations. Taiwan's evolution as a prosperous, Western-aligned democracy creates what Chinese leadership views as a governance model challenge, particularly given their shared language and cultural foundations. Under Xi Jinping, Chinese policy has prioritized centralized control and stability, with official discourse often characterizing this approach as necessary for Chinese conditions. Taiwan thus presents a paradox which could conceivably reinforce Beijing's determination to resolve the situation to its satisfaction.

Taiwan is unquestionably rooted in Chinese heritage. Linguistically and culturally, Taiwanese society is very much part of the tradition and lineage that most people would call

11 Bo Xiao, "Trump and the Coming Cultural Revolution," February 11, 2017.

"Chinese." People from Taiwan mix easily with people from mainland China, although they can usually be distinguished from those who grew up on the mainland from their accent, vocabulary, and patterns of behavior. It would be a mistake to think of the two societies as being completely separate, or hostile to each other. They are not. Despite suffering diplomatic indignities, people on Taiwan tend to recognize and appreciate their ties to the mainland, and many of them are happy living on the mainland to work, invest, and raise families (as I have done myself).

The temperature of the warm feeling has gone up or down with the passage of time and changing politics, but there is a certain comfort level between people from Taiwan and the mainland that cannot be denied. But Taiwan has also evolved as a society and has developed a distinct culture all its own, and a change in its status would be a big shock with unknowable consequences. The resolution of this eighty-year stand-off will be a defining moment for the world.

Over the years, Mr. Peng remained active in politics and held strong views on various security issues involving America, Japan, China, and Taiwan, right up until he passed away in 2023. I met with him for the last time earlier that year. He described the period from around 2008 as the beginning of great nervousness.

Analysts generally agree that maintaining the status quo is imperfect but acceptable to all parties, but Mr. Peng explained that while keeping things as they are may be the goal, it would be a mistake to assume this arrangement can be carried forward for much longer.

"China's military capabilities have changed everything," he told me, as we drank tea in his office in Taipei. "Now that

Chinese missiles fired from the mainland can hit targets as far away as the Philippines, the United States itself is in danger. Will America risk its own security in order to protect Taiwan? With this uncertainty, the status quo no longer exists."

Mr. Peng was right about the missiles. China's land-based missiles can easily reach targets throughout the Pacific and beyond. Mr. Peng was also right to question whether the status quo still exists at all. The fragile arrangement put in place in 1979 between Washington, Beijing, and Taipei has become frayed over time. Under this arrangement, Taipei tacitly agreed not to pursue independence, and Beijing agreed to delay taking the island by force. The United States agreed that there is only one China.[12] Getting to that agreement required imagination and finesse, but since then, much has changed. At the time when Beijing accepted the agreement, China's military was severely outdated. As Mr. Peng pointed out, that is no longer the case.

Taiwanese society has also changed. Mr. Peng, who was very much in the native Taiwanese majority camp, said: "If the KMT comes into power it could lead to disaster." His concern came from the idea that the two main political parties—the DPP and the KMT—are split on how to manage the relationship with China. The KMT accuses the DPP of advocating for Taiwan's independence, saying "If you want to send your sons and daughters to war with China, then vote for the DPP." The DPP says "If you want to give up your freedom and way of life, then vote for the KMT."

Neither outcome is appealing, putting the people of Taiwan in a bind. And the CCP faces a dilemma it cannot easily resolve:

12 Taiwan was not a party to the agreement, which was bilateral between the US and China. When switching diplomatic recognition from Taiwan (ROC) to China (PRC) the US put in place the Taiwan Relations Act that defined its relationship by law, ensuring that Taiwan would be defended, although not explicitly requiring the US to actively defend the island.

its assertiveness is meant to project strength but instead tends to highlight the trouble it has winning hearts and minds across the strait.

CHAPTER 20

Deals and Delusions

Tuesday, November 8th, 2016, is a date that many will recall with absolute clarity—remembering where they were and what they were doing when the unthinkable happened. Because of the time zone it was actually the morning of November 9th in Shanghai when the election results were announced and we learned that Donald J. Trump would succeed Barack Obama as the next president of the United States.

The American Chamber of Commerce was co-hosting an election-watching party in partnership with the US Consulate so our members and others from the community could gather to witness American democracy in action.

I arrived early at the Portman hotel, just as the AmCham staff finished putting up the red and blue bunting around the large ballroom. They had created lifesized cardboard cutouts of Hillary Clinton and Donald Trump, and members were already taking selfies in funny poses. The mood was festive. Large screens carried Fox News and CNN showing each state turn either blue or red as the results came in, drawing a mixture of gasps and cries of glee. The audience included Americans and Chinese, plus a few mid-level Chinese government guests. Our

Chinese friends were fascinated by the spectacle, as nothing even remotely similar exists inside the People's Republic of China, where transitions are highly secretive and Chinese citizens often learn the names of their new leaders only after the new appointments are announced.

About mid-way through the morning, before the final result was known, Hanscom Smith, the Consul General in Shanghai, took the stage to offer brief remarks about America, democracy, and the sacred traditions that allowed for the peaceful transition of power. Hanscom was the quintessential diplomat, educated at Princeton and Georgetown, and he spoke with deliberate precision, never fumbling a word or phrase. Even at the annual AmCham Ball, where I hosted Hanscom and his partner Eric Lu at the head table, he kept his poise and allowed himself no more than a glass or two of wine.[13]

Given the opportunity to speak from an essentially American platform within the People's Republic of China, anyone else might have been tempted to take a swipe or two at China's system of government, perhaps comparing it with American democracy in action, but Hanscom was as disciplined as any foreign service officer could be and stuck to his script.

Hanscom later explained: "We definitely didn't shy away from delivering critical or uncomfortable messages to our Chinese counterparts, but generally did so privately. The election event was designed to showcase American democracy, and we knew that our Chinese guests were sophisticated enough to draw the contrast with China's system. Even in 2016, we also had to be careful about compromising our Chinese guests—we

13 Unlike Taiwan, China does not recognize gay marriage. Until 2001, homosexuality was classified as a mental illness. As a society, China has been tolerant, although perhaps not embracing, of diversity. Most of my Chinese friends simply believe there are more important issues and can't be bothered to think a lot about personal matters like same sex partnerships. In recent years, the CCP has placed more emphasis on social norms, restricting LGBTQ rights as well as women's rights and other freedoms.

never wanted to get anyone into trouble for attending this sort of event."

Business chambers tend to lean Republican, and AmCham Shanghai was no different. However, our internal polls were just as misleading as those back home in the United States. Throughout the campaign the Chamber had been hosting events for members to gather and watch the debates between Trump and his challenger, Hillary Clinton. Electronic clickers, provided by a local tech entrepreneur, gave us real-time voting that showed Clinton holding a strong lead through all three debates.

AmCham members were taken completely by surprise when by about eleven o'clock in the morning it became clear that Trump was the winner. To the surprise of some and the delight of others, Donald Trump won the election and took office on January 20th, 2017.

Trump's first few months in office were rough. He had promised to repeal Obamacare (the Affordable Care Act) in his first hundred days in office and replace it with his own health care scheme. However, months later he and his team were still groping around, leading him to eventually throw up his hands and declare, "Nobody knew health care could be so complicated."

Chinese officials were equally stunned. My friends in government could not fathom how a man with no political or military experience, a volatile temperament, and a disdain for institutions could rise to the top. For China's bureaucrats, leadership requires loyalty, mastery of policy, and years of service. Trump represented everything their system was designed to prevent. "What qualities does Trump have that make him so popular?" one official asked me, genuinely perplexed.

At the street level, Chinese people took American politics less seriously. "Of course Trump is great!" one fellow told me as I was killing time in front of a convenience store. I had struck up a conversation with a couple of *liumang*—hooligans who were obviously up to no good. One of them claimed he was a scrap metal collector, but I got the sense he collected other things as well in order to make ends meet. The other was more vague about his profession. We were next to a bank, and I suspected he was a money changer, which is illegal in China. "He's rich! And his family is beautiful. We love Trump!" He understood celebrity politics well—strength as theater.

Members of the American Chamber were less sanguine, Republicans and Democrats alike. Trump made us uncomfortable, especially when he spoke about China. Throughout the campaign he attacked China relentlessly, saying it was "raping our country" through unfair trade practices, and the Chinese government's economic policies were "the greatest theft in the history of the world." We were worried that Trump's habit of name-calling would not play well in Beijing, where mutual respect is a critical starting point for any relationship.

Fortunately, Chinese government officials understood our political system well—far better than we understood theirs—and generally took the campaign rhetoric for what it was. They were amused as Trump continued to lash out, calling previous American presidents "incompetent" in dealing with China while expressing admiration for President Xi and support for his approach to governing.

Trump's first meeting with Xi came at Mar-a-Lago in April of 2017, and the business community wondered if Trump could just be the unconventional president who would shake things up and change Beijing's pattern of behavior. There was a general consensus that while Obama hadn't necessarily done anything wrong, the relationship was becoming increasingly lopsided in an unsustainable way. Could a transactional approach result in more reciprocity, opening China's markets in the same sectors that were available to foreign competitors in the United States?

Ken Jarrett and I worked closely as a team leading the Chamber. He was still president at the time, and I was serving as the elected chairman of the board, while keeping my private sector job. That gave me the final word, but I often deferred to Ken, especially on matters of government. He had thirty years of experience as a diplomat and deep knowledge of China. Ken and I wrote a number of op-eds, some of which were picked up by the *Wall Street Journal*, and by regional publications like the *South China Morning Post*. Writing on behalf of all AmCham Shanghai members, we came up with a piece to offer suggestions to President Trump in advance of his first meeting with President Xi:

> April 2017 Mar a Lago meeting between Trump and Xi
>
> China's President Xi is not a golfer. He prefers soccer. So there will be no post-game backslapping at the Trump owned golf course near the Mar-a-Lago Club, site of the Trump-Xi summit of April 6-7. But both leaders will be playing a game with even higher stakes—the U.S.-China relationship.
>
> The stakes are high for the business community too. Uncertainty prevails about how much election rhetoric will become reality. Companies on both sides of the Pacific seek clarity about the direction of the relationship as they consider new investments. None of this is good for two economies whose trade and investment flows are increasingly intertwined, with implications for millions of workers and businesses.
>
> The Mar-a-Lago summit takes place against a backdrop of anti-globalization sentiment, a rising

China, and growing frustrations from the U.S. business community about the operating environment in China. The U.S. political transition and China's approaching 19th Party Congress add yet more complexity. But what does the U.S. business community want from the summit?

First, an element of personal rapport between the two leaders would help. They will need to understand and trust each other in the future, and better that they begin now.

Second, real and significant progress is needed on some of the longstanding frustrations of the foreign business community. These include market access improvements in a variety of industries, including financial services, information technology, healthcare, professional services, and agriculture. In the latter case, putting more agricultural products in the Encouraged Section of the Foreign Investment Catalogue would be a good start.

Third, many foreign companies have prospered in China, but it's getting harder to do so. Competition from local companies is welcome—as long as it's exactly that. But there's growing unease—and evidence—that the government is stacking the deck against foreign companies in a variety of ways.

The country's cyber security laws look designed to stifle foreign hardware IT manufacturers' sales as much as to protect the rights of Chinese consumers. China's insistence on technology transfer in certain sectors, a commercial version of pay-to-play, aided China's transition from an agricultural to industrial economy, but is outdated and unfair. Modern industrial policies, however, including Made in China 2025, are formed with local companies in mind, with subsidies on offer to domestic manufacturers. The Chinese government's championing of domestic industries like microchips, achieved through low-cost state-backed loans, gives local companies a clear advantage when competing with privately financed foreign companies.

Past U.S. administrations have tried, with limited success, to overcome Chinese indifference to American complaints about unfair trade practices and market access barriers. President Trump is likely to press the business community's concerns with greater determination, which we welcome. While we do not support a policy of tit-for-tat, growing Chinese investment in the U.S. is a trend that we should leverage to open those parts of the Chinese economy that remain closed or unreasonably restricted to foreign businesses.

One area in which Trump should push for substantive change is China's service sector. Whether due to market restrictions, government fiat or provincial foot-dragging, foreign banks have been clearly impeded from making any credible progress in China. Even industries in which the Chinese government has spoken about improving market access, such as insurance, progress has been glacially slow and the details sparingly few. Restrictions in architecture, law, travel and education are even more outdated and anti-competitive, especially given the maturity of domestic firms.

When both leaders sit down together, they should be reminded of the stakes. A January 2017 report for

> the US-China Business Council, prepared by Oxford Economics, estimates that U.S.-China trade supports some 2.6 million jobs in the U.S., and many more in China. Growing Chinese investment in the US, some of which has restored manufacturing jobs, should continue to be welcomed. So too U.S. investment in China, but on terms more equitable than now.

Our original thought was to make this an open letter or op-ed, but after consulting with people at the Consulate we decided on a more conservative approach, opting instead to circulate our ideas through contacts at the State Department. We had done this before and received helpful feedback through the same channels. Neither of us had experience working with Trump or his senior team, but we knew he was thin-skinned and could react badly to a public statement telling him what we thought he should do.

The goal was not so much to push our specific requests—these ideas were not new. Instead, we hoped the incoming president would view us as a partner, and tread carefully so as not to damage our foothold in the market while implementing his China strategy.

The Mar-a-Lago summit produced warmth, but little substance. Trump seemed charmed by Xi. For a president who admired strongmen, Xi's discipline and control held appeal.

Donald Trump made his first trip to China as president in November of 2017, while we were still learning who from the White House would lead China policy. Many of us assumed it would be Wilbur Ross, the Secretary of Commerce. Ross joined the president in Beijing, but we later learned it would be anyone *but* Ross taking the lead. As it turned out, Trump's China team was a study in contradiction: dealmakers and ideologues thrown together with no clear strategy. China became the purview of

Treasury Secretary Steve Mnuchin and US Trade Representative Robert Lighthizer, from the economic team. They would be supported by well-known "China hawks," Peter Navarro and Matt Pottinger, as well as the ever-present Steve Bannon, a close advisor to Trump even after he was dismissed from his White House post.

Navarro was a Harvard-trained economist teaching at UC Irvine, and the author of *Death by China*, an incendiary book that painted China as an economic predator and political manipulator. Pottinger was a former journalist who had worked in China. He subsequently served in the Marines before joining the National Security Council, after which he was promoted to become Trump's deputy national security advisor.

Wilbur Ross, the Secretary of Commerce, was initially brought onto the Trump economic team largely because of his China experience. Ross's career as a private equity investor spanned decades and included numerous trips and many deals in China. At his core, Ross was a steel man. He made a fortune buying low and selling high, and he was suspected of front-running deals while playing a role in influencing government policy. I don't know about Ross's previous deals, but some weeks into Trump's presidency I received an invitation to a private event announcing the launch of a new private equity fund. It was on WL Ross & Co. letterhead. My name must have been on a list of investors and bankers. I was intrigued.

The Grand Hyatt occupied the top floors of the Jinmao building, a short walk from the HSBC headquarters building in Lujiazui. I found the ballroom and took a seat in one of the front rows. The event was well scripted and ceremonial, with a row of chairs up on the stage. Each speaker took a turn with the microphone, explaining their role in the new $10 billion fund that would invest in undervalued assets in the steel industry.

I felt a tap on my shoulder, and turned to find a former colleague I hadn't seen in a few years. He covered industrials at HSBC while I handled tech and media clients. "Hey, is WL Ross the same Ross as the guy from Trump's..."

"Yup. Commerce," I replied.

"So there's no conflict of interest, and it's legal for him to...?" My friend pointed to the screen showing potential deals in the steel industry, where Ross would have a direct hand in making policy.

"Apparently it is," I said.

"Awesome! We're gonna to do some *deals*!" My friend put two thumbs up and motioned with his hands as if he was reeling in a fish.

This was the deal-making expertise that President Trump was looking for on his China team, until something went wrong. Immediately after winning the 2016 election, steel was high on the new president's agenda. He had gone after the Midwest working-class vote and was eager to deliver results. Trump cut off supplies of steel from Canada and picked a fight with the Europeans, but the big prize was getting tough with China. Ross knew what he had to do, or at least thought he did.

Chinese negotiators also saw an opportunity. Ross was a familiar figure, and after following the campaign rhetoric closely, they must have thought they could collaborate with the new president. The Chinese negotiating team focused on steel and hammered out terms with Ross.

Before Secretary Ross could present the deal to the president, Steve Bannon found out about it and leaked it to Fox News. According to sources,[14] with Bannon's help the hosts and commentators picked the deal apart and went on the air with

14 A Washington insider who declined to be named.

criticism before Ross could bring it to the president. Trump tuned in and heard one of the Fox News personalities call Ross's deal "ill-informed and reckless," while others said the agreement didn't address state subsidies that led to oversupply in global markets. Ironically, these were exactly the issues that would later be pushed out of Trump's trade deal, so they were never addressed. Trump killed the steel deal without even speaking with his own secretary of commerce. This humiliated Ross, and the Chinese negotiators refused to work with him after that. From that point forward, a new team was put in place to work with China, but it was also clear that only one voice mattered in the discussion.

Trump worked hard to create an image for himself as a dealmaker and wanted to use his Beijing trip to bolster his reputation. The call went out to our members to produce something to announce—anything the American dealmaking president could point to as a win. This was a familiar pattern that generally worked out well for companies, working with mayors and governors who made a habit of manufacturing photo ops. The politician cuts the ribbon for the photo, taking credit for bringing investment and jobs to the community. The company gets increased visibility, and a government advocate it can call on for support if the project runs into trouble.

AmCham members were cooperative, and hopeful for better relations and improvements in business ties. Commerce Secretary Wilbur Ross, who had not yet been thrown off the China team, traveled with the president and invited members to meet with him in Beijing, and hinted that a "meet and greet" with POTUS[15] himself might be possible.

---

15 POTUS is the acronym for President Of The United States. It's useful, especially in the State Department and the White House where presidents of other countries are often referred to. Here, for example, the word "president" could have referred to Trump or Xi.

A small group of us—a dozen or so—made the trip from Shanghai to Beijing to meet with Ross, standing behind him while he announced $250 billion worth of deals, most of which were done long before he or Trump arrived in Beijing. It was an impressive headline, but did nothing to help our businesses in China or address the structural problems causing the trade imbalances. We came away cynical about what the new administration might actually accomplish, and slightly disappointed that we didn't meet the president.

Back in Shanghai, the atmosphere at our next monthly AmCham meeting was electric as members gathered to hear our report from the meetings in Beijing, full of hope and optimism for better relations with China. The chamber is non-partisan and works cooperatively with whichever party occupies the White House, but I was in a puckish mood and couldn't help myself as I took the stage to deliver my report to members. I felt I needed to lighten the mood and manage the members' expectations. Due to term limits, I would leave the board anyway, so I wasn't thinking about my next election.

"As you know, we just came from Beijing where we met with Secretary of Commerce Wilbur Ross. President Trump was expected to attend but got called into another meeting." There was an audible sigh of disappointment but I held up my hand to quiet the room. "Instead of meeting with us, President Trump was taken to a VIP room up on the top floor. There, he had a meeting with God." I looked out at the crowd and saw puzzled looks, especially from our Chinese members who were less familiar with American humor. I continued with my report. "God said to him, 'Donald, I see what's happening on earth, and I'm not happy. It's over.' Trump says, 'What do you mean?' God says, 'There will be a flood. You seem to be in charge down there so I want you to go back and prepare your people. Now go.'"

By now I could see people grinning, but they were still puzzled as I continued. "...so Trump comes back to us and says, 'I have good news, great news, and even *better* news. First, the good news—there is a God!' The president went on to say, 'Now the great news—God says I'm in charge. And now the even better news—we don't need to bother fixing health care! Also, I was right about climate change. The climate is going to change, but humans won't be the cause of it!"

The Republican members in my flock didn't appreciate the joke and thought it was disrespectful of me to make fun of the president. They were hopeful that Trump would achieve what he said he would—a better deal for American companies in China. Others, perhaps, sensed the deeper irony: both governments now relied on faith—not in God, but in their own myths of strength.

In general, American companies greeted President Trump's unique approach to China with a mix of skepticism and curiosity, wondering if his negotiating style could actually work. His style was the opposite of traditional diplomacy, and generations of China hands had counseled that the right way was to address issues with China behind closed doors, not in public and certainly not on Twitter. Both leaders were performing for domestic audiences: Trump for the cameras, Xi for the party.

Among the Chinese, Trump was popular, at least at first. Chinese officials kept their counsel on America's domestic political affairs, but ordinary people openly admired the billionaire with the seemingly picture-perfect family. They believed a transactional American president who cared little about China's record on human rights or other ideological niceties could be good for China.

For American companies, the coming years were uncertain. Trump's volatility collided with Xi's rigidity, producing a fragile, transactional relationship that neither side fully controlled. The two strongest economies in the world were now bound together by mistrust. The next four years would prove to be a wild ride, leaving all sides confused, frustrated, and worse.

CHAPTER 21

The Art of the Trade War

"Appear weak when you are strong, and strong when you are weak." From *The Art of War*, by Sun Tzu

"When you're attacked, you've got to strike back hard and fast." From *The Art of the Deal*, by Donald J. Trump

On the first day of his first term, President Trump fulfilled his campaign promise and withdrew from the Trans-Pacific Partnership, an initiative the chamber had supported from the beginning and worked hard to promote. It was a strategic blunder that delighted Beijing. We understood that the pact's power was geopolitical, not just commercial, and it was America's best tool to balance China's growing influence in Asia. We were disappointed but not surprised. Trump's trade war, however, was something different entirely.

Trump, a real estate tycoon and former reality television star, had little experience with international trade, but he declared that America's trade deficit with China was the root of our problems, and proof that China's business practices were unfair. In March 2018, he imposed the first round of tariffs that would eventually cover $550 billion worth of Chinese goods imported into the United States. His actions directly violated America's commitments under the World Trade Organization[16] and drew immediate retaliation from China, setting off a trade war. The conflict hurt both sides—but revealed something important: China's dependence on access to the US market was deeper, and more fragile, than it wanted to admit.

At first, companies adjusted to 15 percent tariffs by reducing profit margins or pushing the costs onto distributors, with little impact on the consumer, and therefore sales. Business could more or less continue as before. By 2018 most American companies had adopted the "in China for China" strategy, so they were making products in China for sale domestically as well as export. Some, however, were hit with tariffs in both directions. Some companies shipped part of what they made in China to the United States, where their customers would need to pay the US tariff, but they also imported machinery and equipment, or material inputs for manufacturing in China. Those companies paid the retaliatory tariffs to China.

When Trump increased the tariffs to twenty-five percent, businesses reacted dramatically, and trade flows became distorted or stopped entirely. Factories re-routed supply chains overnight and trade flows became distorted.

Still, business finds a way. When China imposed retaliatory tariffs on almonds from California, Vietnam suddenly developed an incredible appetite for nuts. Trade flows through third countries followed a clear pattern, closely tracking the measures China and the United States imposed on each other. The big winners were Vietnam, Mexico, and other countries with open ports and access to both markets.

16 World Trade Organization DS543: United States—Tariff Measures on Certain Goods from China.

What mattered most was confidence. People, whether directly affected by the tariffs or not, felt uncomfortable with Beijing and Washington at odds. China was also changing, the regulations were tightening, the economy and investments were slowing. AmCham members, irrespective of their party affiliation or interests, yearned for an end to the trade war. The overriding sentiment was a desire for stability and a return to normalcy, where we could get back to business unhindered by geopolitical tensions. For American firms, it was a lesson in exposure: profits could vanish at a stroke of a presidential pen or from a directive from Beijing.

Congressman Rick Larsen was a busy man. Larsen and his partner in the House of Representatives, Darren LaHood, commanded a presence in the conference room, and at well over six feet tall, towered above the members in my delegation. The two men co-chaired the House Working Group on China, and we met with them regularly on our trips to Washington. LaHood's demeaner was folksy, but Larsen exuded an aura that many found unsettling. "Are we working here, or are we taking photos?" He stopped in mid-sentence to admonish my staffer, who was taking photos of our meeting for the AmCham magazine. She quickly put her camera away.

Our trips to Washington during the Trump administration differed greatly from those under previous presidents. The Trump White House was famously insular, with decision-making concentrated at the top. We continued meeting with the State Department, Agriculture, and other departments, but not with the US Trade Representative. With active negotiations taking place in China a visit from an AmCham delegation was deemed to be too sensitive.

Unlike the rest of Washington, Larsen and LaHood worked well together, and a discussion with them was always one of my favorite stops on DC tours. Larsen, a Democrat, represented a district in the state of Washington, and LaHood, a Republican, was from Illinois. They were extremely well-informed and constructive, but also challenging. After listening for a while, Congressman Larsen turned to me and said: "Yes, Mr. Gibbs, but *what do you want us to do?"*

The two legislators were results-oriented and data-driven, and always reviewed the materials we sent over beforehand so they could pepper us with questions. They also asked about our meetings with the White House, eager to triangulate what they were hearing. They had met often with President Obama and worked closely with his team on the Trans-Pacific Partnership, but that arrangement changed under Trump. Under Trump, Congress was entirely left out of the China policy conversation, and frustration was apparent. After speaking with us for about forty minutes, they stood up and Congressman LaHood said, "Guys, thank you for coming by. It's been an interesting discussion, but honestly, I don't know why you're talking to us. You really need to be talking down the street." He jerked a thumb toward 1600 Pennsylvania Avenue.

Dan Sullivan, a Republican senator from Alaska, had common cause with the chamber and explained the impact of Trump's tariffs on his state. Sullivan had worked previously at the National Security Council before being elected to Congress and expressed frustration with China's lack of follow-through on promises. He believed reciprocity was an important goal but tariffs were particularly damaging to Alaska. Fishermen from his state—sparsely populated and chronically short of labor—would send fish to China to be deboned; the fish would be re-imported back to the United States, with duties levied in each direction. With both sides increasing tariffs in the trade war, this activity became non-economic.

America's lobster businesses suffered as well. After investing heavily to support growing demand from China, the trade war slapped a 35 percent tax on their goods, collapsing revenue for lobstermen. Canada's businesses, on the other hand, thrived. Lobstermen hunting in the same waters sold their catch to China tariff-free while the Americans went bankrupt and sold their boats.

The impact of Trump's trade war on America's automotive industry was especially severe. Bill Russo, a consultant to the industry based in Shanghai, said that GM and Ford were sourcing low-cost components from China, allowing them to pass savings onto consumers and fattening their margins. Trump's tariffs ended all that. Russo shook his head, "If the trade war was a missile aimed at Beijing, the unintended consequence was that it landed squarely on Detroit,"[17] he added.

According to Russo, the tariffs also failed to reshore manufacturing supply chains to the United States, a claim backed up by AmCham's own survey of members. The tariffs did, however, inspire Chinese companies to invest in Mexico and other third-country locations from which they could access the American market, thereby accelerating the globalization of many Chinese firms.

On August 6, 2020, President Trump issued an executive order initiating a ban the Chinese-made TikTok mobile app from the United States. The president's order, based on a national security threat posed by TikTok's collection of personal data, highlighted

17 Ker D. Gibbs: *Selling to China*. Palgrave Macmillan (2023). p. 110

the fact that a Chinese internet business had entered the market and registered over 100 million users in America. But in China, Twitter, Facebook, and similar services have long been blocked, leaving them with only a handful of users who use VPNs to jump over the censorship wall. The glaring lack of reciprocity was nothing new. Even LinkedIn withdrew from the market in October of 2021.

The president's order targeting Chinese social media apps was based on the same logic that China invoked to restrict American companies—data and algorithms could be used to manipulate public opinion, spread disinformation, or create societal discord.

At first, the American business community in China treated it like a joke. Most of us would have liked nothing better than to separate our teenagers from silly, addictive videos, and we secretly wished the president would ban a few more apps while he was at it. But President Trump had also issued an order banning WeChat. In terms of data security, that decision could have made sense, if TikTok made sense, but a ban on us using WeChat would also effectively cut us off from our customers in China.

Trump, supposedly a pro-business president, was hammering Beijing to buy more American goods, just as his predecessors had. AmCham had long advocated for more access to the China market, and our member companies clawed and scratched every day to find more business in China, expanding their market share and capturing a bigger part of Chinese consumer spending.

In China, that spending in now mostly through WeChat. Starting from about 2014, Chinese consumers began using electronic payments on their mobile phones almost exclusively. According to Bryce Whitwam, a marketing guru in Shanghai, "Wallets soon became antiques, something saved for overseas trips, because in China, one only needed to carry a phone."

He went on to explain, "Thanks to the power of WeChat Pay and Alipay, transactions using coins and paper money were eliminated."

President Trump's executive order raised the threat of American companies being prevented from using the payment system that most Chinese consumers used.

I arrived at my office late that morning. Joseph Chan, the chief legal officer of Yum! Brands was already waiting for me. Normally, visitors were asked to wait outside in the spacious community area of the chamber's new offices in the swish business district of Xintiandi, but Joseph was well-known around the chamber so my assistant invited him to wait in my office.

I could see that Joseph had been up all night. "Ker, what the—? How does this help us? What are we going to do?" Joseph and I knew each other well. He was in private practice before joining Yum China and we worked together on deals when I was a banker with HSBC. Joseph still had contacts with Washington DC law firms.

Yum China operates thousands of KFC and Pizza Hut locations, making it the steward of some of America's most successful brands in the country. While its success draws heavily on American brand appeal, the company also made clever moves that kept their restaurants full and its cash registers ringing. The menu carried familiar items like chicken tenders, mashed potatoes, and flavored wings, a particular favorite among Chinese kids. But kids don't come to KFC by themselves—they are usually accompanied by grandparents, who have no taste for American fast food delicacies. Therefore, KFC's menu in the 5,000 or so restaurants included items like chicken-and-seaweed rice bowls, egg tarts, and congee, favorites among older people in China.

Joseph explained other interesting facts about how KFC

operated. As a cash business, Yum China used to employ thousands of people who did nothing but count coins and bills. That is, until mobile payment platforms like WeChat changed all that. "This is an existential threat," Joseph explained. "Without WeChat, how are we going to operate our business?" Joseph was not exaggerating. After the spinoff from Yum! Brands, Yum China was a separate company listed on the New York Stock Exchange, at the time valued at about $20 billion.

The Trump position was that WeChat collected personal data on American citizens, and therefore posed a national security threat. He may also have seen a ban as creating leverage against China in his trade war, but it was also a way for him to play tough against the CCP in a way that didn't affect voters, at least those living in the United States where very few people used the app.

But it did affect us in China, where everyone uses WeChat. Even street merchants and beggars hold out QR codes to accept electronic money transfers instead of cash. The Trump team might not have considered that Chinese consumers have choices. Nike has a huge business selling clothes and shoes in China, but Germany's Adidas has a store right next to it in Shanghai's retail cluster on Nanjing Road, as do the local sports brands, Li Ning and Anta. German and Chinese firms wouldn't be subject to Trump's ban.

Facing this threat from our own government, we quickly formed a task force that met every week to share what we learned about Trump's executive order and plan what to do about it. The executive order directed the Department of Commerce to study the issue for forty-five days and define specific activities and transactions that would be restricted. We were keenly interested in the outcome and hoped to influence it to protect our businesses in China. Unfortunately, the White

House simultaneously prohibited Commerce from discussing the issue. We needed a coordinated effort if we had any hope of influencing the outcome.

All American companies and individuals would be affected, but I focused on the consumer brands that would be most helpful for our lobbying efforts. I soon realized that nobody wanted to be identified. Twenty or so companies joined the task force, but almost all of them demanded to remain anonymous. Some companies—like Apple and Tesla—were notoriously secretive, and most companies preferred to come under the AmCham umbrella when commenting on Chinese government policy, but in this case they refused to be identified as they pushed back against the US government's demands. That left me as the spokesperson for our group to go on Fox News and CNBC to explain the damage that Trump's policy would do to our companies that had worked so hard to earn a position in the vast China market.

In the end, the courts stopped the WeChat ban, but the experience shook us up thoroughly, and revealed how tenuous our position was, stuck in the geopolitical vice.

Toward the end of the first Trump administration, after the 2020 election, I visited Washington and met for the last time with Trump-appointed officials. My meeting was at Treasury with a political appointee, who seemed more interested in sending out his resume than in anything I had to say. He didn't bring a notebook to our meeting. On my way out, I turned to him and asked, "What was the thinking behind the WeChat ban? Cutting us off from WeChat would have caused a lot of American businesses to pull out of China. Did people here not understand that?"

He simply said, "Oh no, Mr. Gibbs, we knew exactly what we were doing." He didn't elaborate, but I took this to mean that the Trump team was willing to destroy American businesses in China, giving up hard-won market share gains and handing the business to our Chinese, European and Japanese competitors. This would be the exact opposite of what Trump was supposedly trying to achieve with his trade war, leaving us bewildered, as China's officials undoubtedly were as well.

Ironically, of the two Chinese platforms targeted during Trump's first-term executive orders, the WeChat ban quickly faded from the headlines. It became bogged down in court challenges, and because it affected only a niche user base in the United States—mainly Chinese speakers—the issue never generated sustained political momentum. TikTok, by contrast, did not disappear. Its scale, cultural reach, and potential to shape public opinion ensured that concerns about data security and foreign influence remained central to the national debate.

Under the Biden administration, those concerns crystallized into bipartisan action. In 2024, Congress passed legislation requiring TikTok to be sold to a US-controlled entity or face a nationwide ban—the first time the United States targeted a major global platform on national security grounds. Lawmakers argued that the app's algorithmic recommendations could be manipulated by Beijing, intentionally or not, at moments of political sensitivity. Ironically, this very suspicion helped prolong TikTok's visibility and relevance; the app remained a political flashpoint long after WeChat had slipped from public memory.

The political irony deepened further when Donald Trump, who had first attempted to ban TikTok by executive order in 2020, embraced the platform during his 2024 campaign. His team credited TikTok—its short-form videos and its reach among younger voters—with helping drive engagement and amplify his MAGA messaging. What began as a national security target became, in Trump's own hands, a powerful political tool. TikTok has survived not only legal scrutiny but also shifting administrations and contradictory political impulses, emerging as both a geopolitical liability and an indispensable channel in American electoral politics.

Trump was a familiar personality type to Chinese leaders. A clever pundit wrote: "If Donald Trump hadn't come along then the Chinese would have tried to invent him."[18] Beijing officials know how to work with—and manipulate—people who are ego-driven, thin-skinned, and have a weakness for flattery.

Beijing managed to keep substantive economic issues out of the so-called phase one trade deal, which essentially amounted to a few large soybean purchases. But even those weren't fulfilled. Trump's presidency ended with America's trade deficit even larger than before, and trade with China more lopsided than at any other point in history. Beijing was delighted that America had withdrawn from the Trans-Pacific Partnership, was backing away from alliances, and shrinking from its traditional role as a global leader.

Even Trump's steadfast supporters within the American business community in China were disappointed with Trump's first four years in office, and we were all horrified as his 2020 election rhetoric descended into name-calling and offensive remarks about our host country and America's largest trading partner.

Looking back at the letter that Ken Jarrett and I had written as Trump's first term began, little from our list had been achieved. Market access had not improved at all, and wasn't even

18 William Overholt, a China expert and senior research fellow at Harvard University's Kennedy School

mentioned in the phase one deal. We had asked about insurance and banking, but trade in services was left out completely in favor of agricultural purchases.

Trump's tariffs failed to "bring jobs home." Instead, they pushed Chinese manufacturers into Vietnam, Mexico, and other third countries—accelerating the very globalization Trump sought to reverse. Both sides ended weaker: the United States economically bruised, and China strategically exposed.

When Trump left office after his first term, US-China tensions were at their highest in decades, but the underlying imbalance remained: China's economic model still depended on exports and access to global markets, while America's response had become reactive, erratic, and often self-defeating. Trump's trade war exposed genuine Chinese vulnerabilities, but it also demonstrated how willing the United States was to absorb self-inflicted damage in pursuit of leverage.

Some of Trump's actions, like his proposed ban on WeChat and TikTok, would have been devastating for American companies operating in China, had the courts not intervened. His first term taught us a hard lesson: the president was willing to impose enormous costs on US firms as he negotiated his deals. Tariffs, app bans, and export controls disrupted supply chains, raised costs, and left many American executives quietly asking whose interests were actually being served.

Over time, it became clear that President Trump was using tariffs as a tool to promote domestic manufacturing and reduce dependence on foreign supply chains. His reasoning centered on revitalizing the American economy by bringing manufacturing back to the US, pushing toward greater self-sufficiency. This approach bore similarities to China's own industrial policy goals. China had long pursued economic self-reliance through initiatives like Made in China 2025, which aimed to reduce dependence on foreign suppliers and foster indigenous industries. AmCham members had consistently raised concerns about market access restrictions, policies favoring domestic firms, and an uneven playing field for foreign companies in China. The Trump administration's policies suggested the US was adopting some similar tools of economic nationalism.

Beijing welcomed the chaos that Trump injected into US policy, but it misunderstood America's resilience. And Washington, in turn, misunderstood China's vulnerabilities—mistaking aggression for confidence. Beneath its muscular nationalism, China faced slowing growth, technological chokepoints, and rising isolation.

This new approach would have to factor as multinational companies reconsidered their business models. China was already becoming a low-growth, low-profit market, but if the US and China both transitioned toward self-sufficiency, the long term prospects for American companies in China would certainly be affected.

But for Americans living and working in China, the biggest change was that under Trump, America's relationship with China became openly hostile. We hoped this was only a matter of style, as Trump takes pride in being brash and unpredictable, and the New York real estate tycoon likes to "shoot first and negotiate later." A hostile opening may not indicate unwillingness to cooperate, although understanding the president's objectives could be a challenge. By the end of his first term, even Trump's steadfast supporters were frustrated with his approach to China.

Donald Trump lost his bid for re-election in 2020, and as he left the White House, I penned the following letter to AmCham members for our magazine:

With the Biden administration taking over in just over a month, now is a good time to look back and assess the last four years of US-China relations. AmCham Shanghai, as a non-partisan organization, works cooperatively with whatever administration occupies the White House. The Trump White House has taken a certain approach to China, putting our members in an almost constant state of crisis. What has been the overall net effect?

Business performance has been good. According to AmCham's annual survey, members still see good growth and profitability, so that hasn't changed. According to AmCham's 2020 China Business Report, 78% reported profits in 2019. Despite a decline in five-year optimism, the vast majority of companies continue to invest in the China market. In fact 92% report no intention to leave.

Market access, a main pillar of the Chamber's advocacy with the Chinese government, has improved somewhat. China lifted equity caps, creating more opportunities for American companies in banking and insurance. American Express has finally been granted a domestic transaction license this year (albeit to the joint venture), but Mastercard and Visa are still waiting. Cloud computing, data centers, and many other business segments remain restricted in China. Overall, not much has changed in terms of market access for firms that are not already here.

Reciprocity and a level playing field for American businesses have been important goals for this administration. The executive orders against WeChat and TikTok's operations in the United States cited national security rather than a lack of reciprocity, but the imbalance is painfully obvious. Dozens of American internet businesses continue to be blocked in China, even as TikTok accumulated over 100 million users in the United States. The WeChat and TikTok bans are still being challenged in the courts, while China shows no sign of movement to allow Twitter or Facebook to operate in China. Reciprocity remains an elusive goal.

The Phase One trade deal was signed in January, although some pundits described it as no more than a ceasefire in the trade war, with the significant issues pushed into a non-existent Phase Two. A third of AmCham Shanghai members report they were unaffected by the Phase One trade deal. Still, the structural changes around intellectual property and currency reform are welcome moves. Discussion around the Made in China 2025 plan has faded, but state subsidies are still very much in place. Genuine reform of state-owned enterprises is clearly not happening.

The targets set by the Phase One trade deal will not be achieved, although corn and pork purchases are up from previous years. Energy purchases will fall far short, but that can be explained by the collapse of global demand and drop in the price of oil.

America's trade deficit, a major issue according to this administration, has actually increased from $735 billion in 2016 to $854 billion at the end of 2019. The trade deficit with China has remained about the same, $347 billion in 2016 versus $345 billion in 2019.

Manufacturing jobs, another goal for the

administration's China policy, have not returned to the United States. According to AmCham's last two surveys, fewer than 5% of respondents reported reshoring production to America.

Overall, it would be fair to say progress has been made in certain areas, but the administration's ambitious goals to correct imbalances in the US-China relationship have not been achieved. The one metric that is clearly worse is the tension and mistrust between the two countries. AmCham members are deeply concerned, with 71% saying that US-China tension is their top challenge in 2020, an 18 percentage point spike from last year.

In this environment, America has chosen a new president.

With this as the current state of US-China relations, AmCham is holding a series of (virtual) meetings with members of Congress, and with career officials in the administration. Tension, bringing with it potential for misunderstanding, is higher than it has been in decades. AmCham has always pushed for fairness and reciprocity in the US-China relationship. A rebalancing is underway. We hope changes can be made without harming our interests, and that the United States and China can forge new patterns of trade and investment that continue to benefit both countries. There are challenges ahead. AmCham will engage with the Biden White House, just as we did under Trump.

I walked into the swish offices of Bain and Company, on the 38th floor of Plaza 66 in central Shanghai. A young woman came from behind the reception desk and took my coat and guided me to the board room. It was set up with notepads and pens, and plates of danish and croissants were placed in the middle of the table. At the end of the long narrow room were two video screens. I could see they were connected, but figures were moving around on the screen so I couldn't make out who they were.

Men in suits stood around, chatting in groups of two or three as the room continued to fill up. I found my friend Yoke Loon Lim, the president of Dow Chemical in China. He was chatting with Eddy Chan, the head of FedEx, comparing their collections of fine wines. The monthly breakfast meeting brought together the CEOs of the major foreign companies, mainly Americans and Europeans. As head of the American Chamber, I was invited as a courtesy and occasionally briefed the group on topics of interest to the foreign business community.

The sharp clink of a spoon tapping a glass ended the conversations, and a tall man at the far end of the table invited us to take our seats. He wore a light grey suit, cut slim at the leg, with a dark blue pocket square. His cuff links looked expensive. Pierre Cohade, the former president of Goodyear in China, was well known by the senior people in Shanghai and often gave talks on strategy and management. He spoke in a soft but authoritative voice with a heavy French accent. "We have a special guest speaker today, our good friend Sean Stein. As you know, he is stepping down this year from his position as the US consul general here in Shanghai, and we asked him to give us a briefing on how he views US-China relations."

Sean was seated opposite Pierre at the far end of the long conference room table, and stood to address the group. He was heavy set, with brown hair and a high forehead. He had already shed his suit jacket, but was wearing his trademark vest over a white shirt. The room was filled to its capacity of about thirty people, plus the two joining via video, all senior executives, and almost all men. It was a mix of Europeans and Americans. Everyone knew Sean, and respected his acumen.

Sean was a career diplomat, with postings in the northern industrial city of Shenyang, as well as Beijing and Washington. Earlier in his twenty plus year career with the State Department he was in Indonesia, where he met his wife. Many of us knew his family, and we wondered how he found time for them while seeming to be at every important event, day and night. He was also a voracious consumer of media. He read everything, even keeping track of Chinese language sources like *Qiushi*, the party's political journal that explained the thinking behind certain policies and directives.

Unlike his predecessor, Hanscom Smith, who spoke precisely and deliberately, Sean was animated and spoke in a quick, staccato style. He always made a point of understanding his audience, so he knew when he needed to explain things for people who were unfamiliar with the world "inside the beltway" and when he could assume a high level of knowledge. This group was the latter, so Sean went quickly through the history of US-China relations, just hitting the top of the waves.

"Bill Clinton decided to separate trade from human rights, and brought China into the WTO. China got rich and America lost jobs, but we got an ally to put more pressure on Russia. Sure, we wanted to see more democracy in China, but it was more important to get China to stop stealing intellectual property and it would have been nice if they actually followed the rules under WTO, but they didn't do any of that."

The room was quiet. A few listeners nodded as Sean summarized decades of State Department work.

"Then came Bush two. He continued engaging, and tried to do something about the trade imbalances. He cared a lot about the RMB, which people thought China was manipulating to make their goods cheaper, but for the most part China didn't pay much attention."

The Europeans in the room mostly ran manufacturing companies that were sensitive to exchange rates. A few of them looked at each other, nodding.

"Obama leaned in on engagement. He kept going with the JCCT and expanded it with the S&ED, but nothing happened."

Pierre interrupted from across the room. "Sean, why don't you explain, for those of us who are not American. Not everyone knows about the JCCT."

"Sorry," Sean nodded. "We had this thing called the Joint Commission on Commerce and Trade, going back to the 1980s when the US and China would get together and talk about all the issues. We would talk about trade, and market access, and a lot of specific things with agriculture. Hundreds of people would fly from Beijing to Washington, and Washington to Beijing. At one point we sent two hundred officials, plus all the security and support staff. We got nothing. We also used to have the SED. Under Obama we rebranded it and added security, so it became the Security and Economic Dialogue. Then *everyone* got involved. We didn't just have State and Commerce. We had Treasury, Defense, Energy, everyone. It got even bigger, but what did we achieve?"

The room was silent.

"Sometime around the end of Obama's first term, a bunch of us got together and made a list of all the most important things we wanted from China. There were about eighty items on two pages that we wrote down and put in a drawer. Then, toward the end of Obama's presidency, we took it out and put a mark next to everything where we got some movement or accommodation. Do you know what we got?"

More silence.

Sean held up his hand in the shape of a zero, pausing for effect before he continued. "So in comes Donald Trump. His team looked at what Obama and Bush and everyone else had accomplished with China and they weren't impressed."

I recalled a conversation with Ryan Haas, an Obama official on the China team. Ryan told me that after the 2016 election he and a few colleagues went to Trump Tower to brief the people who would be working on China for the new president. The conversation about China lasted less than five minutes. They simply weren't interested in hearing what Obama's people had been working on and believed they had nothing to learn. The conversation shifted to baseball.

"Trump's people took the opposite approach. I guess you could call it shoot first and negotiate later, but they started by putting up tariffs." Sean, as a career official, was politically neutral and used the word "they" for the Trump team. He continued to explain the Phase One trade deal and other wins that the administration believed had been achieved, and concluded his speech on the Trump doctrine.

Ken Jarrett, sitting a few seats over from me, put up his hand. "Thank you Sean, for the succinct explanation of the course of events and the Trump doctrine." After finishing his term as president of the American Chamber, Ken had joined the Albright Stonebridge Group, a political consultancy, as a senior advisor. He was a bit older than Sean, and as a career diplomat himself he was intimately familiar with the story Sean had just told, and had played a part in much of it. "Many of us have been curious about it, because his erratic behavior and off-the-cuff remarks on China often don't seem to match policy. That leads us to ask, does Trump himself know about the Trump doctrine?"

This brought chuckles in the room, and people directed their attention to Ken, who was also well-known and respected in the group. Sean laughed along with us. He started to answer, but the atmosphere in the room had changed. The Europeans cared little about Trump's affairs with women, but they could not understand how someone who was so unpredictable and uninformed about history and global affairs could become the leader of the free world. A man sitting across from me mocked the way the US president had shoved aside the prime minister of Montenegro, placing himself in the front and center for the photo. It was a metaphor for how many Europeans felt about the way America exercised power. They were relieved that the chaos seemed to be over and Trump would be gone, but it remained to be seen if America could recover the global leadership position it had lost in the previous four years.

Neither side had achieved what it wanted. The US hadn't reshored jobs, and China hadn't earned respect. Both had exposed their weaknesses: America's political volatility, and China's structural fragility.

For Beijing, the first Trump presidency did not end well. In the final few months, Trump administration officials took turns calling out China's misdeeds in a series of four speeches. National Security Advisor Robert O'Brien led off by accusing China of seeking to remake the world in its authoritarian image. FBI Director Christopher Wray called out Chinese espionage and intellectual property theft, reporting that "the FBI is opening a new China-related counterintelligence case every ten hours." Attorney General William Barr took his turn and focused on economic threats. He criticized Hollywood for accommodating Chinese censorship and accused American companies of becoming "pawns of Chinese influence."

Secretary of State Mike Pompeo gave the fourth and final speech at the Nixon Library on July 23, 2020. He declared that the US policy of engagement with China had failed, and explicitly called for an "alliance of democracies" to counter China. Pompeo's speech differentiated between the Chinese people and the CCP, which to Beijing sounded like a call for regime change. After leaving office, Pompeo made several trips to Taiwan, where he made inflammatory and provocative remarks that were counter to America's long-standing policies.

As a result, Beijing sanctioned Mike Pompeo and twenty-seven other Trump administration officials, saying they had "seriously violated China's sovereignty." The move prohibited them from entering China.

Another of Trump's allies, a sharp critic of China in who's office I had been in a shouting match, was also sanctioned. Senator Marco Rubio had continually criticized China's record on human rights, and suppression of protests in Hong Kong. I hadn't necessarily disagreed with the senator on the facts. I simply pointed out that discussion with Beijing might be more effective if we treated our counterparts with more respect.

Four years later, in January of 2025, Marco Rubio became the US secretary of state in the second Trump administration.

The Bund along the Huangpu River was cold and windy, as it always is in January, but the mood in Shanghai was upbeat. My car, marked with the official AmCham logo on the door, deposited me in front of number 27 Zhongshan East Road. The buildings on the Bund were all vintage, but this one in particular was historically significant. Back in the day, it was the Shanghai headquarters of the British Jardine Matheson company, one of the famous trading houses of the nineteenth century. Jardine was said to have been the most successful of all the opium traders. The building had since changed hands several times.

The Chinese characters etched on a bronze plaque above the double doors read *"luosifu huisuo,"* the Roosevelt Club. I waited for the elevator, an old model made by the Otis Elevator Company, and watched as the dial above the door turned counterclockwise to the ground floor. The club's founder, Tim Tse, greeted me as I stepped out, and brought me into the Presidents Room, an enormous high-ceilinged space with a portrait of Teddy at one end and Franklin at the other. It was a fitting venue for the inauguration dinner, marking the end of Trump and the beginning of the Biden administration. The CEOs and senior leaders of American companies were gathered, enjoying the elegant surroundings and the view overlooking the Huangpu river as they sipped cocktails.

I took my seat at the head of two long tables next to Jim Heller, Sean Stein's successor as the US consul general in Shanghai. Jim offered reassuring remarks about the peaceful transfer of power, despite what had just happened on January 6th, and explained the transitions that would take place within the State Department. The Republicans in our group made gracious remarks about President Biden. The collective mood was optimistic. The chaos was finally over, and we had high hopes that the US-China relationship could return to a more stable path.

None of us could have anticipated what happened next, in Alaska.

Officials in Beijing prepared for their first meeting with America's new administration, hopeful for a more cooperative relationship. China's top diplomat, Yang Jiechi, and Foreign Minister Wang Yi flew to Alaska in March of 2021 to meet with their new American counterparts.

President Biden appointed Antony Blinken, who had served in a number of foreign policy roles, as secretary of state. He and national security adviser Jake Sullivan welcomed their guests at the Captain Cook Hotel in Anchorage, Alaska. If the visitors were expecting to hear something different from the Biden administration than what the Trump team had said, they were disappointed.

In opening remarks, Secretary Blinken echoed Christopher Wray and accused China of cyberattacks. He went on to talk about Xinjiang, Hong Kong, and Taiwan, and the "rules-based international order." He concluded by saying, "The United States' relationship with China will be competitive where it should be, collaborative where it can be, adversarial where it must be."[19]

The team from China seemed only to hear the adversarial part. After opening with a lighthearted remark about the interpreter, the Chinese officials unleashed a counterattack on the Americans. Yang Jiechi, who served as China's Minister of Foreign Affairs back in 2008 during the global financial crisis, said: "I think the problem is that the United States has exercised long-arm jurisdiction and suppression and overstretched the national security through the use of force or financial hegemony, and this has created obstacles for normal trade activities, and the United States has also been persuading some countries to launch attacks on China." Beijing's frustrations with the United States had been building up, and there was particular concern about America's strategy of strengthening alliances, a hallmark of Biden's presidency, which Beijing viewed as "containment."

Yang continued: "What China and the international

19 *Nikkei Asia*, "How it happened: Transcript of the US-China opening remarks in Alaska," March 19, 2021.

community follow or uphold is the United Nations-centered international system and the international order underpinned by international law, not what is advocated by a small number of countries of the so-called rules-based international order. The United States has its United States-style democracy and China has Chinese-style democracy. It is not just up to the American people, but also the people of the world, to evaluate how the United States has done in advancing its own democracy."

The January 6th attack on the US capitol was still fresh, and Yang seized the opportunity to take a swipe at America's institutions. "Many people within the United States actually have little confidence in the democracy of the United States, and they have various views regarding the government of the United States. In China, according to opinion polls, the leaders of China have the wide support of the Chinese people. The opinion polls conducted in the United States show that the leaders of China have the support of the Chinese people. No attempt to smear China's social system would get anywhere. Facts have shown that such practices would only lead the Chinese people to rally more closely around the Communist Party of China and work steadily towards the goals that we have set for ourselves."

Next, Yang brought the American business community into the discussion, although thankfully without mentioning the Chamber of Commerce directly. "The overwhelming majority of American businesses in China have said that China's business environment is good and nobody has forced them to stay in China. They see a profit coming from their presence in China, and they see immense opportunities in China. That's why they are staying in China. And I believe that for our two countries, under the new circumstances, we need to enhance communication, properly manage our differences and expand our cooperation instead of engaging in confrontation."

Yang was correct in saying American businesses were staying in China, but their enthusiasm had been declining for years by 2021, even before the influence of Covid. Overall market growth was low, operating costs were high, and trust in the regulatory environment was eroding. Today, the shift is even more pronounced. Many companies are limiting their exposure to China and curtailing new investments. Slowing growth, rising geopolitical risk, and state interventions have made long-term commitments hard to justify.

The two sides went back and forth on which side better represented "international public opinion" and "universal values," and swapped accusations of cyberattacks, with Yang saying, "The United States is the champion in this regard." The Americans pointed to international cooperation that enabled its mission to Mars. The project of course had excluded the Chinese, as Yang did not fail to point out. The meeting ended on a chilling note, with Yang stating: "We've had confrontations in the past, and the result did not serve the United States well. China will pull through and has pulled through such confrontation."

The business community in Shanghai was horrified. Friends in the State Department told me that after the sharp exchange in public, the private meetings were polite and productive, but the damage was done. According to one source, the Chinese officials were angry and "doxxed" the American interpreter, meaning they released her personal information to the public. She immediately began receiving death threats and abuse on social media from Chinese zealots, who accused her of mistranslating to make the American positions sound more aggressive. It was an odd accusation, since Yang is actually fluent in English and could have translated the meeting himself.

If the Obama presidency marked the end of engagement, Trump represented the beginning of hostility, and the downward slide in relations between the two most powerful nations on earth continued during the Biden era. China's diplomats spoke like conquerors, but they were defending a system that feared transparency, foreign capital flight, and social unrest. The dragon was breathing fire, but its scales were brittle.

Trump's trade war laid bare important structural weaknesses in China's economy, yet the broader strategic effect of his policies actually strengthened Beijing's position. By embracing tariffs, protectionism, and unilateral deal-making, Trump undercut US alliances and abandoned multilateral tools that could have constrained China's rise. These moves not only diminished US leverage but also validated Xi Jinping's longstanding narrative that China must pursue self-reliance, accelerate local innovation, and prepare for a hostile external environment. Meanwhile, the Trump administration's unpredictability and retreat from global leadership created diplomatic space that China readily filled across Asia, Africa, and Latin America. Thus, while Trump exposed aspects of China's fragility, his approach ultimately advanced Beijing's strategic objectives: weakening the American alliance system, normalizing economic coercion as a policy tool, and reinforcing domestic support for Xi's inward-looking development model.

The trade war, which continued through the Biden years and into Trump's second term, cemented a long-running shift in US-China relations, turning structural trends into the baseline reality we face today. Decoupling is no longer hypothetical: China's pivot toward self-reliance and the Global South, combined with US inward-looking politics, has made deep engagement improbable. The trade war exposed China's vulnerabilities, including a dependence on foreign markets, while revealing that America's political volatility can be just as consequential.

Ironically, Trump's confrontational, deal-driven style often mirrored Beijing's control-oriented instincts, accelerating policies hardliners already favored. Today, the relationship is defined by mutual fragility: a dragon whose fire dazzles but whose scales are thin, and a United States whose political turbulence shapes outcomes as much as Chinese strategy. For businesses, policymakers, and strategists, the lesson is clear: deals now unfold not in a predictable system, but in a theater of insecurity, where weakness, not strength, drives both sides' behavior.

PART 6

CONTRADICTIONS

Chapter 22

The Precarious Rise of Officials

Xu Kunlin's star was rising in China's political hierarchy. He didn't speak English, but he was polished and professional, and very much the new model for China's government officials. People like Mr. Zhang, the official in Nanjing who had been so helpful to me, were the old guard and I couldn't help thinking how different this new breed of officials had become. Unlike Zhang, who was constantly smoking and drinking, Mr. Xu was tall and fit, and projected confidence and optimism about the future.

China's old guard was fading, replaced by technocrats who projected confidence, but whose confidence masked a deeper anxiety: in China's system, one misstep—one accident, scandal, or dip in metrics—could end a career overnight.

Mr. Xu broke free from the cluster of people surrounding him and crossed the room in my direction. I was balancing a glass of wine in one hand and a stuffed mushroom in the other, which I quickly got rid of. "Ji huizhang!" Mr. Xu called me *huizhang,* my chamber title, as he grabbed my hand and shook it. "Why haven't you come to see me? It's been a long time!"

We met when he was vice mayor of Shanghai before he

became party secretary of Suzhou, a neighboring city and important manufacturing center. We had exchanged letters when I congratulated him on his promotion, but before I had a chance to visit him he was elevated again to become governor of Jiangsu province. Recently, Xu was promoted again, and as of September of 2025, he became the party secretary of Liaoning Province and a member of the standing committee of the provincial party committee. The process ensures the Communist Party leadership maintains ultimate control over key government appointments, with the People's Congress providing the constitutional legitimacy through a formal electoral mechanism. It is common for officials to move between positions in government and the party, and could be a good thing for their careers.

Mr. Xu continued to pump my hand, asking about my family and my career, but he would soon be pulled away to greet other guests. The event was a reception hosted by Jiangsu Province at the end of Shanghai's CIIE—the China International Import Expo, a massive trade fair that started as an annual event in 2018.

The CIIE, now China's flagship trade fair, was designed to showcase openness but the event itself reveals a constrained system obsessed with obedience and control. Participation is obligatory, access exhausting, and attendance a test of political loyalty. Behind the choreographed efficiency is a rigid hierarchy where outcomes are scripted, and risk-taking could be fatal. China's governance model looks disciplined; in practice, it is brittle.

I hated attending, as even gaining entry to the massive CIIE complex was an odyssey by itself because of security, traffic controls, and the sheer size of the crowds. I had to compete for space and air with 400,000 attendees, but it was essential to see and be seen by dozens of mainly provincial-level government officials—people like Mr. Xu.

In Shanghai, Xu was one of eight vice mayors in the city government, each holding a different portfolio, but his new role as head of Jiangsu province showed that he was clearly on a fast track for promotion. If he did well in Jiangsu then his next appointment could very well be up to Beijing. This would be by no means easy. With a population of 80 million, Jiangsu province is the size of Germany, with per capita income already quite high. Jiangsu's economy is vital to China, with a wide range of industries, including automobile manufacturing, electronics, and more.

In the Chinese system, promotions are managed by the party's Organization Department, a powerful body that assiduously keeps track of performance. Mr. Xu would be evaluated based on everything from tax revenue to how school children performed on national exams. A major accident, like a chemical plant explosion or a train derailment, could end the career of a party official even if nothing they had done or not done could be traced to the incident.

Jean Liu, a senior executive with a large education company in China, explains it this way: "Senior officials normally started as entry-level civil servants and worked their way up to positions of power and influence. Officials, and the bureaus they work in, are measured by KPIs ("key performance indicator," a common metric for evaluating individual contributions to a business), just as company managers are. The difference is that KPIs set for government officials and bureaus are often inflexible, even artificial. And they change from time to time, depending on the priority du jour. When working with different levels of officials and the bureaucracies they work for, we must try and understand their KPIs. Otherwise, we will never understand why some of our requests fall on deaf ears."

Keeping track of officials is a challenge, since no one stays long enough to form an independent power base. Promotions are constant, rotations relentless, and the system suppresses initiative and candor. Officials learn to avoid risk—and in the process, avoid responsibility. The system looks efficient, but it is ultimately driven by fear—fear of failure, fear of blame, and above all, fear of losing control.

Regarding promotions, Jean says: "Government officials get reassigned all the time. The Chinese government has excellent cadre succession planning, better and more consistent than any corporate human resources succession planning I have ever known. Civil servant talent is recruited at the entry-level through formal exams and interviews. Young officials then hone their skills and political savvy through on-the-job training. Mid to senior-level officials are rotated and reassigned as they move up the career ladder—a process that gives them a chance to work in different fields and locations and, equally important, little chance of forming cliques. Senior state-owned enterprise and university leaders are also considered government officials, and often shift back and forth between government positions and enterprise or university leadership roles."

Mr. Xu and I had met many times, but in official meetings or dinners, with little opportunity for meaningful discussion or personal rapport. He read his talking points and I read mine; at times, my role as head of the chamber was to put members in front of officials and then get out of the way. AmCham had the power to convene, but no control over policy or resources to make changes, just informal influence often best exerted by members.

Our annual "Government Appreciation" dinners were a highlight of the year, drawing over 300 members and dozens of Chinese government officials. The chamber staff carefully managed the seating arrangements, inviting the US ambassador to make a speech and accompany the Shanghai vice mayor and

other dignitaries at the head table.

"Appreciation" in the name of our events may be a bit of a misnomer. The speeches indeed included a great deal of fawning and pleasant words, and at least one member company expressed concern that sponsoring an event like this could get them tripped up with the Foreign Corrupt Practices Act. (We checked, and were told by counsel that with no quid pro quo, it doesn't apply.) But the dinners were highly functional as well. The eighty or so working-level Chinese officials were carefully placed at tables with member companies with business with their departments. The architecture firm Gensler, for example, hosted a table at which an official from the City Planning Department would be seated. Exxon Mobil would be with the Department of Energy, and so on.

Most of the Chinese officials remained for the entire evening, but the vice mayors had a habit of leaving immediately after their speeches. I suspected this was a deliberate protocol move, not wanting to elevate foreign chambers to a higher status, although it's true that government officials at that level would often attend two or even three dinners in one evening.

This bothered Bob Theleen, who as AmCham chairman made several memorable speeches at these dinners. He shook his head, saying "The mayors would run from the room like they saw a ghost! What are they afraid of?" His question cut deeper than he realized. The answer was simple: visibility. High-ranking officials avoided informal contact that might later be used against them if they were accused of impropriety.

Our sponsors paid handsomely for the privilege of attending these events (and to support the chamber) but they could only buy proximity; meaningful connections were rare. In China's political culture, access is ritual, not a relationship. Business executives would have appreciated more than just an opportunity to shake hands and drink a few toasts. Chinese government people always seem to have "run out" of business cards, which is convenient because they don't want to be contacted directly. They much prefer that contacts be made through assistants who will vet and ensure that no surprises land on their boss' desk.

In contrast, Max Baucus, President Obama's ambassador to China from 2014 until 2017, was famous for offering his business card and connecting to people on WeChat, no matter their rank or title. Thousands of Chinese names—and quite a few foreign ones—were in his phone contacts, which he managed himself. Baucus attended several of these dinners during his term in office and he and his wife, Melodee Hanes, always stayed late into the evening, mixing with Chinese and American guests.

Max and Mel moved among the thirty or so tables, each with ten guests that included one or two Chinese government officials, drinking toasts, exchanging pleasantries, and taking selfies. Baucus, previously a senator from Montana, loved this Chinese tradition, which nobody told him about before coming to China. He told me that he had to learn a lot on his own. When he first arrived in China he knew about chopsticks and other basics, but he was unfamiliar with some of the subtleties that have elevated Chinese eating traditions to a fine art.

According to Baucus, a party secretary was hosting a dinner in his honor, but as he tucked into his entrée he looked to his left and right and saw empty chairs. "How rude to leave me alone like this!" He thought to himself, until he looked around the room and saw his host moving from table to table, chatting and drinking as he went. Ambassador Baucus left his desert untouched, picked up a glass, and headed for guests at the nearest table, who were delighted to see him embrace their tradition.

Mr. Xu and I developed a relationship—I won't say friendship, since high-ranking officials like him don't make new friends, certainly not with Americans like me—more or less by accident at one of these dinners. Normally, the arrival of two VIPs is carefully managed so that one is never kept waiting for the other. Diplomats sometimes snub each other this way, driving home the point that one side is more desperate for a meeting than the other, or as revenge for some slight in another context, but the AmCham staff managed to stay carefully neutral and not get caught up in those matters.

We had booked a room near the grand ballroom for our VIP guests. The ambassador's control officer was supposed to contact the chamber staff to let us know when to bring the vice mayor into the room. The ambassador's car was late. The control officer called, but the junior staff member who took the call was afraid to tell me the bad news. Vice Mayor Xu was already in the waiting room expecting the ambassador and his entourage to arrive at any moment. Instead, he had me.

Mr. Xu was warm and gracious, but impeccably careful. Someone is always watching in China. To my relief, he made no issue out of being kept waiting for a half hour or so, as I did the best I could to keep him entertained. He recalled the speech I had given the previous year that mentioned my Chinese mother and my daughter, both of whom grew up in Shanghai, and how important the US-China relationship was to my family. He didn't offer details about his own family, but we chatted about travels around China and agreed that foreign investment brought mutual benefits to our countries and that Shanghai was quite welcoming as a place for foreigners to live and conduct business. Years later, when we met again, we still shared a warm personal feeling, but the environment had changed, and the number of foreigners in Shanghai was a fraction of what it had been before.

When Xu Kunlin took the top job in Suzhou in September of 2020, he was succeeded in the Shanghai vice mayor position by Madam Zong Ming, a capable administrator with a background in architecture and history. She was the editor of a beautiful book that described Shanghai's historical buildings, with photographs and helpful captions explaining their original purpose and historical significance. The city of Shanghai is proud of its history and has preserved many buildings that date back to the 1920s and 1930s and even earlier, placing a *tongpai,* or "brass plate" on an outside wall indicating its significance. Unfortunately, this task was assigned to the Buildings and Construction Department instead of an entity that would have more appreciation for culture or history, so most of the brass plates indicate if the construction was stucco or brick, which is less helpful for people interested in who lived there, what they did, and why it was important.

Vice Mayor Zong and I had met several times already, when she sent over an invitation for the American Chamber to bring member companies to a meeting. We met at the Hengshan Hotel, not one of the five-star international hotels where chamber events were usually held, perhaps emphasizing that she was the host and we would be on her turf, which we very much were.

The AmCham staff sent over a dozen or so company names. Her office accepted all but one, and we later found out why. The meeting was carefully choreographed, and her office already knew what issues each company would likely raise. The rejected company had a problem they knew they couldn't solve, so it was better if that company simply didn't show up.

Our meeting was intended to be at the working level with little ceremony, but I was met at the main entrance of the hotel and escorted into a large conference room. It was set up with two long tables facing each other, with seats behind each for assistants and note takers. There was a name card and a microphone in front of each seat at the table.

Vice Mayor Zong opened the meeting with brief remarks, and then invited me to speak. I began the way all meetings with Chinese officials begin: by thanking them.

No matter that the Chinese government is deliberately opaque, and that foreign companies suffer all kinds of abuse, including selective enforcement of regulations, procurement policies that favor local companies or state-owned enterprises, or investigations that unreasonably target foreign companies. Even commercial disputes could give local companies the ability to place an "exit ban" on a foreign executive, preventing them from leaving the country, almost always resulting in immediate capitulation.

This wasn't the time; diplomacy required performance. "Thank you, Vice Mayor Zong, for your leadership and support." I spoke in English, giving the translators something to do, and to set the pattern for the one or two non-Chinese speakers in my group. "American companies here in Shanghai benefit from the business-friendly policies of your government, as well as the infrastructure that has developed so well in recent years..." This was all true enough. Nobody in the room would disagree, as I mentioned a few facts from our recent business climate survey—just the positive ones of course—before introducing the company representatives. One by one our companies took the microphone, said a few words about their business, and mentioned an issue on which they needed the government's help.

The vice mayor was flanked by city department heads, and she handed out assignments in real time as each problem was described. One of the companies reported that an environmental study was taking too long and was delaying construction on a new facility. A department head spoke up, explaining that the environmental study wasn't a problem, but they were hesitant to approve a second factory because of a report that one of the company's other factories was emitting odors that affected local schools. The head of the Shanghai Municipal Education Commission said he would look into the problem to assess its seriousness and report back. The company representative said he would present a report explaining that the new factory was different and that smells would not be an issue.

Another company had problems bringing in specialized equipment for a new factory and was directed to the Shanghai Municipal Office for Port Services. This was the vice mayor's way of assigning tasks and delivering results. It was impressive, and revealing. The process was not about solving problems creatively, but managing them administratively. Every act of "responsiveness" was another exercise in control.

After the meeting, I asked an AmCham member if he thought Chinese officials were helpful. His reply: "If a guy has a hold of your balls he can make you do whatever he wants. When he lets go of your balls, is he being helpful?"

I learned later that the German Chamber of Commerce and the European Chamber were also invited to similar sessions. Clearly, the vice mayor had KPIs she needed to deliver on. Western business leaders tend to avoid government entanglements, but in China it pays to cultivate relationships with local officials. The local mayor or party secretary can be helpful or detrimental, but a line of communication to them could be helpful either way. Successful managers in China invest time getting to know them, and find out what they need to accomplish for their next promotion.

Officials like Xu and Zong rise because they master the art of projection: competence, confidence, harmony. But underneath lies insecurity. Their success depends not on innovation or trust, but on avoiding failure. And in China, that is the ultimate fragility: a nation that fears chaos so deeply it strangles the very adaptability that made it powerful.

CHAPTER 23

Covid-19 and Control

2019 had been a busy year for me and for the chamber, and I looked forward to getting away during the Chinese New Year to spend time with my family. We were vacationing in Penang, Malaysia, staying at the legendary Eastern & Oriental Hotel. The E&O was a colonial-style hotel built in 1885, when British spice (and opium) traders were mixing it up with Southeast Asian merchants.

The hotel was also the backdrop in one of the scenes of Michelle Yeo's "Crazy Rich Asians" movie, which was a sensation among my Chinese American friends but drew a "meh" inside China. Audiences in China were bored with stories about ostentatious lifestyles and the crass behavior of the super-rich, both on-screen and off, but Chinese Americans were thrilled with the all-Asian cast and a dreamy star that they could identify with. I asked one of my local friends in Shanghai about it but she simply blinked and said: "What are you talking about? ALL our movies have Asian casts. That's just the first *Hollywood* movie with an all-Asian cast!"

Before I left China for the holiday in January of 2020, I had been hearing murmurs about a troubling situation in Wuhan.

Public health officials were scrambling to identify the cause of a mysterious illness making people sick across the city. Early reports described a pneumonia-like condition, and the similarities to the 2002 SARS outbreak, Severe Acute Respiratory Syndrome, were unsettling. I remembered how the first cases of the 2002 SARS appeared in Guangdong province, but the Chinese government delayed reporting them for months. By the time the World Health Organization issued a global alert, the virus had already spread to other cities in China and throughout Asia, eventually infecting over 8,000 people in 30 countries, and killing at least 700 people. We were about to get hit with something much, much more severe.

I was lounging by the pool when my phone rang with the news that Wuhan was shut down.[1] Nobody was allowed in or out of the city of 11 million people.

I rushed to contact the AmCham staff from where I was in Malaysia, pulling as many of them as I could back from their holidays. We needed all hands available to collect reliable information and get it out to our members as the virus—and government measures to control it—headed toward Shanghai. Rumors and misinformation were already rampant, making AmCham a critical trusted source for news and helpful advice. I didn't yet know whether Shanghai would also be locked down, but it was clear that business would be affected.

I went on Fox News to sound the alarm, warning that supply chains could become interrupted. As it turned out, all businesses—especially restaurants and bars, but also factories and offices—were kept closed, and the government shut the international border on March 28[2]. The ports came next, shutting

1 On January 23, 2020, Wuhan was closed to traffic coming in or out, and would remain locked down for the next 76 days.

2 The precise order was: "Temporarily suspended entry for most foreign nationals."

down supply chains just as I had predicted. I thought seriously about staying out of China, not knowing how the situation would play out, but I returned to Shanghai just before the border was closed. I would not leave the country again for the next two years.

We soon had good communication channels established with Chinese government sources, as well as American authorities, and the Chamber became a hub for information and coordination of resources to battle against what soon would become known as Covid-19.

In those early days Shanghai had very few cases of Covid, but the situation in Wuhan was dire. They were quickly running out of masks and gowns, which doctors and nurses needed in order to care for the sick. People were dying in the street. Healthcare professionals worked around the clock, grabbing sleep when they could and even sleeping on the floor. In acts of extraordinary self-sacrifice, some professionals traveled from other cities and provinces to help in Wuhan.

Not knowing what else we could do to be helpful, AmCham worked with member companies to secure additional supplies of PPE—the personal protective equipment that was so badly needed—and ship them to Wuhan. Most of the masks and gowns were made in China, but local inventories were low, so the supplies had to be acquired and shipped from the United States. AmCham member companies, moved by the heroic efforts of the healthcare workers in Hubei and elsewhere, donated cash in the hundreds of millions of renminbi and contributed even more in products and services to fight the epidemic.

Cameron Johnson, a long-time Shanghai resident and an expert in manufacturing operations and sourcing, happened to be in Seattle, and bought up whatever he could find from Home Depot, Lowes, and Target stores. "I brought ten large boxes to the Post Office. I never knew PPE could be so heavy! People asked why I needed all the masks, but when I told them what they were for, everyone was cooperative and eager to help."

Soon after, despite the travel bans, the Covid virus arrived in the United States and shipments of PPE were needed in the other direction. AmCham became a logistics coordinator to locate and secure supplies and ship containers of PPE to hospitals in the United States. This was more difficult than it sounds, since Chinese regulations for donations are strict, and we were required to pay a fee to a local firm. In the end we were able to get it done and secured space on cargo planes donated by AmCham member companies.

AmCham also began maintaining a list of companies that could help with acquiring PPE and other materials and assisted FEMA—the Federal Emergency Management Agency—on a pro bono basis to conduct due diligence on potential suppliers. Johnson, back in China, became AmCham's resident expert on securing supplies of PPE to send to hospitals in the United States. "The first factory I visited produced auto parts. They got into mask-making because they were shut down and the local government asked them to make PPE instead. Factories that previously made electronics were better, since they understood about cleanroom environments."

The effects of the lockdown in Shanghai at that point were actually minimal, and short-lived. The government quickly put thermal imaging temperature checks at all the chokepoints around the city, including malls and office buildings. Rapid testing was made available in every neighborhood and business center. The well-coordinated efforts were remarkably effective, with a compliant population and available technologies.

If a person tested positive for Covid, everyone they had been in contact with could be identified within minutes. If they took a train in the last few days, then everyone who sat within several rows of them was notified immediately and required to self-isolate and get tested. One member of my staff got a knock on her door at ten o'clock at night. Earlier in the evening she had taken a rideshare car; before picking her up, the driver of the car had driven past a hospital where a Covid case was reported. She was simply asked to take a test and self-isolate until the result was available. Easy. The system worked—but only because the population obeyed. Compliance wasn't optional; it was cultural. From the outside, it looked like discipline. From within, it was fear masquerading as order.

The foreign business community was in awe of the efficiency and effectiveness, with few complaints about the obvious impact on privacy and personal freedom. We watched the situation in America unfold, shaking our heads about the squabbles over mask mandates and debates about vaccines. True, people in China have been conditioned to obey government edicts, and the foreign population likewise has implicitly agreed to conform to Chinese sensibilities.

China's Covid measures caught the attention of Congressman Rick Larsen, who spent a great deal of time thinking and talking about China. He represents a district in the state of Washington, where China is by far the state's largest export market, representing about 20 percent of the total. The state sells apples, cherries, and of course Boeing airplanes. Larsen, as mentioned earlier, also co-chaired the House Working Group on China, together with Congressman Darren Lahood. Members of the American Chamber met regularly with Larsen and Lahood, and scheduled a Zoom call in November of 2020, almost a year into the global pandemic.

"I want to hear about China's Covid controls, and how it's affecting American business over there. Can someone give me a report on that?" Larsen tended to bark out questions. As one of the high IQ lawmakers in Congress, he could digest information with incredible speed. He had no tolerance for half-baked ideas or arguments without data. He was also tall and intimidating, even on Zoom.

With about a dozen senior executives on the call, we quickly went around the screen and explained that Shanghai's Covid lockdown was severe and tightly enforced, but it was short. For about six weeks beginning in February of 2020 offices were empty, factories were shut down, and stay-at-home orders prevented people from leaving their apartment compounds. One person per household was allowed a quick trip to the store for food and necessities, but the streets were otherwise deserted.

Having been through the SARS epidemic in 2002, the controls were not entirely unfamiliar and China's Confucian value system created the framework for individual sacrifices for the common good. China's highly digitized environment also provided a ready infrastructure for contact tracing.

"Yeah, yeah, yeah," Congressman Larsen snapped. "I know all about contact tracing using mobile phones. Don't forget, guys, Washington is a high-tech state! We have an app, and *seventeen percent* of people in my district already use it." There was a long silence on our end of the call. Delegation members typically fight for air time, but nobody wanted to tell Congressman Larsen that seventeen percent was nowhere near a number to be proud of.

China's compliance rate was 100 percent, and mandatory. China's efficiency came at the price of freedom. America's freedom came at the price of efficiency. Each system revealed the other's weakness.

In China, there could be a mountain village somewhere that had no electricity (and probably no Covid), but everywhere else in the country the contact tracing app provided one hundred percent coverage, with one hundred percent compliance. It was simply not possible to move around the city without showing a green QR code on your mobile phone. The code turned red if you (which is to say, your phone) had been near someone who tested positive for the virus. Yellow indicated you had been to a region considered risky, and your movements would be restricted. Larsen listened, but he was unconvinced that China's system would work in America.

As long-term residents of China, we had become accustomed to a system that imposed restrictions. Restaurants shifted from dine-in to delivery, and factories and offices were allowed to re-open, provided they had sufficient masks, hand sanitizer, and equipment in place to monitor possible cases of Covid.

The restriction on travel was a different story, and disproportionately impacted resident foreigners, who suddenly couldn't make business trips to headquarters, travel home to visit family, or bring children to visit grandparents. We were stuck. To be precise, nothing prevented us from *leaving* China; the problem was getting back in. This resulted in many families becoming separated, as the working spouse stayed behind while the rest of his or her family returned to their home country.

Returning to China became an odyssey. A two-week quarantine would await the intrepid traveler who made it that far. Visas were suspended and flights were nonexistent or impossible to book. The chamber became a clearing house for re-entry procedures, starting with the "PU letter" from the Ministry of Foreign Affairs. We never did learn why it was called a PU letter, although it could have come from the word *putong*, meaning "ordinary," written across the top. The letter would need to explain why this particular person needed to be in China, and how their presence would impact the Chinese economy. If the person was in charge of an investment project, managing a large number of workers, or was otherwise vital for some kind of economic activity, then a visa was likely to be approved. Spouses were rejected, as were certain categories of workers, for no apparent reason. At one point we were told that lawyers need not apply, but teachers were welcome.

I had dozens of meetings with Chinese government officials, including Vice Mayor Zong Ming and officials from the Ministry of Foreign Affairs. My appeals to loosen the travel restrictions so families could be reunited were met with nods, but I could tell there was a huge gap in how we viewed the situation. Workers in China are accustomed to hardships, with many going home only once a year, which is why Chinese New Year is such an important holiday. Millions of migrant workers fight for train tickets, since the annual holiday is their only chance to see their children, or aging parents.

The second issue was with vaccines. The locally developed vaccines were apparently safe, but not very effective. BioNTech reached a deal with a local firm, Fosun, to manufacture the Pfizer BioNTech vaccine in a facility just outside Shanghai, but approval from China's regulator was still required. Rumors were flying about when it would be approved, and who would be eligible to take the first doses that became available.

In order to get to the bottom of it, I met with Vice Mayor Zong Ming on March 3, 2021. She was flanked by officials from China's Centers for Disease Control and Public Health Bureau, and we were told that the BionTech vaccine would be available in China "in June." The Chamber immediately began registering our member companies and their employees—including families—so we could get the jab as quickly and efficiently as possible when it became available. It never came. Chinese authorities refused to approve the foreign vaccine, leaving the population vulnerable. Politics—and Chinese pride—triumphed over science. Control over cooperation. Fear of foreign vaccines was fear of admitting weakness.

I spent the next two years begging China's government to reopen the borders, relax travel restrictions, and approve a foreign vaccine. The *South China Morning Post* published my op-ed calling for the US and China to work together on mutual vaccine recognition and to put in place the kind of vaccine passport system used in other countries. We even delivered a letter to Premier Li Keqiang, asking him for cooperation on these issues. Despite our generally good relationships and sustained efforts, we made little progress with the authorities. To them, family separation was an inconvenience, not a tragedy. Control came first.

And then, Omicron. In November of 2021 the new variant was identified in South Africa but quickly spread to the United States and throughout the world, including China. The new strain was less deadly but far more transmissible than Delta or other strains. There seemed to be no way to stop it, causing a shift in strategies for how to deal with the public health crisis. Most countries shifted to aggressively protecting the most vulnerable members of the population, especially the elderly, while relaxing futile attempts to contain it.

Not China. The party continued to insist that the zero-Covid policy was "safe, scientific, and correct." The World Health Organization called it "not sustainable."

China's stubborn adherence to zero-Covid is an example of what can happen under a system that lacks diversity and transparency. The doctor who first alerted colleagues about the virus in December of 2019, Li Wenliang, was accused of "spreading rumors" and punished by authorities. The government later apologized, but not before Dr. Li died of Covid-19.

Dr. Zhang Wenhong, a prominent infectious disease expert,

advocated for a more balanced approach to Covid, especially in reaction to the Omicron variant. He was immediately targeted for investigation, widely believed to be politically motivated. Others, like Zhang Zhan, a citizen journalist, were jailed for speaking out about China's handling of the pandemic.

Before Omicron, Shanghai had taken a relatively relaxed approach to Covid. The controls were followed, but life was pretty much normal as long as masks were worn and travel restrictions were observed. The first cases of Omicron changed everything. The new variant spread aggressively and within days, over 10,000 people tested positive for the virus and weeks later, over 100,000 people were confirmed positive. Still, deaths were rare. The new variant was far less lethal than previous ones.

Nevertheless, the order from Beijing sent Shanghai into lockdown. For about ten weeks, people were confined to their homes, except for Covid testing, and the entire city of 23 million people was shut down. Authorities had done little to prepare, resulting in food shortages, especially in less affluent parts of the city. Babies went without formula, the sick had no medicine.

Finally, public displeasure reached the boiling point when ten people died in an apartment fire in Urumqi, a city far from Shanghai but also in zero-Covid lockdown. According to reports, some people were locked in their homes and firefighters were prevented from reaching the blaze because of zero-Covid controls, unleashing a wave of anger across the country.

In December of 2022, Chinese authorities suddenly reversed the policy and inexplicably went to the opposite extreme, removing all Covid measures. The virus had anyway, in the end, escaped.

Ironically, the effectiveness of China's controls also left the population with no natural immunity since so few people had actually contracted the virus. Vaccination rates were low, mainly because people didn't feel the need but also because of information—and misinformation—about its effectiveness and side effects. I took the locally developed vaccine myself and had no problems, but others reported side effects and the government did little to allay fears or encourage people to take the jab.

The elderly in particular were concerned about side effects. During the initial rollout in early 2021, anyone with serious heart disease or poorly controlled diabetes was advised to consult doctors before vaccination, and older adults were initially excluded from China's vaccination program due to limited clinical trial data in this age group. Vaccination for those over 60 didn't become available until June 2021. Foreign vaccines such as Pfizer and Moderna were never made available to people in China.

The sudden change in policy resulted in the entire population being exposed to Covid, with a staggering number of people getting sick within a very short period. Most people recovered quickly, but many vulnerable elderly people died. Hospitals and morgues were inundated.

A family friend visited me in my apartment in Shanghai, some time after Beijing finally lifted the zero-Covid policy in December 2022. "There was nothing we could do with the body," she told me, fighting back tears. Her father-in-law, who was living with her and her two children in their Shanghai apartment, had contracted Covid and died. The morgue was full and turned her away. "We kept him with us in the apartment for six days, but after that it became too much. We took him out to Chong Ming Island..." My friend's voice tapered off as she described her trip to the sparsely populated island about a two hour drive north of Shanghai. "Please don't ask me any more about it..." The island was at the mouth of the Yangtze River, where ocean currents carried everything out to sea.

After the Shanghai lockdown of 2022, the city's party secretary, Li Qiang, was promoted to become China's premier, effectively number two below Xi Jinping, and Vice Mayor Zong Ming lost her job. Nobody I spoke with could explain the rationale for either decision, but I heard from her office that there was blow-back from our conversation about approval of the foreign vaccine. After AmCham announced the result of our meeting to the members, the *Wall Street Journal* picked up the story. It's hard to say if that, or our letter to Premier Li Keqiang, could have led to her removal.

In the end, the party proved what fragility really looks like: a system so focused on control that it relents only when control fails. China's Covid response exposed the deeper truth behind the image of a disciplined, unified state: a system that can enforce control with extraordinary precision, yet lacks the ability to adapt. Bureaucracy splintered under pressure, the healthcare system buckled, and the party's inability to admit mistakes exacerbated a public health challenge. Zero-Covid succeeded only for a while. It could not be contained indefinitely, and when it escaped, the system's rigidity became its undoing. Middle class attitudes were impacted and supply chains seized up. In the end, the way the pandemic was handled did not show the power of the dragon so much as highlight its fragility: a system capable of immense mobilization, yet strangely inflexible.

Before Covid, US-China relations were already on a downward track, and the pandemic accelerated it. Washington complained that Beijing withheld information about the virus until after it was too late to contain it. Beijing said the virus may not have originated in China at all, coming up with an alternative story about the US Army being responsible. Worst of all, America's president descended to the level of a racist schoolyard bully, calling the virus "kung flu," a meme that would be picked up by his supporters and lead to violence against Asian Americans. Viewed from Beijing, Trump's ugly name-calling revealed a weak leader who was out of ideas.

Chapter 24

Friends Fall

In July of 2021, AmCham received a message from Beijing that Vice Foreign Minister Qin Gang would be visiting Shanghai, and could we please arrange for him to visit a few foreign companies?

I had met Mr. Qin before in Beijing, but as far as any of us could remember this would be the first visit from someone of his rank to visit us from Beijing. It was a great honor, and members were excited. Rumors were circulating that Qin was about to be named the successor to Cui Tiankai, the long-serving Chinese ambassador to the United States.

Cui was a fluent English speaker, unlike other officials of his generation, having worked as an interpreter at the United Nations before joining the Foreign Ministry. During trips to Washington the chamber would always request an audience with Ambassador Cui, but a meeting with his deputy was the best we could achieve. We hoped our previous meetings with Qin could help us work more closely with one of China's top officials managing the relationship with America.

The event space in our new offices could hold about ninety people, but the chamber staff felt thirty was the right number to be seated comfortably, and we proceeded to make a list. These tasks were never easy. We had the usual diversity requirements, but if the head of Ford was invited then we had to include GM; with Coke came Pepsi, and so on.

As required by protocol, I met the vice minister in front of our building, a modern high-rise office tower in Xintiandi. The building management had been notified of our important visitor so they could clear away traffic and streamline the security. An elevator was held at the ground floor so the vice minister and his entourage could be whisked up to our offices.

Mr. Qin greeted me warmly, and we moved quickly upstairs where I walked him through our offices and introduced him to the staff. I showed him our history wall, a project that emerged as a byproduct of the activities for the 100th anniversary of the Chamber and the masterwork of my predecessor, Ken Jarrett. It's a clever collage of historical photos that chronicle major events of the last century from the perspective of American business in China, and US-China relations in general. It was a visual reminder of how deeply intertwined our countries had become—and how much that relationship was now in doubt.

We have a photo of Carl Crow, the journalist who wrote the landmark book *400 Million Customers,* as well as pictures of 3M's first investments, and of FedEx entering the market in 1984, supplied by long-time AmCham member and FedEx executive, Eddy Chan. Murray King provided photos of Shanghai Disneyland, another seminal event for American business in China, and for cultural exchange between the two countries. With 50,000 guests entering the park each day, millions of Chinese children form their first impression of America from a mouse, a duck, and a pirate of the Caribbean.

The vice foreign minister arrived with a modest entourage of six or seven people—Mr. Qin's flawless English made a translator unnecessary—most notably including a woman by the name of

Hua Chunying. She was the spokesperson for the Ministry of Foreign Affairs, and well known as a wolf warrior whose job it was to "punch back" at the West. She said things like Canada's foreign minister "can't help speaking without thinking,"[3] and used Twitter constantly to criticize the West, especially the United States. The Twitter feed under her name was clearly managed by her staff, since she didn't speak English, at least not with me. Our conversation was pleasant enough, but I wondered what her role was since it's not common for a vice minister to travel with the ministry spokesperson. During our meeting she sat to Mr. Qin's right and frequently spoke in his ear, presumably making sure he stayed on message, which he did.

Qin delivered the expected remarks, including a strong rebuke to us as the business community for not standing up to our government. "Decoupling is the wrong way to go," he told us, in a firm, almost accusatory tone. "How is this good for you, and if America is a democracy, then why are you letting this happen?"

It wasn't my place to point out that the export controls were stopping American-made microchips from going into Chinese missile guidance systems. Still, I couldn't resist pointing out the contradiction.

"You are right, Mr. Vice Minister, that you won't find anyone in this room who favors decoupling," I said. "But with respect, I have to ask you, who started it?" Mr. Qin looked sternly across the table at me. I hoped I hadn't gone too far, but our previous conversations had been candid, just not in front of so many people. I suspect Madam Hua also understood much more English than she let on, since she seemed to understand exactly what I was saying, and scowled at me as I pressed on. "What is

3 *South China Morning Post*, "Sarcasm is China's latest weapon in battle with Canada over detainees," January 18, 2019.

your Great Firewall, if it's not decoupling?"

The room froze. Qin looked at me without expression. Hua looked daggers in my direction. The Chinese diplomats were right, that US export controls on advanced technologies were driving a wedge between the American and Chinese economies, forcing companies to bifurcate product development. But it was also true that Beijing, by censoring the Internet and effectively keeping foreign companies out of China's technology ecosystem, had managed to silo its digital economy (thus the term, "Great Firewall"), keeping it separate—effectively decoupled—from the rest of the world. Beijing had already built a digital wall around its economy, shutting out non-Chinese firms while demanding access to foreign markets. China's control came at the cost of isolation—an illusion of self-reliance masking deep vulnerability.

I offered this as a comment to the vice minister in a way that didn't require a rebuttal, and I saw Madam Hua saying something in his ear.

Later in the day, I escorted Mr. Qin to tour the GM showroom, where he could play with the car maker's advanced technologies and sit inside its newest vehicles. GM has a joint venture with Shanghai Automotive Industry Corporation (SAIC), a state-owned company. The head of the SAIC side of the joint venture made an appearance but then stepped out and allowed the GM executive to lead the tour.

From GM we moved to Honeywell, which has an enormous business in China and many joint ventures, but unlike GM, its main business is wholly owned. Mr. Qin tried on some fire safety gear and admired the displays of Honeywell's wide range of industrial products. Honeywell develops technologies that are important in advanced manufacturing and automation, which China is eagerly adopting in order to keep moving upward in the value chain.

After the tour we ended up in a conference room, where we could discuss Honeywell's business in China in more detail. Madam Hua and most of the group had peeled off, leaving Mr. Qin alone with me and one or two senior people from Honeywell. By then it was clear to me that he was preparing himself for Washington, where he would represent China as the new ambassador. He was keenly aware of how difficult the job would be, and between the tours he peppered me with questions about America and our politics.

After watching Honeywell's slick corporate video and listening for a while, Mr. Qin was clearly impressed with the size and success of Honeywell's business in China and remarked: "You have a nice business here… wouldn't it be a shame if it could not continue?" I don't believe he intended, or if he was even aware of how his question sounded like a mob boss collecting money for protection, but the Honeywell executive glanced at me with a worried look.

I don't know if "threat" is the right word, or perhaps "foreboding prediction" is more accurate, but I had heard concerns like this expressed before, just never from such a senior leader. Some months earlier, I visited the Foreign Ministry in Beijing with a list of items to discuss, mainly of a tactical nature—visas, customs procedures, and the like. A deputy director from the North America Division met me in a small conference room. "Mr. Gibbs, I understand you have some requests, and a letter to deliver." Our agenda items had been discussed already at the staff level.

As I recall, I was planning to invite Han Zheng, China's vice premier at the time, but who had previously been mayor and party secretary of Shanghai, to attend our annual dinner. The deputy director accepted my letter of invitation. Mr. Han declined, and delivered a statement of support for the American

Chamber instead. Vice Mayor Zong Ming read the letter aloud as part of her speech, and I felt palpable relief from the hundreds of AmCham members in attendance. They were bothered by the increasing tension between the United States and China, but as long as China's vice premier still supported AmCham and our presence in China, there was hope.

"That's fine," said the Deputy Director, "but first I have something to say that you need to hear."

President Trump's special brand of diplomacy had taken its toll. The Chinese official spent the next forty minutes telling me—his voice often trembling with emotion—how he and others like him in the ministry believed that having a relationship with America was a good thing for both countries, and that he personally didn't think America had ill intentions toward China. "But we are reaching a limit," the deputy director said. "We are approaching a point where I am having a difficult time internally defending that position, and explaining why a relationship with America is still good for China."

He wasn't specific about what issues would push him and his colleagues too far, but it seemed to me that the tariffs were less important than the fact that Beijing wasn't feeling respected, and that people in Washington didn't seem interested in listening or understanding China's perspective. The economic issues were less important than emotion, pride, and loss of face. Beijing's insecurity was boiling over. Qin Gang, on his way to becoming China's ambassador to Washington, seemed to be delivering a similar message.

My European colleagues warned me that when Qin was posted to London he took fierce positions and was anything but diplomatic. They called him the leader of the pack of wolf warriors who were punching back and putting the West in its place. That may have been true, but I saw him as a man who listened. He may not have agreed with everything I said but he never shut down a conversation or belittled my positions, even while telling me I was wrong.

On my next visit to Washington, which would be my last as president of the American Chamber, I contacted his office to see if he would accept a meeting. He had only been in the role for a few weeks and I knew he would be busy, but to my surprise he not only accepted the meeting but he invited me for dinner at his home. So I bought a moderately priced bottle of California wine, gathered a few AmCham members, and in December of 2021 we visited the home of China's ambassador to Washington.

Chinese people generally entertain in restaurants or clubs, so this was my first experience dining in the home of a Chinese official, not that the ambassador's residence is an ordinary home. Security was surprisingly light, but the tony DC neighborhood seemed quiet and safe. Even more surprising, he asked for advice. American officials ask people all the time what they should do, which is normal in a democracy. I had never heard a Chinese official asking for advice, certainly not from an American. But we were in his home and he seemed at ease.

I was as frustrated and disappointed as he was with the United States and China being at each other's throats, and I certainly didn't believe it was my place to tell China's ambassador what to do, but I wanted to be helpful. I pointed out that the benefits of trade can be difficult to touch and feel, and the effects of globalization were uneven, causing many Americans to become anti-trade, and there is no country more closely identified with trade and globalization than China. "For better or worse," I told the ambassador, "in a democratic system, Washington is a reflection of what voters are thinking." I advised him to spend time away from Washington. "Here in the capital you already know what people are going to say, and they know what you're going to say, or at least they think they do."

I suggested that he tour the country, just as Max Baucus had in China, and connect with ordinary Americans. I knew his job as ambassador would be to read speeches that were written in Beijing, and that the issues vexing our countries depended on decisions that would not be his to make. He was hand-picked by Xi Jinping, and was expected to be a loyal footsoldier and communicator.

Whether it was because of what I said or because he liked baseball I'll never know, but he managed to get out of Washington DC and tour a good part of the country. He threw the opening pitch at a major league baseball game and took a shot during halftime at an NBA game, which amazingly, went straight into the net. Qin's speeches and media appearances were harsh, but I believed he genuinely wanted harmony between our countries and that he would bring that message to ordinary Americans. I wished him well and had hope for his success.

Some months after our dinner at his home we met up again, this time at a conference in Chicago, where I spoke on a panel. He was the keynote speaker and guest of honor. I took the opportunity to invite Ambassador Qin to visit the campus of the University of San Francisco, where I was teaching, and he graciously accepted. Before we could schedule the visit he was promoted to become Minister of Foreign Affairs, and recalled to Beijing. It so happened I traveled to China myself that summer, but just as I contacted his office to arrange a visit, Minister Qin mysteriously disappeared.

The blogosphere lit up with rumors. Qin Gang was seen on June 25, 2023 in Beijing, but his public events after that were cancelled. After weeks of speculation, a spokesperson put out a vague mention of a "health issue," which nobody believed. It was well known that he had had an affair with a Chinese journalist, and that they had a baby together. The woman traveled back to China at about the same time. She also disappeared.

The man once trusted by Xi himself had become a liability. In a system built on conformity and control, that was not acceptable. Qin Gang's story is the story of China's diplomacy itself: confident in public, anxious in private—strong in image, fragile in practice.

China's relentless leadership changes, like so many other features of the system, reveal a state that projects confidence but seems to operates from a position of insecurity. A government that must continually cleanse its own ranks to enforce loyalty is one that has never resolved its internal fractures. The revolving cast of vanished ministers, sidelined generals, and silenced diplomats underscores a deeper truth at the heart of the "Fragile Dragon": China's strength depends on control, not stability; on fear, not trust. The more tight the grip on the system, the more brittle it becomes. The pattern suggests a political system that prioritizes political alignment over institutional autonomy, centralizes rather than distributes authority, and emphasizes loyalty in key appointments. Rather than demonstrating strength, recurring purges raise questions about institutional stability within highly centralized governance structures. Systems that concentrate authority, restrict information flow, and rely heavily on individual leadership face distinctive challenges: reduced early warning capacity, limited ability for self-correction, and succession uncertainties. The very features designed to maintain control—centralization, narrow trust networks, emphasis on political reliability—create potential vulnerabilities, particularly during transitions or crises.

CHAPTER 25

Into the Dragon's Lair

It was ten o'clock on Friday night. The caller didn't identify himself, but he spoke with a tone of authority that my IT systems manager recognized immediately. School teachers use it, police officers use it, and communist party officials use it when they expect absolute obedience.

The American Chamber publishes a weekly newsletter, a monthly magazine, and maintains a website with content across various commercial topics. We aren't a publisher, and we certainly are not a news organization. The business license hanging on the wall puts the Chamber in a vague category that permits "consulting services," which could mean just about anything. In China, every entity with a website needs an ICP license as an "internet content provider." The ICP license application requires a technical point of contact. He's the guy who maintains IP addresses, manages email accounts, and maintains spam filters. In this instance, his job was to take calls from the Cybersecurity Administration on a Friday evening.

"There's a problem with your content…" The caller was firm but polite, almost like a neighbor calling to say you'd left your lawn sprinkler on, and it was flooding the sidewalk.

"What's the problem with our content?" My IT manager needed more information, but he knew better than to challenge the caller's authority. Better to listen first.

"I'll send you the list. You have two hours to take it down."

It was July of 2020, and relations between the United States and China had gone from bad to terrible. Still, I had no reason to think the American Chamber of Commerce had anything to worry about. On Monday, we got another call, this time during business hours, with a simple message: a time and a place, and an order to report to a man named Li Bing.

I arrived at the lobby of an office building in the Xuhui district, on the main drag of Zhaojiabang Road, close to other government offices. The address was marked clearly enough but otherwise, there was no sign in front and a surprising lack of security or access control. I arrived early and found the room. It was small, with no windows. Cameras were set up from four angles. A man was seated, head down in his laptop.

"Are you Li Bing?" I asked.

"No." The man didn't look up but kept poking at his keyboard. He seemed to be setting up some kind of form, perhaps to take notes. I took a seat across from him and took out my notebook. I was eager to find ways for the meeting to seem normal, which it wasn't. A moment later, a second man walked in.

"Are you Li Bing?" I asked.

"No."

A third man entered the room and took a seat between the other two, opposite me. I didn't ask, but he was clearly in charge. He began by showing me his badge. From across the table, I could see shiny metal and a big red star inside a black folding case, but that's all. If his goal was to intimidate me, then it was definitely working. The face behind the laptop didn't have a badge. Next, the man in the middle—I assumed this was Li Bing, the man I was ordered to see—told me to hand over my phone, which was Mr. Laptop's cue to bring out a cloth bag. He held it in front of me as I placed my phone inside.

My phone was protected with a password, but it occurred to me that I might be about to find out if the story was true, that Apple had agreed to provide the government with a back door to see inside phones, in exchange for continued access to the Chinese market. The US government made the same request, which Apple rebuffed. In any case, I knew there was nothing on the phone that could incriminate me. I just felt naked without it.

Next, Mr. Li directed my attention to the cameras, as if I could fail to notice them up on their tripods with huge lenses pointed right at me. "Our session will be recorded." I thought about asking if I could get a copy, but I kept quiet.

"You are here because you are the *fa ren* of the American Chamber of Commerce." The *fa ren* is the legal representative of a company or organization. Legal liability is a big deal in China. Some Chinese bosses list their driver or some other junior person to be the *fa ren,* but they don't always get away with it. At best, the ruse can give the real boss a day or two to plan strategy after authorities start poking around. Exit bans have been used to keep the legal representative of companies from leaving China until disputes are resolved, which is a powerful motivator to capitulate. "Is that correct?" Mr. Li's tone was authoritative and direct. I answered that he was correct, that I was the legal representative of the Chamber.

"The American Chamber of Commerce has a website and publishes content that can be seen by the public?"

"Yes," I replied. "We are a membership organization and produce content for our members, but much of the content is also available to the public."

"You are in violation of the Cybersecurity Law of the People's

Republic of China. I'll explain later what that means." He paused and pushed a single sheet of paper across the table. "Sign this."

I took a moment to read the two-page letter, printed on the front and back. Mostly it was legal and bureaucratic mumbo jumbo, except for the operative phrase: "I admit to committing a crime." I hadn't asked any question up to this point, but I looked across the table and asked: "Can I have a lawyer review this before I sign?"

"No." Mr. Li did not elaborate.

"Can I take a copy of it after I sign so that I can review it with a lawyer later?"

"No."

I thought about what it would mean, to have a document admitting to a crime. What would be the next step? Handcuffs? Or would the document be filed away, to be used against me later in some unrelated context?

"I can't sign this," I said, hoping Mr. Li would not take offense. I explained that I didn't believe I had committed any crime. The American Chamber operates legally in China and is committed to abiding by all laws and regulations. As the *fa ren* (legal representative) and CEO of the organization, it was my most basic duty to ensure that the Chamber followed the law in every aspect. I meant it. AmCham had a high profile and I was careful, even making sure the AmCham car never got a parking ticket. I had fired a driver because I couldn't get him to stay under the speed limit.

As I sat before Mr. Li and his colleagues, I was acutely aware that the US State Department had issued a warning[4] to American citizens in China that we could be "subject to arbitrary detention." The State Department's use of the term "arbitrary"

4 BBC, "US issues fresh travel warning after China detentions," January 4, 2019.

caused some division within the foreign business community. None of us denied that detentions were taking place, but there was disagreement over how arbitrary they were. With limits on the information we have access to, and the awareness that all information in China is controlled, it was usually possible to see the link between some kind of action and the detention. I needed to find the link.

"Look," I pleaded. "Whatever we've done that got your attention here, I want to make sure we don't do it again. Can you please explain what the problem is with these articles?" For the word "explain," I used the Chinese phrase *"qing jiao,"* which means "please teach me," demonstrating my humility and willingness to comply if they would just tell me how. They had given us a list of about a dozen items. One of the articles was written by a Washington DC-based economist and made a passing reference to Taiwan as a country—a definite no-no in mainland China—but the others seemed to be a random collection of articles on various business topics, but one of the items was the cover of our monthly magazine. We had already removed the articles from our website, but I printed out copies to bring with me. I picked up the cover photo and moved it to the center of the table. It was a picture of the leader of the country in which we operated. There was nothing unflattering or remarkable about the photo.

"I just want to know what we did so that we won't do it again," I said.

I'd been there for several hours already. I was scared from the outset, which of course, was the objective. There were no windows, but I knew it was dark outside and wondered if they planned to detain me overnight.

Mr. Li glared at me, angry that I would ask such a question.

"Ni ying gai zhidao!" You should know! This non-answer put a stop to my line of questioning, and Mr. Li again tapped on the document he wanted me to sign. He explained that there wouldn't be any consequences (it was a relief to know I would not be leaving in handcuffs), but he needed my signature on the document. I was tempted to suggest that I would sign his document if he would sign another, confirming what he'd just said.

"But I haven't committed any crime," I replied in a meek voice with my most humble demeanor, imagining myself prostrate in front of a magistrate in a Qing dynasty court. "Signing a document saying I have would be a lie."

"Of course you've committed a crime. Otherwise, why would you be here?" Mr. Li's logic was unassailable.

Despite numerous back-channel inquiries, we never did learn what had prompted the CAC to come looking at the American Chamber. The chamber has good working relationships up and down China's complex system of government. In Shanghai, we meet regularly with the mayor's office, as well as commerce, customs, and other departments.

The law Mr. Li referred to, once he got around to explaining it, actually governed news media organizations. To be more precise, we were accused of acting as a news organization without registering as one. Non-news organizations are not permitted to write about the military (no problem there, I thought to myself), or government (in a country where the government plays such a strong role in the economy, that could be a problem), or economics. I didn't say it out loud, but I considered asking Mr. Li, "You do know that we are a chamber of *commerce*, right?" How could we function without mentioning the government or the economy? Applying these standards, pretty much any information we made available to our members could be considered an illegal act.

I had been in the room for four hours without a break. Mr. Li finally agreed to alter the text to say I had "mistakenly failed to observe a regulation." I signed the confession and was allowed to leave, but not before being instructed to write a letter of apology explaining what I had done (I could take the weekend to figure it out). I needed to assure them that I would provide proper training to everyone at the Chamber who was responsible for content. Lastly, I had to certify that I would personally review everything the Chamber published so that I could be held personally responsible. Individual blame and accountability are very important in China, and it's what people are most afraid of.

It was late at night by the time I was allowed to leave, mentally and emotionally drained from the experience.

To this day I don't know what prompted the incident, but the experience put into context the spate of detentions that have taken place since. A number of foreign journalists and business executives have been arrested, detained, or simply disappeared, creating much stress among foreigners living in China. Some say it's nothing unusual. Criminal acts are punished everywhere, as they should be. Others wonder what evidence there is that a crime has occurred, or what the charge is in the first place. China's justice system is opaque, with ninety-nine percent of court cases leading to a conviction. I was glad to still have my freedom, something I will never take for granted again.

After my encounter with Mr. Li and the CAC, the US embassy began giving me briefings about my security. The RSO, the Regional Security Officer, advises the ambassador on matters of security, but he also exchanges information with American companies, and contacted me through the consulate. He was a large man with broad shoulders. I could tell he was ex-military by the way he spoke, but he didn't elaborate.

I didn't want my colleagues to become alarmed. About half of the AmCham staff were Chinese citizens, and I knew that some of them were occasionally approached by someone from the government for private conversations. I never thought much of that, and assumed they just wanted to know what we were up to. However, an office visit from American security personnel could make the staff feel uncomfortable being caught in the middle, so we met in a nearby coffee shop.

"You're an unlikely target," he told me. "Whatever the goal is, they can probably achieve it with a lower profile target that will be less complicated. But it pays to be prepared." He told me to remove anything from my apartment that I would have to go back for in case a fast trip to the border became necessary. Any document, object, or item of personal value that I couldn't leave without should be removed ahead of time. "Keeping a go-bag in your office or car might be a good idea," he said, although we agreed things hadn't yet reached that point and very possibly never would.

Far more likely was the possibility of an AmCham member being detained, as reciprocal to the PLA (China's military, which reports to the Communist Party, is called the "People's Liberation Army," or PLA) individuals who had been detained in the United States. AmCham members in China came from a variety of backgrounds, with a good number having served in various branches of the US military. Some were still members of the National Guard, which could be interpreted as the equivalent of the PLA, depending on the circumstances.

Toward the end of the first Trump administration, a decision was made to round up a number of suspected Chinese spies in the United States and deport them. The US government claimed to have evidence that the Chinese consulate in Houston was being used as a hub for espionage operations and theft of intellectual property, and ordered it closed. Naturally, the Chinese government retaliated by closing the US consulate in Chengdu, and blamed the United States for escalating tensions.

The United States also detained six Chinese citizens and accused them of lying on their visa applications. One in particular was a medical researcher who applied for a visa to enter the United States and work at UC Davis. She was granted the visa, entered the US, and was proceeding with her research until a photo surfaced showing her in full military uniform. It would not be difficult to imagine Beijing similarly scooping up an American citizen in China in order to make a point.

My friend Bob Theleen used to say that any sentence starting with: "China is…" would certainly be wrong. He was referring to the contradictions. China is modern and chic, but at the same time, it follows long-held traditions and beliefs. Chinese people are shrewd at business and unstoppable entrepreneurs, yet the country is formally self-described as socialist. The government imposes heavy censorship, yet expects innovation and creativity from the workforce. Foreign investment, ideas, and expertise played a significant role in China's development, and local officials continue to appreciate the boost they get from foreign companies in achieving their goals, even as officials at the national level push back on American leadership. China has become hostile to the West while seeking a greater role in the global economy. The streets are safe and free of crime, yet at times the government itself can be the source of fear, as people who thought they had no reason for concern have been detained.

Foreign Minister Qin Gang's disappearance was odd. That

summer, in 2023, one of my Chinese friends visited me in my apartment, eager to tell me what happened. I had to tell him to keep his voice down, and we put our cell phones in my Faraday bag. I learned about these devices from the embassy security briefings. The bag is made of conductive material and constructed in a pattern that blocks signals coming in or out. They are used in a variety of situations, including construction sites where a mobile phone signal could accidentally detonate explosives. Neither of us had reason to think our phones were bugged, but it couldn't hurt to be careful.

"He was poisoned." My friend was from Shanghai, but seemed to have good contacts in Beijing and had often impressed me with his insights. "They're saying he was turned by the Americans." My friend was not a conspiracy theorist, nor was he paranoid about Americans. His career had mainly been with Chinese tech companies, where he was very successful, but he also mixed easily with foreigners and spoke English with near-native fluency. His theory was that Qin wasn't an American spy, but that he had provided the introduction to corrupt Chinese military officials, and that Americans had paid those people for information.

"The Russians discovered it. They have better intel on the United States, and they came to Beijing to expose it." The theory made sense. The Russian deputy defense minister had been in Beijing the day before Qin's disappearance. Also, China's defense minister, Li Shangfu, was accused of corruption at around the same time, along with his predecessor. Something was going on, and the story—or parts of it—could be true. My friend went on to say Qin was given a choice between slow torture or drinking poison, and that he had opted for the latter. The story sounded more and more far-fetched to me. I was later told by a different source that Qin was alive, but had suffered a mental breakdown resulting from interrogation. I didn't know what to believe until finally, an authoritative source uncovered what had apparently happened.

Lingling Wei wrote for the *Wall Street Journal*, and had a remarkable ability to get the inside story about the murky and secretive goings on in Beijing. During Trump's trade war it was relatively easy to follow the American positions. The chief negotiators, Treasury Secretary Mnuchin and US Trade Representative Robert Lighthizer, briefed the media regularly and it was often possible to get staffers to reveal bits and pieces of what was going on behind the scenes. Beijing was different. Vice Premier Liu He was running the show and ran a tight operation. Liu had a complicated job finding the middle ground in his own camp between hard liners who were fed up with the West and advocated a break, versus those who saw China's future continuing to be tied to the United States. I spoke with Lingling frequently during the trade war, both on and off the record. Somehow, she filed stories about what the Chinese team was thinking that turned out to be correct, time and again.

Lingling was born in China, and at some point in life she decided that she wanted to become a journalist—a real journalist—and for that, she needed to leave China. She studied at New York University, got a job at Dow Jones, and eventually became a US citizen. In 2011 she became a China correspondent for the *Wall Street Journal* in Beijing. She covered business and the economy, and developed a reputation for fairness and accuracy, collaborating with veteran colleagues like Bob Davis and Jim Areddy. Together, the team provided invaluable information that the foreign business community relied on, giving investors confidence that they knew what was going on.

In 2020, she was expelled from China. At about the same time the Chinese consulate in Houston was closed, and the United

States expelled a number of Chinese journalists. Hundreds of Chinese nationals had been given press credentials and special visas to work and report from the United States, but they never filed any stories. Finally they were asked to leave. Beijing retaliated by expelling almost all of the American citizens working for major news outlets in China, adding Lingling Wei to the list.

She continued reporting from New York, and after investigating for a year she finally got to the bottom of what happened to Qin Gang. According to Lingling, Qin Gang's crime was connected to the affair he had with the journalist, but it wasn't because of the baby, or the fact that the child was a US citizen, born in America.

The journalist, Fu Xiaotian, had a glamorous lifestyle, hobnobbing with the rich and famous, as well as powerful people in government positions. Eventually, she was accused of improper connections to British intelligence. Lingling reported that information about Fu did in fact come from the Russians, who passed it to Beijing. In the Chinese system, an "improper connection" could mean anything from delivering documents in a black bag, to being cozy with an individual who years later lands in an awkward spot.

Qin Gang's crime was apparently the latter, although Beijing has not explained it fully. Qin was not reinstated, but he remains a member of the party and is referred to as "tongzhi," or comrade, indicating at least some level of acceptance, if not trust.

My own crime, and the reason for my detention, has never been fully explained. After consulting with a number of people who tend to know about these matters, the only theory that makes sense is that it was a power play, designed to remind me that foreigners play a limited role in China. Officials as high up as Vice Premier Han Zheng speak publicly about how welcome foreign investment is, and how much they value the presence of our companies, but at the same time, the party doesn't want anyone to forget who is in charge.

Conclusion
Looking Back and Moving Forward

As the end of my term as president of the Chamber drew near and I prepared to come home in 2021 after nineteen years living in Shanghai, my mother again made a rare, but firm, request. I was to travel to our ancestral home in Hubei province and visit the graves of my grandparents. In China, a special holiday is dedicated to this activity, called *qingming*, or "tomb sweeping." On that day the roads are jammed as people head for the cemeteries to clean headstones and burn paper money for their ancestors to use in the afterlife. I would need to do that, but my mother also wanted a copy of our family *jiapu*. A *jiapu* is a book containing the names and birthdates and a list of male heirs going back hundreds, and in some cases a thousand years or more. She also wanted me to visit the local archive to see what I could learn about my grandfather.

My mother had barely met him herself. She was still a child when her father died, and she was raised by various relatives. My mother grew up during the Japanese occupation, and China's civil war. That period of China's history was messy, with many families split apart.

It was a busy time for me, but the request did not seem optional. So I prepared myself for the trip to the small town of Yingshan, a two-hour drive from the city of Wuhan. I saw no need to make a big deal out of it. My plan was to find my way there, look up a few relatives, snap some pictures, and be done with it.

Fortunately, the government relations team at the American Chamber reminded me of the political sensitivities, given the changing nature of the US-China relationship. A member of the staff pointed out that while I may see myself as a blood relative with every right to go poking around in my family's hometown, others might see the visit differently. How long would it take for someone in the village to look up my name, find my picture on the internet next to an American flag, and alert authorities to put an immediate stop to my investigation of what could be considered state secrets? That would not do.

Therefore, my AmCham colleagues made official inquiries to get permission for my visit. I was still hoping for a low-profile trip without official dinners or meetings. I had enough of those in Shanghai and was looking forward to wrapping up my duties and returning home. So I went alone to the offices of a branch of the Foreign Affairs Office in Shanghai, where I would explain my mission.

The office was in a beautiful historic building of European design, with a long driveway leading to a canopied entrance. The director, Mr. Sha Hailin, whom I'd met many times both in an official capacity and in social settings, met me at the door and greeted me warmly. He was a stocky man with a full head of grey hair that belied his athletic prowess. He and I had played ping pong together a few months earlier in an exhibition match to celebrate the 50th anniversary of "ping pong diplomacy." We were paired in a doubles match, which we won thanks to my skill at staying out of his way while he slammed the ball across the net. For a man in his sixties he was remarkably spry.

He brought me up a creaky wooden staircase to a conference room that could have been the set of a 1930s Shanghai gangster movie. There was a fireplace at one end, and glass-enclosed bookcases displaying pictures of dignitaries and objects commemorating various meetings and events. I took a seat on one side of the long conference table. Mr. Sha sat opposite me, flanked by several staffers.

"Mr. Ji, I hear you will not continue as president of the Chamber. We should have a dinner for you." We spoke in Mandarin and he used my Chinese name. Dinners are the preferred mode of expressing almost anything in China, from hello to goodbye, thank you, or "I want something." I enjoyed Mr. Sha's company and wouldn't object to a dinner with him, but with only weeks left in my term my schedule was already full. The Chinese language has a rich lexicon of vocabulary to avoid obligations and deflect praise, and when needed, to escape long drawn-out dinners with drinking and toasting. I thanked him for his offer and made the necessary noises to avoid setting a date.

"So... what was it you wanted to talk about? Your office didn't tell us." Mr. Sha made a face, pretending to be hurt and slightly confused. Chinese government officials avoid taking meetings without knowing exactly what's on the agenda and what will be said. Surprises are not welcome in the People's Republic. I had not provided much in the way of detail because this was a personal matter and I didn't want my staff getting too deeply involved, but that was all about to change.

I explained briefly what my mother had asked me to do, making clear this was a family obligation, not some pleasure trip to the countryside. This went over well, as everyone in the room understood and was also bound by the Confucian principles that turn a parent's wish into the child's command. Mr. Sha and his staff were supportive but cautious.

"I see," said Mr. Sha. "What is your grandfather's name? Can you write it down?" The spoken Chinese language is extremely compact with many homonyms, so things need to be written down in order to be unambiguous, especially proper names. I wrote out the characters and slid the paper across the table. "Li Cishan? Your grandfather's name is not Ji?" My mother's family name is Li but children, especially males, generally take the father's family name. It's not unheard of to do otherwise, but this often implies some kind of drama, like a child born out of wedlock. My parents came up with a clever solution. The Chinese character for "Ji" is the same as "Li," with only one stroke added. Therefore my name keeps a connection to the Li family, but Ji has a sound similar to the front end of my father's family name, Gibbs.

"What I need, Mr. Sha, is a letter of introduction so the local authorities know that I'm on a personal trip for my family, nothing more. This has nothing to do with the US government or the work of the… "

"Ohhhh…." The young man sitting at the far end of the table hadn't said a word, which was normal. Junior staff in China don't speak unless spoken to, and his head was down over his phone as he poked through the results of his search. "We know *exactly* who your grandfather was." He said it in a way that I couldn't tell if that was a good thing or a bad thing, and I recalled my grandfather's complicated relationship with the KMT and the CCP. I waited as the phone was passed around on the other side of the table.

Mr. Sha removed his glasses and squinted at the small screen and frowned as he read the text. Finally, he looked up at me and said in a solemn voice, "Your grandfather was a very important man. Of course we will help you, Mr. Ji."

He went on to explain that according to the source his young subordinate had found with a few clicks on his phone, my grandfather had worked alongside Chen Duxiu, a co-founder of the Chinese Communist Party, to start the journal *New Youth*,

Shanghai's first Chinese language magazine. In the 1920s and 1930s, foreigners ran Shanghai and all its institutions, including the daily newspapers. "In fact," continued Mr. Sha, looking around at his colleagues to confirm, "I believe *New Youth* was founded in this very building!"

I was never able to confirm that, but *New Youth*, also known by its name in French, *La Jeunesse*, was one of the most influential publications of its day. Some of the short stories written by Lu Xun, the pioneering Chinese writer and intellectual, first appeared in *New Youth*, as did articles by Mao Zedong.

My mother said nothing about this when I was growing up. When I asked her what my grandfather did she replied vaguely, "Oh, he was a lawyer." I suppose that was accurate, but I learned later that he was one of the most important attorneys in Shanghai, and head of the "Lawyers' Guild," which to my understanding played a role not dissimilar to a chamber of commerce.

Several weeks later, after much back and forth between the Foreign Affairs staff and AmCham, I made the trip to Yingshan. I was treated like royalty. Two black cars met me at the township border and escorted me to the State Guest House, bypassing the ordinary hotel that my staff had booked. For the next three days, every meal and every minute of my day was planned and scripted.

That evening I met the party secretary, Mr. Zheng Guanwen, the top government official for the county of Yingshan. Gifts were exchanged (arranged by the AmCham staff, thankfully), photos taken, and impromptu speeches made. The whole thing was over the top and I felt embarrassed, knowing I was a much less important person than they were making me out to be. Banners were put up reading "Warm Welcome to President Ji Kaiwen (referring to my AmCham title) Returning Home." I was touched nearly to tears, and I knew that my mother would be happy. I also couldn't help but think how different this version of China was, far from Beijing and a world away from the Foreign Ministry's "wolf warriors" who seemed to take every opportunity to spew venom at Americans.

The next day I was taken to the Yingshan County Martyrs Memorial. The director, Mr. He Baisheng, was waiting at the entrance. He escorted me to the top of the stairs and guided me to a portrait of my grandfather. One of my cousins had prepared a wreath for me to place at the site.

Once finished at the Memorial I was taken to the Archives, where again I was met at the entrance as if I were a head of state. The director, the party secretary, the curator, and the entire staff met me at the door and posed for a photo. Inside, they gave me a stack of books with my grandfather's essays and spent the next few hours with me, explaining his life and work.

China is full of contradictions. I have on occasion been recognized as a native son, yet in other circumstances I have been treated with suspicion and even detained. China's diplomats have trusted me to deliver messages, yet conversations with them often reveal little about what our conflicts are really about. Still, we must take every opportunity to understand how the issues look from Beijing's point of view, not just our own, if a path forward can be found.

From 2022, I took up a teaching position at the University of San Francisco, and have since then spent most of my time in the United States, while occasionally traveling back to my home in Shanghai. I traveled around the US, giving talks on China and promoting my first book, *Selling to China: Stories of Success, Failure, and Constant Change*. The 2022 midterm elections were approaching, setting the stage for the Biden-Trump rematch in

2024, and I found that the groups I spoke to were more interested in the larger geopolitical questions than the operational advice that was the subject of the book, which I edited and co-authored with several of my AmCham colleagues. My notes from those talks, and the many questions and comments that emerged from them, formed the basis for this book.

One of those trips took me to Omaha, where I was invited to speak to a group of private equity investors on the sidelines of Warren Buffet's annual shareholder meeting. Their concerns were mainly about China's post-Covid economic recovery, but also about whether the country had become effectively uninvestable for various reasons.

I responded with a picture of a struggling Chinese economy hampered by consumers who had to a considerable extent lost confidence in the decision-making that had guided China for the past decades. The swaggering consumers of the late 2000s and early 2010s who were traveling the world buying up property and luxury goods from Paris to Sydney had been replaced by cautious households facing uncertain prospects.

"For the first time in decades," I told the investors, "people in China don't necessarily see a bright future ahead of them, and even people who have managed to hang onto jobs aren't feeling wealthy. When people don't feel optimistic they don't buy cars or refrigerators, leading to a downward spiral in the economy." That remains the case today. China's recovery remains weak, and foreign investors have mostly stayed on the sidelines.

It was my first time in Nebraska, and I took the opportunity to get out of the city and meet some farmers. I wasn't sure what to expect, as I waited beside a dirt road that divided rows of corn extending in all directions. The hot, humid summer weather had not yet arrived and I felt the gentle breeze that pushed the rows of corn back and forth. Windmills poked out of the fields in seemingly random locations, in contrast to the neatly planted rows and the precise geometry of the pivots that carry water from wells to plants.

The pivot system consisted of a long pipeline supported by A-shaped trusses mounted on wheeled towers. Each tower was fitted with an electric motor that drove the wheels in a large circle, delivering water evenly across the crop. Depending on the size and speed, a full cycle could take several days to complete.

I had arranged through a friend to meet the land owner, who drove up in an enormous Ford F-150 pickup truck with oversized chrome wheels. He was a big man, but he still had to climb from the cab and drop several feet to reach the ground. He wore boots, jeans, and a plaid shirt; we chatted as he handed me a pair of boots.

"So you're from China? A long way from home, aren't you?"

I explained that I was living in China, but that I'm American, and I was curious to know what people in Nebraska thought about China, our relationship with the country, and the politics of Trump's trade war. I knew that Nebraska was a deeply red state, so much so that the color divide wasn't between red and blue, but between red and green—red families drove tractors made by International Harvester, but green got their equipment from John Deere. I had no idea what a Nebraska farmer might say about the communist nation, or how much he knew about China. As turned out, quite a bit.

"Do I hate China? Hell no. I love China. One out of five of these rows is going to China," he said, waving an arm toward his crop as we walked toward his well, and the gas generator that powered it.

After winning the election, President Trump wasted no time putting China in his crosshairs. Unlike his first term, which focused on the trade deficit and IP protection, he fixated on

China's involvement in bringing fentanyl to the United States, declaring a "national emergency" in order to invoke IEEPA to impose tariffs on goods from China. IEEPA, the International Emergency Economic Powers Act, was the same legislation he had used in his executive orders against TikTok and WeChat during his first term. This was the first in a series of salvos not just against China but nearly all of America's trading partners, including staunch allies like Canada and Japan.

In the early period of Trump's second term, his approach to trade—and China in particular—was marked by confusion, volatility, and a lack of strategic clarity. Tariffs appeared and disappeared in rapid succession, sometimes within a single news cycle. One week the administration announced sweeping duties on a new category of Chinese imports; the next week the president suggested they might be delayed, reduced, or scrapped entirely. This erratic signaling made it nearly impossible for firms to plan inventories, manage supply chains, or price long-term contracts. Importers—who actually paid the tariffs at the border —found little comfort in Trump's insistence that "foreign governments" were footing the bill. US Customs and Border Protection's own data showed that tariff revenue came overwhelmingly from American companies and consumers, not China.

Even the president's objectives were difficult to discern. At times he framed tariffs as a punitive measure designed to make Chinese imports prohibitively expensive and force manufacturing back to the United States. That interpretation implied a sweeping reshoring campaign, one that would require long-term investment in infrastructure, workforce training, industrial clusters, and permitting reform—none of which the administration advanced in any systematic way. American manufacturing employment edged up in the early years of the first Trump term but had largely plateaued by 2019 and showed no sustained surge that would justify a strategy of raising import costs without complementary domestic reforms.

At other moments, Trump suggested the tariffs were simply a bargaining tool—leverage to secure better trade terms while preserving two-way commerce. But if the goal was improved market access, the erratic nature of the measures made negotiation harder, not easier. China responded in kind, targeting U.S. agriculture, aviation, and autos, and pushing American exporters into a cycle of retaliation that Washington never translated into a coherent agreement. U.S. exports to China declined in several key categories during the first trade war, and the early second-term moves risked repeating the pattern.

Most importantly, none of the structural issues that manufacturers in America have complained about for decades—high labor costs, rigid union rules in certain sectors, complex permitting, environmental reviews that can stretch for years, and fragmented industrial ecosystems—were meaningfully addressed. Raising tariffs without tackling these constraints did little to improve the competitiveness of American factories. According to the National Association of Manufacturers, more than 70% of firms cited workforce shortages and regulatory burdens as primary obstacles to expansion, far outweighing competition from imports. Yet these areas saw little progress.

The result was an atmosphere of uncertainty that neither strengthened US industry nor produced durable concessions from Beijing. By elevating tariffs without a clear strategic pathway—whether toward reshoring or toward negotiated liberalization—the administration created pressure without purpose, costs without a corresponding plan, and headlines without grounding in long-term economic policy.

Trump's second-term approach to China has been far more personal, interventionist, and improvisational than his first.

In his first term, Trump's China strategy was shaped by a comparatively large and experienced team, although some did not last long in their roles. Rex Tillerson, the ExxonMobil CEO with decades of experience working with foreign governments, was replaced as Secretary of State by Mike Pompeo. John Bolton, Nikki Haley, Wilbur Ross, Steve Mnuchin, and Robert Lighthizer. They all brought long résumés in diplomacy, finance, trade, or national security, and were well qualified to advise the president on China policy.

Matt Pottinger—who began as the National Security Council's Senior Director for Asia and was later promoted to Deputy National Security Advisor—played an especially influential role on China. He met several times with delegations from the American Chamber of Commerce. While we didn't always agree with his hawkish views on China, we respected his depth and experience with the subject matter. Pottinger had spent seven years as a *Wall Street Journal* correspondent in China, became fluent in Mandarin, and later enlisted in the US Marine Corps, serving multiple tours in Iraq and Afghanistan. His unusual combination of on-the-ground China reporting, military experience, and policy expertise gave him a level of credibility and domain knowledge that made him one of the most respected voices in the administration shaping China policy.

That team was also anchored in identifiable goals: reducing the trade deficit, forcing market access, and pressing Beijing on intellectual property. In the second term, the policy has narrowed around Trump himself, producing a China strategy that is less a coherent program than an ongoing series of transactional moves. He has threatened blanket tariffs on all Chinese imports while simultaneously carving out bespoke exceptions for companies like NVIDIA, and even demanding that the US government take equity stakes in firms such as Intel. These gestures—part punishment, part favoritism—leave businesses unclear whether the aim is truly reshoring manufacturing or simply renegotiating better terms through pressure and presidential discretion.

The result is profound confusion over US objectives. Trump speaks of bringing factories home, yet routinely signals that what he really wants is leverage to strike deals—tariffs as bargaining chips rather than tools of a long-term strategy. For American companies, this creates an unpredictable environment: one day they are told to reduce exposure to China; the next they are granted licenses to keep shipping high-end chips there, provided they cut Washington in on the deal. In practice, the policy mimics China's own style of state intervention—opaque, discretionary, and leader-driven—while weakening the institutional predictability that once gave the United States a competitive edge.

During his first and second terms, Donald Trump has amplified Washington's long-standing concerns about China's rise, but he has also governed in ways that increasingly resemble Beijing's own approach to economic management, suggesting a certain acceptance of Beijing's approach.

Rather than reinforcing America's institutional strengths, he has embraced tools—tariffs, investment screenings, supply-chain commands—that he wields less as instruments of national strategy than as expressions of personal authority. Decisions that once rested with agencies, interagency processes, or Congress now flow directly from the White House. In this, Trump mirrors the Chinese system more than he challenges it. His open admiration for Xi Jinping's centralized power is not just rhetoric; it is reflected in the way he governs.

This book has shown that the parallels run deeper than policy mechanics. As an earlier chapter noted, the resemblance to Mao is striking: the elevation of the leader's personal will over institutions, the demand for loyalty over competence, the instinct to divide society into supporters and enemies. The Cultural Revolution was an assault on bureaucratic restraint; MAGA channels a similar populist fury toward the "deep state," media, and political opponents. Trump's second-term threats—blanket tariffs, direct intervention in semiconductor supply chains, demands for equity stakes in private firms—echo Maoist improvisation, where the state expands to match the leader's ambitions. As Mao blurred the line between personal politics and national purpose, Trump folds economic strategy into his own transactional worldview.

This drift toward centralization does not strengthen America; it tilts the contest onto terrain where China holds natural advantages. Beijing's hybrid coercive model—formal export controls combined with murky administrative pressure, customs slow-rolls, whispered orders, and sanctions without clear off-ramps—works precisely because its system is designed for ambiguity and political discretion. China can impose costs without legal challenge, mobilize industries by fiat, and sustain economic pain without electoral consequences. The United States cannot—and should not—compete by imitating a system built on opacity and coercion. When America abandons predictability, the rule of law, alliance coordination, and an open investment climate, it forfeits the very strengths that made it successful. The consequences are already visible in Southeast Asia, where Trump's episodic diplomacy and tariff threats contrast sharply with China's continuous commercial engagement. A rivalry defined by who can be more centralized or punitive favors the country engineered for that style of governance.

The United States wins when it reinforces its own advantages: competitive markets, transparent rules, broad-based innovation, deep alliances, and a system that attracts global talent rather than repels it. Guardrails in critical technologies are necessary, but they must be embedded in a coherent strategy rather than deployed as bursts of personal authority. America's role should continue shaping the trading system, building coalitions, and harnessing its entrepreneurial energy. If the contest centers on dynamism, openness, and alliances, then the future for America is bright. The path forward is not to out-China China but to double down on an approach that has always made America strong.

China itself illustrates why imitation is misguided. Beneath its commanding posture lie deep vulnerabilities—demographic contraction, mounting debt, inefficient state enterprises, and weak institutional feedback loops that limit policy correction. Many of Beijing's most assertive policies reflect insecurity rather than confidence. WTO accession and decades of foreign investment fueled extraordinary growth, but the benefits were uneven, producing domestic distortions and foreign political reactions that now shape the debate around "de-risking." China's drive toward self-reliance is a response to external pressure and internal fears, yet it risks slowing innovation and raising structural costs. The outcome is a system more brittle than it appears, not necessarily more resilient. China's rise has produced both real strengths and real vulnerabilities—in the economy, politics, society, and geography—and Beijing's current policies respond to perceived threats as much as to real ones.

Misreading China—overstating its strengths while overlooking its weaknesses—is dangerous. It encourages an escalation of threats, fuels counterproductive US responses, and risks locking both countries into a confrontational cycle that neither can easily escape. China competes vigorously with the United States and is in many ways effectively challenging the current international order, but it is not an unstoppable juggernaut. Clarity about China's genuine capabilities and limitations is essential. Exaggeration leads to poor strategy; understanding leads to effective policy.

For the past four decades, the United States and China have lived in relative peace, and the commercial relationship has made both countries more prosperous than they would have been otherwise. As a market, China still holds vast opportunities, and our relationship has brought other benefits as well. Our universities have attracted talented students, scholars, and researchers from China, many of whom stay in the United States to start companies, create jobs, and pay taxes. Commerce between our nations has stocked our shelves with affordable products and created wealth.

Chinese society has benefited tremendously as well from a stable and productive relationship with Western nations, although pride and CCP propaganda compel the Chinese to assign credit elsewhere. China, now unshackled by poverty, enjoys the benefits of surplus and contributes to the fields of art and music, impossible during more turbulent times.

The last four decades have demonstrated that cooperation between the United States and China is possible and highly productive. Working together would lead to advances in how we manage everything from climate change, global pandemics, managing the Arctic, and other areas of mutual interest. Resolving our issues would undoubtedly lead to the best possible outcome, and usher in a new age of prosperity for both nations. It's entirely possible, and highly desirable, for the two countries to find a path forward that each can comfortably live with.

The path forward for American businesses will be

complicated, but with understanding on both sides that path can be successful. Business has always played an important role in diplomacy, as far back as the days when Lord McCartney and his American counterpart, van Braam, tried to open trade between the West and Qing dynasty China. They failed in part because of myopic arrogance on the part of the Qing court and partly because they did not come with products that China wanted or needed, at least in the eyes of the court.

Foreign companies will need to navigate the narrow corridor between what China wants and what the United States will allow. They must learn from the opium wars and Lord McCartney's mistakes and choose products and services wisely. Fortunately, in a market as large and innovative as China, this leaves huge opportunities in health care, environmental technologies, consumer products, and many other sectors.

Foreign companies will also need to adopt strategies and corporate structures that position businesses "in China with China," as explained in an earlier chapter in this book. Given how developed and competitive the market has become, the best approach could be a partnership or joint venture rather than competing directly against entrenched local players that have inherent advantages. Owning a piece of a successful business is better than owning all of one that fails, as eBay did. The good news is that local businesses—like Orange Hotels, where I was a part owner—have become very high-quality with good management and strong growth.

Lastly, foreign businesses need to be structured in a way that minimizes loss in case of disaster. Companies need to adopt strategies to move assets off the balance sheet and avoid being forced to write them off if continuing the business in China becomes untenable, as would be the case if war was to break out over Taiwan or the South China Sea. This gives businesses less control but minimizes downside risk. Sadly, a conflict between the United States and China is not an impossibility.

As discussed at the beginning of this book, *the Chinese system cares deeply about national security, sovereignty and respect,* any formula or construct that puts America and China into a harmonious relationship would need to accommodate the CCP's requirements in those areas. China wants to be respected as a significant power in Asia, and in a position globally that corresponds to its economic importance.

The United States has security interests of its own, and obligations to adhere to. It also has commercial and strategic interests in the region that it is unlikely to back away from. America is not going to accept being kept out of the South China Sea, and abandoning Taiwan would send the wrong message to all US allies and have political ramifications within the United States. It's unlikely that Washington and Beijing will ever view human rights in the same way, but as both countries go through leadership changes, anything is possible.

Direct military conflict between the United States and China is of course the worst possible outcome. There are multiple ways in which this could come to pass, with the most likely one being military action from the mainland on Taiwan. Short of war, two great powers can damage each other in all kinds of ways, dragging other countries down in their wake. A continued antagonistic relationship will continue to disrupt global trade and bifurcate markets.

With each passing day, we seem to find new reasons to dislike, distrust, and disengage from each other, moving us closer to open conflict. Therefore it is critically important that we make every effort to understand and communicated with the other side.

The gap in nuanced understanding of China has always

been the backdrop for our conversations about China. That doesn't mean necessarily that the Chinese system is criticized unfairly—much of the criticism is justified. It just means that it is misunderstood because not enough people on the American side know enough about how China really works. The Chinese diplomat, Ji Chaozhu, was Zhou Enlai's translator for his meeting with Henry Kissinger in 1971. In Ji's book, *The Man on Mao's Right,* he recounts the first formal words exchanged between the two statesmen at a top-secret meeting in Beijing.[5] Kissinger opened his remarks by saying "many visitors have come to this beautiful and, to us, mysterious land..." Zhou reportedly held up his hand and said, "When you become familiar with China, it will not seem as mysterious as before." According to Ji, who was interpreting for both men, Kissinger was visibly startled by the breach in protocol. But he set aside his prepared talking points and the two began forging a relationship of trust and mutual respect that historians agree was key to normalizing relations between the United States and China.

Sadly, half a century later China is still a mysterious land. In part this is because the party is deliberately opaque. The leadership makes decisions behind doors that are closed to outsiders, which in this case includes the Chinese people. The changes taking place in China add to our difficulties as the China we thought we knew is fast becoming something else entirely. China is nothing like us. That doesn't make it wrong, or bad, just different. And we need to understand it as a precondition to co-existing peacefully. The alternative is unimaginable.

China has changed, even in the relatively short time since I first arrived. In 1985 Chinese people knew little about the world beyond their borders, or how to run a business. They were curious

5 "The Man on Mao's Right," by Ji Chaozhu (Random House, 2008)

and optimistic, and eager to cooperate with new friends from the West. China was opening up and they were experiencing more freedom than they ever thought possible, and there was every reason to believe the country would continue on that trajectory. But China is a complicated place that changes fast. Its history has never been smooth, and the current period is no exception.

Acknowledgments

This book would not exist without the help and support of a number of people and organizations. The American Chamber of Commerce in Shanghai was my platform during my years living in China, as a place for learning and connecting with people, and for meeting with government officials from the United States and China. I am grateful to the members, the board, and the staff of this great institution that has been so helpful to me personally, as it continues to play a vital role in US-China relations.

The National Committee on US-China Relations (NCUSCR), led by Steve Orlins and supported by people like Jan Berris and her staff, plays a similar role based in New York. Similarly, the US-China Business Council (USCBC) does incredibly important work in Washington DC. I'm grateful to Craig Allen, Melinda Xu, Elizabeth Rowland, and the entire staff of the USCBC.

Other organizations that have been helpful to me, hosting events for the exchange of ideas about China, include the Carter Center, the US Heartland China Association, the Chinese General Chamber of Commerce, and many others.

The University of San Francisco (USF) supported this book, providing research materials and other resources. In particular, I wish to thank the School of Management Dean Otgo Erhemjamts, Professor Xiaohua Yang, the founding Executive Director of the Center for Business Studies and Innovation in Asia-Pacific, and Professor Wei Menkus, the Director of the Center for Asia Pacific Studies. My colleague at USF, Peter Lorentzen, read the entire manuscript carefully and suggested a number of changes. The book is better for it. My USF research assistant,

Anchal Khandelwal, helped with research and fact-checking. Ms Khandelwal and others helped make corrections to the manuscript, but any mistakes that remain are mine alone.

I also want to thank the other foreign chambers and diplomatic missions in Shanghai. The non-American perspective was always instructive and I'm grateful to them for inviting me to events. Whether as a speaker or participant, I always learned something from the programs. I especially want to thank Joerg Wuttke, who for years was my counterpart with the European Union Chamber of Commerce in China. I learned a great deal from Joerg and appreciated the close cooperation between our chambers, especially during the covid pandemic.

I am grateful to my many friends in government, both American and Chinese. As discussed elsewhere, naming Chinese government officials in a book like this and calling out their specific contributions to it could create problems. Here, I will thank Xie Feng, the current Chinese ambassador to the United States, as a representative of the larger body of government officials who have always treated me with consideration and respect. I am deeply grateful to have been hosted in their country, and for everything I have learned from them.

Equally, American government officials have helped me in countless ways, but I especially want to thank the US ambassadors to China who spent a great deal of time with me and with other AmCham members. Max Baucus, the ambassador under Obama from 2014 to 2017, was a true partner to the Chamber and is now a special friend. Ambassadors Gary Locke and Terry Branstad were also extremely helpful to our community and to me personally, as were the Consular officials, including Hanscom Smith, Sean Stein, and Jim Heller.

Bob Theleen and RT Peng were special mentors and my close friends. Sadly, they both passed away as I was writing this book, so they didn't have a chance to change any words or see it completed, but their ideas are deeply embedded in the chapters. Bob and I were close, even as we argued about politics, and I miss him every day. He taught me a lot about China, and how to think about its place in the world. His widow, Jenny Hsui Theleen, helped me recall Bob's stories that appear in the book, and contributed ideas of her own. RT Peng was my first boss in Taiwan and from him, I learned about the local business culture, and picked up a few tricks to play when things got really tough. He taught me persistence, laughing about his favorite Chinese phrase, *"si ma dang huo ma yi,"* meaning to give medicine to a dead horse. We saved a horse or two, winning projects that appeared to be lost. Words can't describe how much I miss him, and how grateful I am to have known him. His daughter, Lana Peng, helped me review the parts of the book that mention him, for which I'm grateful.

Bob Ching, my boss at the Boston Consulting Group, guided me toward a career in China. I look up to him and we remain close friends to this day.

I have many friends in Taiwan and I wish to thank them all, but I'm particularly grateful for the friendship and advice from my UC Berkeley classmates, Yifen Chen and Josephine Chiu, as well as my long-time friend John Cho. Certain members of my wife's family in Taiwan have also helped me with their insights. I won't name them here, but they know who they are.

A number of people either appear in stories or helped write them down, for which I am grateful. Some have declined to be named, and others I may have inadvertently left out, but they include: Denis Simon, Norwell Coquillard, Stan Ryan, Joseph Chan, Ben Kinnas, Zach Noling, Pierre Cohade, Brinton Scott, Yoke Loon Lim, Eddy Chan, Julian Blisset, Mike Rosenthal, Tim Fenton, Andrew Au, Brett Krause, Frankie Gao, Kevin Yi, and

Ed Tse.

Special mention goes to Ken Jarrett, who is celebrated as a highly respected figure in the China watching world. Over the decades, he helped me decipher this complicated and confusing country, and my experience in China would have been very different without his guidance. Ken read the entire manuscript (twice!) and advised me on important diplomatic nuances and corrected some historical facts (but any that he may have missed are my own mistakes).

Alan Beebe, Tara Joseph, Harley Sayedin, and Ben Wang were my counterparts running the AmChams in Beijing, Hong Kong, Guangzhou, and Chengdu respectively. Hsien-Hsien Lei and Laura Younger, the leaders of AmCham in Singapore and Tokyo, respectively also deserve recognition. I learned from each of them, and I want to thank them for their collegiality as well as their contributions to this book.

Tim Tse, the founder of the Roosevelt Club, has been a special friend. He opened his elite social circle to me, which is full of colorful characters, and we enjoyed many nights of long conversations and excellent wine. I'm quite sure that many of Tim's friends would not want to be named in a book like this, but they know who they are, and I thank them for sharing their knowledge and insights.

Some of the ideas in this book first appeared in another book, *Selling to China,* which was a collaboration of co-authors. Unsurprisingly, some of their stories found their way into this one. They have all been amazing partners to work with, and I want to thank Mark Fischer, Dan Krassenstein, Jean Liu, Bill Russo, Bryce Whitwam, Don Williams, Marie Williams, and Kenneth Yu.

Sean Stein deserves special mention. We met when he assumed the role of Consul General in Shanghai, and we became friends through collaborations between the Consulate and the Chamber. We confronted a number of challenges together, including the trade war and the global pandemic.

William White was one of the first foreigners I met when I first traveled to China in 1985. He had already been living in China for several years before I arrived, and helped shape my study of the country and its people.

A number of my China-born friends are still living in China and would not wish to be named. It's impossible to predict what ideas might be acceptable in China today, but could become problematic for some reason in the future. I am grateful to them, as I am to those who agreed to be named: Henry Shen, Jiang Wei, Bo Shao, Wu Hai, Di Yao, Frances Sun, Haisong Tang, Brian Qiao, Su Weichou, Joe King (Zhu Qing), Tony Ling, Pin Ni, Zoe Liu, Dan Wang, Palmer Wang, Qingyi Yin.

My American-born Chinese friends have contributed to this book in different ways, helping me think through what it means to be American and Chinese. Larry Wang has worked in talent recruitment and training for his entire career and knows more than anyone about how this group fits into the complicated US-China equation. Other Chinese Americans who helped with the book include Lenora Chu, Hurst Lin, Alan Tien, Jeffrey Chen, and many others.

A number of people read early drafts and helped guide my thinking on the book. They include: Andres Batista, Mike Pope, Till Vestring, Brian Burns, Bob Marshall, Linda Tsao Yang, and Brook Wessel. Bill Duff, a former State Department official, reviewed certain chapters and helped refine the parts involving the South China Sea and security. Phelim Kine made helpful comments on Xinjiang and Human Rights.

Stuart Rauch, a former colleague and professional writer, read the entire book carefully and critically, fixing organizational issues and inconsistencies. His suggestions made the book better.

Frank Tsai, founder of China Crossroads, has been helpful to me as he continues to courageously organize public lectures in China. Yuelin Yang also organizes talks and roundtable discussions, which are rich environments for people like me to test ideas and hear alternative views.

Orville Schell, a scholar and author of many books on China, encouraged me to write as soon as I had left China. Similarly, Fraser Howie and Scott Rozelle were very supportive, for which I thank them. Perry Link was my teacher in the 1980s and has continued to guide me. I am grateful to them, and to all my many teachers.

Writing a book is difficult, but getting it published would be nearly impossible without help and guidance from friends. I'm grateful to David and Ginny Freeman, the founders of the Sonoma Valley Authors Festival, for their support and friendship. Their annual event in California's wine country is one of the true gems of the San Francisco Bay Area. Big thanks also to Cheryl Popp, the owner of Books by the Bay in Sausalito, and to her colleague Jeff Battis. Each book we purchase from a local bookshop is a brick in the foundation of a well-informed society.

My editor, Graham Earnshaw, helped with his meticulous corrections and professional expertise, but he also has domain knowledge that was invaluable along the way. We did not always agree on interpretations of history, but he helped me get a number of facts right. Any errors that remain are mine, not his.

I have not included a bibliography here, although dozens of books contributed to how I think about the subject. Those that I quoted from are credited with footnotes, but I drew heavily from a few books that deserve special mention. Chris Miller's book, "Chip War," was specifically helpful for the chapter on Taiwan, and Bill Hayton's book, *The Invention of China*, taught me much that I didn't know about 18th and 19th-century history. Ji Chaozhu's book, *The Man on Mao's Right*, provided a helpful quote for the final chapter, but more importantly, it gave me a template for how to look objectively from both sides of a conflict between countries. Ji was a complicated figure. He was born in China, educated in the United States, then returned to China to serve in the Korean war, then later as a diplomat. He loved his country, but also had great respect for the United States. His book serves as a reminder that whether it's the United States or China, we love our country because it's our country, not because it's perfect. As citizens, we criticize and challenge ourselves every day so that we can change our country and make it better.

My wife Amy and daughter Amelia supported me throughout this project and encouraged me to finish the book. My cousins, Tom and Cristy Rathjen, were incredibly supportive and connected me to their social circle, helping me gauge what readers would be most interested in.

Lastly, I wish to thank my parents, Donald Gibbs and Loretta Li Yun-zhen. Everything I have, I have because of them. Whatever I know, I know because of them. This book is all about my parents, and a result of their work, sacrifices, and wisdom. I am eternally grateful.

About The Author

Ker Gibbs' career spans Asia and Silicon Valley over more than three decades. He worked for The Boston Consulting Group in Shanghai, then for Apple and other tech companies. As an investment banker at HSBC, he advised technology and media clients in Beijing, Shanghai, and Taipei.

Mr. Gibbs currently teaches at the University of San Francisco while writing and giving talks on China. He edited and co-authored his first book, *Selling to China: Stories of Success, Failure, and Constant Change*, published by Palgrave Macmillan (2023). He has written op-eds for the *Wall Street Journal, South China Morning Post*, the *San Francisco Chronicle*, and other publications.

He holds a BA in economics from UCLA and an MBA from UC Berkeley. He lives in San Francisco and Shanghai.

